Excellent Established Eternal

The Power of God's Covenant

BY
CONNIE FAUTH

The Power Of God's Covenant
ISBN: 978-1-939570-18-5

102 Theodore St
Washington, IL 61571

Published by Word & Spirit Publishing.
P.O. Box 701403
Tulsa, OK 74170

ACKNOWLEDGEMENTS

Because it has been my privilege to write this book, I want to acknowledge all who have encouraged me since 1975. First, I acknowledge my Lord Jesus Christ. Bible topics would have been no more than another history study without the privilege of being born again and baptized in the Holy Spirit. Second, without help received from family, my life would have been short-lived and unfruitful for the Lord.

Dad, Mom, Buddy, and Harold loved me and taught me so much from the time I was born. Uncle Edwin (Doc) and Aunt Thelma (Pug) were a blessing when they shared their peaceful home with me so many times. Uncle Norman (Bunny) and Aunt Clodene (Elvis) and their appreciation for life are still an encouragement to me. My deceased husband, John Williams, who taught me not to be intimidated as I ministered. All these dear ones have held a special place in my heart, though they have been gone for a long time. I shall not forget their love.

Jack, my youngest brother, and I have been celebrating the goodness of the Lord together for over a year. He is a remarkable man and able to testify in spite of great loss. Perhaps one day he will take the time to write his memoirs. Thanks Jack for your kindness, generosity and encouragement. We have some time left to witness of our Lord and Savior and a lot to look forward to.

A special thanks is extended to my husband, Curtis Fauth, for his encouragement to pick up my manuscript and resume work on this book. Curt, thanks for being there for me. You are remarkably kind and patient. I love you, husband, classmate, and friend. Your dad, Carl, your mom, Dorothy, your sister, Jeannie, your children, Doug and Lynne, and their families, all mean a lot to me.

I also want to acknowledge my children, who are God's blessings to me. We have enjoyed good times and weathered storms together. They have God-given wisdom that has helped me travel areas that I may never have otherwise traveled. My grandchildren have also added grand joy to my life, as most grandparents would understand.

I would especially like to acknowledge:

Renee – thanks for your insightful timely phone calls and cards.

Rod – thanks for your faithfulness and protection through the years.

Robb – thanks for your perseverance in staying close in spite of widespread business matters.

Grandchildren – I love you all dearly. Rather than mention you individually, it seemed wise to thank you in this way. All of you are special to me. I challenge you to live your life doing God's will wholeheartedly. It is by far the most joyful and healthy way to live.

Thanks also to my publisher and editor, and to all involved in putting my notes into book form.

CONTENTS

PREFACE

This study was birthed many years ago, in the mid-1970s, when I heard a minister by the name of Malcolm Smith teach on the subject of blood covenant. Immediately, my spirit was stirred, and I embarked on a quest to learn more on my own. A few years later, when I was a student at Illinois Central College, a professor of creative writing took an interest in helping me compile and complete my original manuscript. He encouraged me to find a publisher who would work with me to get my manuscript into print.

I was finishing my second semester of an independent study in 1982 when my personal life endured strong winds. Without the principles I had learned through my study of covenant, my walk with the Lord would certainly have been unfruitful. But the mystery of the kingdom of God became progressively clearer to me as I weathered those storms.

Eventually, my manuscript was packed away as I moved about, caring for the changing needs of my family and other personal matters, but my notes continued to grow. When my husband suggested I begin work again on my manuscript, I welcomed the encouragement and resumed writing.

Death and life, war and peace, and appreciation of freedom became real to me at a very early age. My earliest childhood memories center around the absence of my father, due to his military service during World War II, and the tragic death of my younger brother, who was not quite two years old when he passed away. I was only three when Buddy fell and hit his head on my mother's rocking chair . . . and nothing seemed to be wrong until the next morning when he did not wake up.

This terrible loss, coupled with the devastating effects of the war, forever changed the course of my family's lives. But intertwined in those painful memories are others—of a little church in our small town, Fairview Church, where I first felt the stirring of faith in the Lord; of the angel who stood beside me as I regained consciousness after a dangerous fall; of the first time I attended a revival service as a young child and responded to an altar call—seeking the peace I was sure was waiting for me there.

Looking back through the years, I can see how God's love, grace, and mercy became progressively real to me. Even before I knew who He was, He was ministering to me and to my family, healing our wounds, providing for our needs, and lovingly guiding our feet onto the path of righteousness.

God has opened His arms and made provision for all mankind through the better covenant. His faithfulness to covenant is incomprehensively abundant. The better covenant too little understood and too often confused in most churches is still the bond of the God-kind of love extended to all. He loves each individual.

Covenant was my first in-depth study after being born again in 1975 and I first preached on covenant at Fairview Methodist Church in 1978. Since then I have been privileged to preach and teach covenant in a multitude of sermons and studies. Diverse backgrounds—Apostolic, Presbyterian, Christian, Baptist, Mennonite, Catholic, Lutheran, and Independents—have been receptive to the biblical clarification gained when covenant principles were brought forth. An understanding of covenant solidified and made more comprehensible many seemingly unrelated incidents in the Bible and more thoroughly defined the provisions and promises of both the Old and New Covenants.

This is a timely subject for today's Christian. Faced with a continuous barrage of assaults against the reliability of scripture, the Christian needs an overview of the Bible that unites, rather than isolates, Bible precepts. Prayerfully, this book will help regain the fervor of faith experienced by the first century believers. They had an understanding of scripture that enabled them to grasp quickly and effectively the teachings of the Holy Spirit as He ministered through those called into the ministry. I believe one reason they were able to comprehend the mysteries of Christ was because covenant principles were familiar to them.

Each day thousands are genuinely born again into the kingdom of God with a desire to know more about their Lord Jesus Christ. They desire to understand how it was possible for Adam's sin to affect all men, what made Abraham, Isaac, and Jacob so special, why God parted the waters when Joshua led Israel into Canaan, and precisely to whom and to what is God faithful. Clarification of these basic biblical principles is greatly needed by the majority of the Christian community.

I do not write as a theologian, rather as one who has seen the goodness of the Lord shown forth in His Everlasting Covenant recorded from Genesis through Revelation. The mystery of the faith and the value of a pure conscience became a reality to me. I struggled for a couple of years when I staggered and almost fell. What I learned of covenant helped me determine when I heard speakers and encountered oppositions what was of God and what was not. God kindly showed me to value what He said above all else. His loving-kindness was before me and I walked, with a lot of help from the Holy Ghost, in His truth. May God bless you as you read of the covenant principles set forth here.

INTRODUCTION

Many years have passed since I first began my study of covenant, and I have come to appreciate the phrase "the word of the Lord" infinitely more now than what it meant to me then. Not long after becoming born again and filled with the Holy Spirit of God, I had already read through the Bible once or twice and the Teacher had helped me understand where, and how often, I had missed the mark. He helped me to learn to enjoy Him. He had begun a good work in me. But when He began to show me how frequently *covenant* was referred to in His Word, I began studying in earnest. That study continues to this day and has led me to write this book.

Words have always been important to me. When I was a child, my Aunt Peggy had a big library-style dictionary full of word characteristics that was worthy of a big city library. When I would visit Aunt Peggy's home, her patience, excellent tea, and that big dictionary were my focus. Words intrigued me. One of my discoveries when searching that dictionary was the lengthy word "antidisestablishmentarianism." I was mesmerized at the time and that word is still stuck in my memory bank, even decades later.

Perhaps words have been a strong interest of mine because another part of my being is exceedingly inquisitive. Searching for where things belong is part of my nature, and words have always seemed like puzzle pieces that together make up a great, mysterious picture. What I didn't realize when I was younger was the critical influence of history in bringing that picture into focus.

I had given some attention to history, but it did not catch my interest fully until later in my life, when I began Bible training. It had always seemed to me that understanding history was equivalent to memorizing dates and events. But an excellent instructor at RHEMA Bible Training Center triggered my active interest when he said, "You cannot understand history until you understand church history." That put me on a history track and moving fast. The aggregate of past events, especially as related to World War II began to fit together for me like pieces of a large intricate puzzle. I stayed focused on the light at the end of the tunnel and kept moving.

I had long listened to the important men in my life—my dad, my two brothers, my two sons, and my husband—share their interest in history. But now the puzzling comments of my dad and uncles came alive for me. They had told stories of fighting for freedom while in the military; of Pearl Harbor, and of time spent in Germany and Japan. Then, with Bible-based dignity, they came home ready to resume homeland and family matters. The seriousness of their conversation stirred in me. I realized that what I had heard was not an issue of dates as much as a firsthand account of what would soon be looked back upon as a critical part of world history. History echoes individual voices.

Antidisestablishmentarianism came to my attention again recently and I understood why this particular word and its definition still intrigue me—it fits within an important place in history. "World history" has become more interesting to me than "word history." The history of words is not my strong point, though I certainly find tidbits interesting when I stumble upon them. But it has been inspiring to find my interest in words and history combining specifically in my covenant studies.

EFFECTIVE COMMUNICATION

Successful communication depends a great deal on the definitions of and placements of words. In this book, you may, if any of my dad's ability with word pictures resides within me, see where Bible puzzle pieces fit together. The perplexing abstract images that have come forth from thousands of transmissions of messages may begin to find their rightful place in your own attempt to put together Bible-related puzzles.

Before proceeding I want to pull from a very new dictionary for clarity on the word "concept." *Concept,* a noun, is an abstract idea; a general notion; a plan or intention; an idea or invention to help. *Conceive,* a verb, is to become pregnant with; to form or devise; to form a mental representation. But in a 1951 Thorndike Barnhart dictionary, the definitions place the emphasis a little differently. In the older version, *concept* is a general notion; an idea of a class of objects; an idea. *Conceive* is a form in the mind; to think up; imagine; to have an idea or feeling, to think; to put in words; express. Lastly, conceive is simply "to become pregnant." The modern age has messed with the old definitions and misconstrued too many basic principles.

Though definitions are helpful in understanding a concept, in our fast-moving worldwide attempt to communicate with one another, new words appear frequently and are difficult to keep track of. Old words are redefined to suit the concepts of a new age. Systems, languages, transmitters, and receivers are needful. Abilities are vast and specialists of every kind are critical. The digital system alone has various components, theories, and applications. Hearing and speaking the same language is not all that is required. Help from the Holy Spirit of God and His accurately translated written word are essential.

The systems, transmitters, and the receivers must be in sound operation for messages to be clearly relayed. Speaking the same language, as well as using excellent dictionaries and other study aids are important for clarity as members of the family of God transmit and receive the heart of God's Word. Components and applications each have multiple options. And so I have found the topic of covenant immensely diverse. Covenant covers a subject thousands of years old. Definitions and proven study aids were invaluable as covenant grew in importance for me. I have realized that going into the world requires following, hearing, and doing according to the Word of the Lord God Himself.

Dictionaries and reference aids will vary depending on the version and publisher and publication date. If my dictionary is older than yours, let my attempt to communicate be grasped by consulting an older dictionary. Though older may not always be better, it surely merits checking out where the gospel is concerned. Hopefully the reality of 1 Thessalonians 5:23 and Hebrews 4:12 will help you understand the effectiveness of the word of God. Let your spirit, soul, and body comprehend the sanctifying work of the God of peace. Ask the Lord for wisdom and dare to continue reading.

SPELLING VARIATIONS

The spelling of *beriyth* may change from time to time. The Hebrew word *beriyth*, which is translated covenant in the King James Version of the Bible, is alternately spelled *beriyt, berith*, *bereith*, or *bereeth*, depending on the references used. Quotes may include one of the variations but primarily the Hebrew word will be spelled *beriyth*, which means a "formal, solemn, and binding agreement: a written agreement or promise usually under seal between two or more parties."[1]

Covenant typifies God's abundant provision for man's salvation. The reality of covenant is a significant component in the world, both currently and historically, and its social significance around the world will be shown in the pages to come. Understanding covenant is especially vital for Christians, but important to all who long to know the truth. Together, let us begin the journey of discovery.

Chapter 1

THE CONCEPT OF COVENANT

The word *covenant* appears more than 370 times in the *King James Version* of the Bible. A blood covenant is the most solemn and binding of all the different types of covenants, which I believe will become progressively clear as we continue this study. This is because Jehovah Himself condescended to make a blood covenant with Abraham. (Genesis 15:18)

The dignity and seriousness of *beriyth* is illustrated by the solemn act of passing between pieces of flesh. The awfulness of taking a three-year-old heifer, she-goat, and ram, and a turtledove and a young pigeon sounds serious enough for me. Seldom have I heard sermons using Genesis 17:9-12. Serious, indeed, but dignified when the Lord credited Abraham's faith as righteousness. The dignity and seriousness of blood covenant will become clearer as we continue to explore the purpose and need for *beriyth* (Genesis 15:6-12; 17:2-21).

God promised to bless Abram with as many descendants as there were stars in the sky and to bless him with all the land he had been walking through. When Abram asked for proof God said, "'Take me an heifer of three years old, and a she goat of three years old, and a ram of three years old, and a turtledove, and a young pigeon.' And he took unto him all these, and divided them in the midst, and laid each piece one against another . . ." (Genesis 15:9-10).

It may not be easy to see the significance of what God was saying to Abram—especially when we are thousands of years and thousands of miles removed from the time and place of that covenant-making event. But as details are brought forth in later chapters the overall significance of this portion of scripture should become clearer.

What happened brought forth a nation that would eventually be divided. Kings would differ, fight, sometimes seek the Lord, and too often they went their own way. Covenant was still understood, but the peer pressure of surrounding nations led by kings seemed to them to be a better way. After all, then their leader could be seen and dismissed according to their own whims.

Generations after God made covenant with Abraham, God had Jeremiah declare judgment for transgressing covenant:

> *"And I will give the men that have transgressed my covenant, which have not performed the words of the covenant which they had made before me, when they cut the calf in twain, and passed between the parts thereof, the princes of Judah, and the princes of Jerusalem, the eunuchs, and the priests, and all the people of the land, which passed between the parts of the calf; I will even give them into the hand of their enemies, and into the hand of them that seek their life: and their dead bodies shall be for meat unto the fowls of the heaven, and to the beasts of the earth."*
>
> —Jeremiah 34:18-20

Abraham's descendants failed repeatedly to submit to covenant stipulations. The dignity, the seriousness, and the consequences of disregarding the stipulations of covenant were demonstrated and pronounced by Jeremiah and multiple other prophets in the Old Testament. According to *The Amplified Bible,* transgressors of covenant could expect to be made like the sacrificial animal if they were found to be disobedient to the covenant stipulation. The participators in covenant willingly and boldly declared, "if I break this agreement it will be done unto me as it has been done unto this animal." Thus a solemn agreement was made. This certainly testifies of the seriousness of the Covenant the Lord condescended to make with Abraham.

Those in Jesus' day typically read about Abram's covenant from the Septuagint. (Ruth 1:17; 1 Samuel 14:44; 20:13; 2 Samuel 19:13). The Septuagint was the Greek version of the Hebrew Scriptures. In the Septuagint, *beriyth* was translated *diatheke*, or the Greek word *rom* which was translated for covenant in the New Testament. In the King James Version of the New Testament, *diatheke* is alternately translated covenant and testament. Thus we have the Old Testament and the New Testament or the Old Covenant and the New Covenant. To study covenant is to study the Bible. To study the Old Testament is to study the Old Covenant and to study the New Testament is to study the New Covenant. Contained within the Old and New Covenants are the steps taken to make covenant, the mutual responsibilities of covenant partners is defined, and the blessings for obedience and the consequences for disobedience are unveiled. The Old Testament speaks of covenants between men as well as covenants between God and man.

TYPES OF COVENANTS

Blood covenants are the most solemn and binding of all covenants and will be the type primarily spoken of in this book unless otherwise indicated. There are equal and unequal covenants within the arena of blood covenants.

The covenants God made with Abraham, Moses, and David were unequal covenants. Indeed, except for the Better Covenant, all covenants between God and men are unequal. The covenant Ruth made with Naomi is an example of an equal covenant. An equal covenant is one in which both parties are able to contribute significantly to the well being of the other. An unequal covenant is one in which one party does all the giving. The Adamic Covenant contained a promise that would be the source of redemption for all men. God promised Adam a redeemer that would bruise the serpent's head, thus forming the Adamic covenant. Covenant, according to *Vine's Expository Dictionary,* is literally a coming together, "which signifies a mutual undertaking between two parties or more, each binding himself to fulfill obligations, it does not in itself contain the idea of joint obligation. . . ." Binding together could be done with an equal or an unequal covenant. There are several Bible examples of unequal covenants, some of which will be addressed later. Examples of unequal covenants are historically documented and confirmed by numerous archaeologists. They can serve to help me paint a more complete picture for you as we explore puzzling views of the scriptures. Perhaps those longing to know the truth will be able to see rather than just hear what is on my heart as I write.

HITTITE COVENANTS

In 1906, Hugo Winckler, a German archaeologist, began excavations in Asia Minor.1 Digging underneath a palace in the village of Boghazkoy he found approximately 10,000 clay tablets. Included in these tablets were some relatively intact remnants of equal and unequal covenants. These tablets came from the extensive Hittite Empire.

The Hittites were a nation that gave their name to the entire region of Syria. Their empire was founded around 1800 B.C. and collapsed around 1200 B.C. Hittites are frequently mentioned in the Bible from Genesis through the book of Nehemiah. They, like all the primitive societies, had an understanding of covenant and they used unequal covenants to govern their conquered countries and groups of peoples.

Archeologists discovered examples of equal and unequal covenants with variations. According to their specific needs and desires the covenantor and the conventee determined what the details would be. Most contained personalized preambles, stipulations (general and specific), blessings and curses, a list of witnesses. In unequal covenants suzerains ruled over their vassals, those whom they conquered.

A suzerain was a superior feudal lord, in an unequal covenant, to whom faithfulness was necessary. Fealty, or intense faithfulness, was required of a vassal, the conquered for whom an unequal covenant became one option. Another option was certain death unless mercy was shown by the usually unmerciful conqueror. Once the Hittites conquered an area, they would choose someone to serve them as a subordinate ruler in the conquered area. These subordinate rulers then became vassals after vowing homage and fealty. Subsequent protection from their lords became the privilege of the vassals.

The vassals ruled with a degree of freedom in an unequal covenant. They were, however, always accountable to their conquerors, their suzerain.[2] The Hittites laboriously recorded these covenant treaties on clay tablets. From these ancient covenants we gain insight into the typical forms of and obligations of covenants. A Hittite suzerain covenant commonly included a preamble, a historical prologue, stipulations, a list of witnesses, as well as a list of blessings and curses.

THE PREAMBLE

The preamble of the Hittite covenants began with the phrase *these are the words of* and was followed by identification of the suzerain. A typical identification would include the title, appellatives, and genealogies of the suzerain. The conqueror would be honored and glorified with sufficient adjectives and accompanying pomp to make him appear formidable. He certainly was to be feared. He had proven his power over the defenses of the captured group of peoples.

With the authority to use the *word of* the conqueror, the suzerain vassal or partner was granted the privilege in specified areas on the behalf of the suzerain. Within prearranged limitations specified in the stipulations of the covenant, the conquered ruled for the suzerain. As the vassal traveled about his appointed area he would herald and enforce the regulations, laws, taxes and military summons of the suzerain with whom he had a covenant. With delegated authority the vassal would declare the word of the area's conqueror. Those who heard the word of the suzerain had heard through the chosen, appointed representative and knew that disobedience meant retaliation. Usually that meant death.

In response to disobedience, the conqueror would send soldiers to reinforce the vassal's declaration of the suzerain's commands, or his word. The covenant partner of the vassal would be expected to enforce his word and be certain it was obeyed. The vassal was the authority in residence, part of the occupying army, backed by the power of the conqueror and his army, his mighty forces.

Approximately 1280 B.C., a covenant, or treaty, was made between the Hittites and Egyptians. Though this seems to have been an example of an equal covenant, the preamble followed the typical pattern of covenants and treaties. The preamble of that treaty, as translated by John A. Wilson, seems a rather comical read today but surely would have been a causal agent for covenant faithfulness.

> The regulations which the Great Prince of Hatti, Hattusilis, the powerful, the son of Mursilis, the Great Prince of Hatti, the powerful, the son of the son of Suppi . . . the powerful, made upon a table of silver for User-maat-Re, the great ruler of Egypt, the powerful, the son of Men-maat-Re, the great ruler of Egypt,

> the powerful, the son of Men-pheti-Re, the great ruler of Egypt, the powerful; the good regulations of peace and of brotherhood, giving peace . . . forever.[3]

Reading this portion of the preamble one realizes that the Prince of Hatti and the ruler of Egypt were powerful, at least in their portion of the world system. Familiarity with the mighty attributes of the Prince of Hatti and the ruler of Egypt discouraged approach and attacks by their mutual enemies. Covenant between Egypt and Hatti was prompted by a common threat from the "Peoples of the Sea" and provided a united defense against the violent raiders. The foe was a confederate host, including Shirdanu, Philistines, Achaeans, and Danaana. They had entered into a covenant also.[4] The preamble of the covenant between the Prince of Hatti and the Ruler of Egypt, when finished, was followed by a historical prologue.

Whether the covenant was equal or unequal, the steps were similar. The prologue and the stipulations may have varied somewhat, but were primarily the same. In a historical prologue a lengthy description of previous relationships between the participants was given. Many of the Hittite covenants were unequal and between a conquering suzerain and conquered vassal. The acts of benevolence by the suzerain would be emphasized.[5] The conqueror would remind the vassal and even reminisce about how he had conquered and befriended his covenant partner. The suzerain would recall how he had promised to establish the vassal in a ruling position of authority. All who would read and hear the covenant would be reminded that the suzerain had fought off opposition so that the vassal could be established as a subordinate ruler. A detailed account of defense maneuvers, for the sake of the vassal, would be recorded. All would be made aware that the conqueror and the conquered were acting as a single unit for the successful rule of the designated area. The suzerain and the vassal had an unbreakable agreement. They had a covenant relationship. After a lengthy historical prologue the covenant would include the stipulations.

STIPULATIONS

The stipulations were the obligations of the vassal as defined by the suzerain. The conditions and requirements of the covenant, a legal document, were specified.[6] Included in the stipulations were the promises of the suzerain. The promises varied, but they usually included a promise of defense and aid. Though the contents of the Hittite covenants varied, they frequently contained instruction to befriend the suzerain's friends and be an enemy to his enemies. Included was an admonishment to *hate whom I hate* and *love whom I love*.

Covenant stipulations included the military obligations of both the vassal and the suzerain. In an equal covenant between Haullusites, the Prince of Hatti and Ramses II of Egypt, the stipulation included being a loyal ally:[7]

> If an evil rumor originates in the Hatti land that someone is to rise in revolt to the Sun and you hear of it, leave with your foot soldiers and your charioteers and go immediately to the aid of the king of the Hatti land![8]

Covenant partners were required to be swift in responding to appeals for military aid. They were to answer any military summons and to engage wholeheartedly in military campaigns commanded by the suzerain. It was forbidden for a vassal to enter into alliances with other kings. He was admonished not to murmur against the suzerain. The vassal also was expected to trust the suzerain to honor his word and to believe what the suzerain said in spite of appearances to the contrary. The stipulations included instruction for the deposit and public reading of the treaty.

WITNESSES

Hittite covenants included a long list of witnesses. The people who had been in attendance when the covenant was made, were listed as witnesses. The Hittite gods were called upon to witness the making of the covenant and their names were carefully recorded. Then all the natural elements were beseeched to witness the covenant. In the treaty between Hattusillis and Ramses II, the mountains, the rivers, the springs, the great Sea, heaven and earth, the winds and the clouds were called on to witness the treaty. When the witnesses had been recorded, a list of blessings and curses was made.

BLESSINGS AND CURSES

Blessings were the just reward of one obedient to the covenant terms. Curses were the just penalty of disobedience. The witnesses were expected to be instrumental in carrying out the blessings and curses depending on the obedience or disobedience of the covenant partners. In the Hattusilis and Ramses II Covenant, the gods were called on to be witnesses:

> The words of the treaty and the oath that are inscribed on this tablet—should Duppi-Tessub not honor these words of the treaty and the oath, may the gods of the oath destroy Duppi-Tessub together with his person, his wife, his son, his grandson, his house, his land, and together with everything that he owns.
>
> But if Duppi-Tessub honors these words of the treaty and the oath that are inscribed on this tablet, may these gods of the oath protect him together with his person his wife, his son, his grandson, his house and his country.[9]

With the blessings and curses listed, the written portion of the covenant was completed. Hittite vassal treaties were given final validity by being recorded.[10] The recorded covenant was then deposited, according to the stipulations, in the sanctuary of the gods who had been called upon to witness the covenant. Periodically, as previously agreed upon, the covenant was taken from the sanctuary and read aloud, usually one to four times each year,[11] as a reminder to everyone involved that a solemn agreement had been made.

The Hittites painstakingly recorded their covenants. Thousands of those covenants have been translated by scholars and are available for study at libraries around the world. Those translations confirm the antiquity and universality of covenant.

> Modern excavations have produced treaty documents and agreements of many kinds written on stone or baked clay tablets from sites reaching from Babylonia . . . to Asia Minor, Palestine and Egypt, and extending in time from the third millennium B.C. to the middle of the eighth century B.C.[12]

The Hittites, Egyptians, Hebrews, Greeks, and Romans were just some of the civilizations that made covenants, individually as well as nationally.

GREEK COVENANTS

Greeks called a covenant partner a "guest-friend."[13] A guest-friendship, a covenant bond, extended for generations afterwards. The duties of their bond included giving of valuable parting gifts when one was a guest in the other's home. It included taking of an oath. An oath was deemed by the Greeks to possess a sacred binding force.[14] If such an oath was broken, it would bring dire vengeance on violators.[15] They vowed in the presence of witnesses and their god or goddess to be faithful, hospitable, and protective to their guest-friend.

ROMAN COVENANTS

To the Romans a covenant was referred to as a *bona fide*, *bona* meaning "good," and *fide* meaning "faith." A promise made in good faith without fraud or deception was a covenant between individuals or groups. To *fide jussion* was to confirm by promise. It was an act of being bound as surety for another.[16] It was a covenant, a solemn agreement.

> Rome, in truth, conceived fides to be the underlying basis of all international relationships, and public conduct. Sometimes the bona fides was expressly guaranteed by a special clause or stipulation, reinforced by a solemn oath; more frequently it was implicit. The violation of the oath was universally considered a deliberate offence against the gods themselves, who exacted vengeance by pursuing to destruction not only the malefactor, but also his family, deemed to be tainted with his perfidy; it was likewise an offence against human law. All races of antiquity recognized bona fides to be an indispensable attribute of private, of public, and of international dealings, indeed, of all conceivable transactions.[17]

The Romans had great respect for the oath, which kept their faith in their embassies and magistracies intact.[18] During Rome's early period, *bona fides* were a fundamental principle of their international transactions, which served as a guide for public officers and for ambassadors.[19] *Bona fides* were also an indispensable condition in the case of a treaty or armistice.[20] But in the later part of their reign, the Roman people began placing less confidence in their *bona fides* as officers, ambassadors, and others in positions of authority began choosing not to keep their word—thus violating their oaths. This undermining of the principle of "good faith," or covenant, in their society played a big role in the fall of the Roman empire, for they had become untrustworthy to all.

Nonetheless, the concept of covenant, known in the Roman Empire as well as throughout societies in every other part of the world, continued. According to research done by H. Clay Trumbull,[21] the American Indians, African tribes, European and Asian groups were still making blood covenants in the mid-1800's. His research blanketed the world—data was drawn from Africa, India, China, Borneo, Germany, Western Europe, and North and South America. It was his conclusion that blood covenant is the closest and most sacred type of covenant. He gave evidence that proved traces of blood covenant can be found on every continent. He also noted that even untrustworthy fellows, who in other agreements might be untrue, were trustworthy when bound by a blood covenant because of its sacredness.[22]

STANLEY AND LIVINGSTON IN AFRICA

In 1869 H.M. Stanley was given the assignment of finding David Livingstone, a famous explorer and missionary to Africa. Livingston was thought by many to have died during his work there, and James Gordon Bennett, founder and owner of *The New York Herald*, gave his journalist, Stanley, the job of finding out whether or not Livingston was still living. In the process of finding Livingston, Stanley discovered that many tribes in Africa still cut covenant. Stanley, like Livingston, soon became familiar with the covenant-making procedures of the African tribes they dealt with. Both of these men cut covenant with representatives from different tribes throughout Africa.

A large portion of their success in Africa can be attributed to the fact that they had an understanding of covenant. Because of the solemn binding of blood covenant, neither Stanley nor Livingstone ever knew it to be broken. Indeed, if one was to break covenant, his own near relatives would actively seek his death.[23] E.W. Kenyon said:

> "The vilest enemies become trusted friends as soon as the covenant is cut. No man takes advantage of the covenant or breaks it. It is so sacred that the children to the third and fourth generations revere it and keep it. In other words, it is a perpetual covenant, indissoluble, a covenant that cannot be annulled."[24]

Stanley became acutely aware of the effective bonding of covenant as he interacted with the natives along the Congo river. He left Zanzibar to explore the African Congo in 1874 and found the villages along the banks of the river mysteriously deserted. Evidence indicated the occupants had hastily retreated just before Stanley's arrival. Their fear of his party was understandable, for slave traders frequented that portion of the Congo, and they had instilled terror and hate. The fact that Stanley was a peaceful and generous traveler was an enigma to the villagers. They just didn't get it. After more than a week of passing vacant villages, as they progressed deep into the heart of Africa, war drums began resonating from the dense jungle foliage.

Throughout the day the drums beat out the location of Stanley's party to the natives stationed along the river. Cautiously Stanley and his men continued their winding course along the Congo. Suddenly shouts resounded from every tree, hill, village, and bay along the river, when unexpectedly a " . . . huge canoe with more than sixty paddles dashed out of one of the bays."[25] With the clarity of a commanding officer, Stanley instructed his men to fire their guns. They were to sink the canoe but they were to avoid, if possible, injuring the natives. The gunshots capsized the canoe. During the subsequent plunge, one was killed. But most of the warriors, with diminishing aggression, hastened for the banks of the river and disappeared among the trees. Stanley's men helped several of the terrified natives aboard Stanley's canoe.

With these living witnesses of Stanley's honorable intentions, peace negotiations with the natives began. The prisoners were made to stand upright in the boats as Stanley's party continued traveling along the

Congo. Their outstretched arms were covered with Stanley's peace offerings of precious beaded necklaces so that all the natives could see the desirability of negotiating with the strangers.

While considering Stanley's intentions, the natives silenced the war drums. The jungle again became mute. Cautiously, Stanley drew close to a deserted bank, chose some perfect necklaces and flung them on the sand. Hastily and fearfully a woman ran out, grabbed the beads and with equal haste fled back into the foliage of the jungle. "Yet, according to the unwritten code of native habits, this meant peace. The presents had been accepted."[26] Within a few minutes the formerly deserted bank was crowded with men, women, and children excitedly receiving their own personal gifts. The hostilities were forgotten. Stanley knew however that " . . . all this would be good-for-nothing if the ceremony of blood brotherhood were not performed to make the new friendship sacred and everlasting."[27]

With solemn dignified seriousness, Stanley and the chief came together to negotiate a covenant. The Bible says a lot about solemn assembly and solemn feasts. Could it be serious-mindedness exists only as a byline for the scornful? Does it only come forth in the ranks of thieves? Is it only a part of gang initializations? Have we reached a point where we are completely void of understanding? If Jesus was laughed to scorn before he raised the young girl from the dead, let today's scornful be warned. God is alive and well and His better covenant is everlasting.

The Lord knows the way of the righteous. Where does that leave the scornful insisting on remaining impudent? Sophistication may be the downfall of many, but Stanley did not allow that to deter him. (Exodus 23:1; Numbers 10:10, 15:3; Psalm 1:1-6, 2:1-12, 92:3).

> The medicine man came . . . he cleared the bush of evil spirits that might spoil the ritual; thereafter he made an incision in the

> arm of each of the future brothers and smeared some blood from one wound into the other. Now they were brothers, bound to help and protect each other, and woe to whichever broke this pact![28]

The covenant was then celebrated with palm wine and plenty of food. Now Stanley and his party were welcomed guests of the very people that had, just the day before, tried to kill them. Faithfulness originates with God and is often found in unusual ranks.

Before Stanley left his covenant partner's village, the chief sent ahead a message of the peaceful intentions of his blood brother. For many months after the covenant was made Stanley continued his journey along the Congo River. He was always welcomed. Villagers received him because he was a blood brother of the chief with whom Stanley had made covenant. This was the first of more than fifty covenants that Stanley cut with African tribes. He made so many blood covenants that his arms were sore from the many incisions.[29]

In 1882, while building a road along the Congo River, Stanley took up a sledgehammer to teach the natives how to use it. Stanley showed them how strong the blow should be and how to strike from the right angle. Stanley's finesse with a sledgehammer was astounding to the Africans who began respectfully calling Stanley "Bula Mataribulla" meaning "breaker of rocks."[30]

Because of covenant relationship, Stanley's name lived on long after his death. With love and respect those who had known his covenant faithfulness often remembered and even sang about him. Even decades afterward Bula Matari was affectionately remembered. The natives would often soothe the baby elephants separated from their mothers for training.

> *Sleep, my brother, do not cry.*
> *Sun went down, moon rides the sky.*

Dream now of juicy papayas.
Eat bananas, grow and play,
That you be strong and one fine day
Can work for Bula Matari.[31]

COVENANT – A UNIVERSAL CONCEPT

Blood covenanting is a universal concept that is a vestige of God's original revelation to Adam. The Adamic covenant is a common heritage of all men who have not yet received the provisions made by the Second Adam. Though covenants are called by different names, they retain many common characteristics.

Throughout the world, covenants have been negotiated, promises made, gifts and names exchanged, and sacrifices made. Incisions were usually made in the covenanters so that their blood could be drawn, mixed together, and then consumed. The scar from the incision was a token of the covenant that had been made. Typically blessings and curses were proclaimed, memorials were established, and wine and bread or a meal were shared, witnesses were called upon, and covenant oaths were taken. The result was a binding, solemn agreement. To break covenant meant death for the transgressor. Though covenants universally have contained most of these elements, not all covenants contained all of them. The type of covenant made varied with the need and the degree of commitment one was willing to make. Blood covenant demanded complete commitment.

BLOOD COVENANT REMNANTS

Today's societies still retain remnants of blood covenant. In the United States one of the remnants of blood covenants can be seen in the institution of marriage. All marriages begin when two people realize they have a desire to have a more involved relationship. They begin to discuss (negotiate) and make plans to wed. Promises and provisions are made. The wedding ceremony is scheduled and witnesses are called. Vows are exchanged in this modern version of a blood covenant, for a lifelong commitment. Marriage, likewise, requires total consecration. Memorials are established when wedding rings are exchanged. The binding force of an endless covenant is symbolized by the exchanging of wedding rings. The wedding ring is a remnant of the marriage covenant ceremony.

> Among the Copts of Egypt, both the blood and the ring have their part in the covenant of marriage. Two rings are employed, one for the bride and one for the bridegroom. At the door of the bridegroom's house, as the bride approaches it, a lamb or a sheep is slaughtered; and the bride must . . . step over the covenanting-blood as she enters the door, to join the bridegroom. It is after this ceremony, that the two contracting parties exchange the rings, which are as the tokens of the covenant of blood.[32]

Because the wedding ring is a covenant-token, many people will not remove their rings while their marriage covenant is unbroken.[33] In the marriage ceremony wine is frequently drunk with the right arms of the couple intertwined so that each drinks out of the other's wine goblet. In our society the wedding cake and wedding banquet is a remnant of the covenanting memorial meal. A meal that is symbolic of giving nourishment and provision to one's covenant partner. Marriage is the most intact, but not the only, blood covenant remnant still present in modern society.

TAKING AN OATH

Another of today's blood covenant remnants is the practice of raising a hand in court and solemnly declaring "I swear to tell the truth, so help me God." This remnant comes from the days when the cut of covenant was made, frequently in the hand or wrist, and the hand was raised toward heaven with a declaration before the covenant witnesses that the covenanter would keep the promise made. Included in that ritual was the understanding that if something other than the truth was spoken the witnesses had authority to recompense the lie. As the hand was lifted, blood from the cut would drip down the arm, usually into a goblet, to be consumed by the other party in the covenant agreement. "The universal custom of lifting up the arm to God in a solemn oath was a suggestion of swearing by one's blood . . . as in the inviolable covenant of sacred friendship."[34]

SHAKING HANDS

In addition to the covenant remnants of the marriage ceremony and the swearing in at court there is the covenant remnant of hand shaking. Handshaking comes from the days when the hand or wrist was cut and the hands clasped to mix the blood, thus making a blood covenant.

> So simple a matter as the clasping of hands in token of covenant fidelity is explicable, in its universality, only as a vestige of the primitive custom of joining pierced hands in the covenant of blood-friendship. Hand clasping is not, by any means, a universal, nor is it even the commonest, mode of friendly and fraternal salutation . . . But, even where hand clasping is unknown in salutation, it is recognized as a symbol of the closest friendship. Thus, for example, among tribes of North American Indians where nose rubbing is the mode of salutations, there is, in their

widely diffused sign language, the sign of clasped, or interlocked hands, as indicative of friendship and union.[35]

OTHER REMNANTS

There are a multitude of other remnants of blood covenants in our present sophisticated society. Some of those remnants include terminology as well as acts. Phrases such as "I give you my word," "he promised," "sign your name in blood," "he is the head of . . . ," "I pledge allegiance," and "he joined" are just a few covenant-related terms which are still current. Some of them are as ancient as time and surely will continue into eternity in some form or another. (Acts 7:5; Hebrews 6:13,16; James 5:12; Genesis 9:16, 17:7,13,19; Leviticus 19:12; Ezekiel 37:26).

Phrases and words are often tossed about with little to no thought. Many do not know how to be a faithful friend. Promises are made flippantly and often too little effort is put into faithfully following through on one's word. Children and adults have heard so many empty promises and have heard the counsel of the ungodly so often, they consequently can become scornful themselves. (Mark 9:42-47).

To break one's promise is equivalent to breaking covenant. It is appropriate—even necessary—to consider the word of the Lord. It is vitally important to study, read in context and amen the Lord's word, His covenant. Arrogance and inattentiveness is unbecoming to everyone. When the word of the everlasting, better covenant is preached or read it is wise to let your ears hear. (Matthew 18:7; Luke 6:38-39; Romans 1:24-25; 1 Corinthians 9:12; 2 Thessalonians 2:2; Psalm 1:1-6; Hosea 5:15; 6:1-7).

There are so many remnants of blood covenant ingrained in societies around the world. It is to our advantage to strive for a clearer understanding of the principles involved. In the Old and New Testaments, it was God who initiated covenant. To accurately clarify blood covenant it is needful that we go back to the beginning of His Word.

Chapter 2

A BIBLICAL VIEW

When I was a young girl, Bible reading was not part of my home life. I don't recall whether or not we even had a Bible when I was a child. Now, however, after years of reading the panoramic Alpha and Omega Bible view of life, it is by far my preferred book.

I was born in a backwoods area of Cape County, Missouri. My parents' families attended Fairview Methodist Church primarily and Baptist churches secondarily. Both Mom and Dad's families were kind and loving and I was free to be a child. The puzzle pieces of the adult world were not part of my world yet.

My thoughts were more inclined toward simple matters—like how to step on the rocks to cross the creek on my walk to school. Some of the rocks were slippery. Some tops were more rounded. Having lost my assignment papers in the creek once, I learned which stones to avoid. I walked the mile to a cousin's home and we continued from there across a field in front of Fairview Methodist Church to another cousin's home. Together we zigzagged our way to school, which was three miles from my home. It was a joy to talk and play on the way to school. Every home was welcoming.

Dad and three uncles had returned home after World War II and we were in an upbeat time and place. Fairview Church was our social center and it was a fun place to go. Weekly services and ice cream socials were a bit of heaven on earth. Fairview was the place where news spread. Attention was given to those in need. The elderly growing feeble, weddings being planned, babies being born, the new pastor coming in was news. The more troublesome national and international events were primarily kept in the circle of older family and friends conversing in the yard.

My beginnings in that rural setting was the foundation from which a longing for truth and the things of God never stopped growing. "What is truth?" is a big question for most people. It seems there are too many puzzle pieces stored in pockets and file cabinets than are properly placed. When I was born again, began reading my Bible, and was soon filled with the Holy Spirit; pieces began to come together. I saw the life of God in the scriptures. I began to habitually fellowship with Him. When I studied covenant, the puzzling "whys" were continually answered as I read, studied, and prayed.

THE ORIGINS OF COVENANT

Beginning with the book of Genesis, several covenants are alluded to even within the first three chapters. One was a covenant made within the triune Godhead, Elohim. Another was the Edenic covenant made between Elohim and sinless Adam. The marriage covenant between Adam and the woman Eve was still another example. The covenant with death began when Adam transgressed the Edenic covenant. Still another covenant spoken of in the first three chapters of Genesis is the Adamic covenant. That solemn agreement involved a promise made by Elohim to sinful Adam. The Adamic covenant was prompted by God's loving-kindness for Adam, in spite of Adam's sinfulness. God conceived covenant principles.

ELOHIM

In the beginning God . . . I have heard it said that if you will not believe the first four words in the Bible, it's questionable whether you will believe anything else written afterwards. *Those that come to God must believe that he is, and that he rewards those that diligently seek him.* God did not call and anoint men to write the Bible to prove He existed. He wrote it for the edification of the ones who believe He exists. The Bible is written for believers not for unbelievers. Belief in God is a matter of faith. (Genesis 1:1)

Do you believe, want to believe, or have never heard who God is? Any number of questions can be a first step toward finding answers. Let your will direct you as you search to find His will. *In the beginning* is the place attention can be directed to find answers in His written word. It is a matter of taking God at His Word and adding your own desire to know truth. Begin your search for truth with questions and you will come to know *in the beginning God.* There, in the Holy Scriptures, is where insight is gained into His covenant, holiness, righteousness, truth, grace, and mercy. In Genesis God began to place a record so that men could discern what is of God and what is not. But the marvels of God's characteristics cannot be comprehended without faith and diligent searching His Word with the help of His Spirit. (John 1:14; 8:32; 14:6; 16:13; 18:38; 7:16-17)

The Bible is for the one who knows that *in the beginning God* or for the one who at least is willing to come to inquire of the Lord. Those who diligently seek the Lord are rewarded by means of His Spirit, His Covenant. His Everlasting Covenant has been activated by His mercy and great grace. (Genesis 1:1; 6:8; 7:5; 9:8-17)

> The first reference to God in Scripture uses the name Elohim: "In the beginning God [Elohim] created . . ." (Gen. 1:1). This name for God is a reference to the supreme Being, the original

> Creator, the perfect Being, the eternal One. Just as most religions describe their divinities in terms of ultimate power (i.e., God), Elohim focuses on several aspects of power, strength or creativity.
>
> Elohim appears 31 times in the first chapter of Genesis, because there His creative power is emphasized. "God saw" (1:4), "God called" (v. 5), "God said" (v. 6), "God made" (v. 7), "God blessed" (v. 22) and "God created man in his own image" (v. 27).[36]

Currently fundamental Christian doctrines and teachings are more extensive than can be adequately explained here. The teachings do include elements concerning creation, salvation, grace, mercy, and every word used to try to explain the goodness of God. World religions branch from the basic principles of covenant the Lord Himself set forth. Though partially retained and polluted by sin, covenant concepts are evident around the world.

The Christian Bible makes covenant comprehensible. Its basic principles are expounded upon in Genesis through Revelation. Few, if any, fundamental Christian doctrines are seen in textbooks on world religions. The pollution of sin has been even worse than Agent Orange. That fact is very real to me. When I made Jesus Lord of my life, my world religion books became nothing more than clutter to me. At their worst, they tempted me to disregard the written Word of God. After being born again I longed to know my Lord Jesus Christ better. The Word of God, Genesis through Revelation, became as a cool breeze on a hot day as I began and continued reading my Bible.

Like sprigs, wild trees, and tares, false doctrines have sprouted in the midst of a lot of churches. Sprouts and weeds become like animated leeches sapping essential nourishment from the plants and trees Adam was to have tended. Adam's strength was sapped away by disobedience. The ground became as rocky soil covered with thistles. Like Adam, we have followed suit. Leaning on our own understanding we try to build without the necessary elements.

The Word of God is the right seed and prepares the heart to be good soil. Separated from the vine, more harm than good is done when lives are not properly prepared, weeded, and pruned. Fundamental doctrines in truly Christian churches include the teaching that God created the world. Assurance of basics, however, is often twisted. Many teach basic doctrines with a twist designed to indulge some erroneous tradition. Believers are to follow the Second Adam not the First Adam. (Matthew 13:3-10; 15:1-14; Mark 4:3-9, 24; Luke 8:4-8, 18)

I hope to show that Jesus Christ is the son of the Creator and is indeed God in the flesh, without falling into any doctrinal rut. Dr. Vic Reasoner said, in an artfully constructed way, many have "pushed their tray through the theological cafeteria, accepting a helping of whatever sounded good." I do not want to walk on that path. Like the new believers at Berea to whom Paul and Silas preached, I have received the Word of the Lord with all readiness of mind, and searched the scriptures daily to discern what is of God and what is not. My study of covenant helped me place puzzle pieces in the right place and the goodness of the LORD became clear to me. (John 7:16-17; Acts 17:11)

Let your heart rejoice, receive the word with readiness of mind. But go on afterwards to seek the Lord in His written Word daily, not just periodically to prove or disprove what has been written in my compilation of notes. Seek Him with your whole heart. Choose Christian books that are scripturally sound and continue to follow Jesus. I have heard it said that lambs follow the sheep but sheep follow their shepherd. Following Jesus takes some maturity. Begin to feed on meat so you can continue to grow. (1 Corinthians 3:2; Philippians 4:8; Hebrews 5:12; 6:13-14; 1 Peter 2:2; Revelation 22:6-7)

Trying to avoid a rut may be as childish as playing around a slippery, muddy creek bank and hoping you don't fall into the green, polluted, slimy pond below. The pond filled with sticky green algae is a picture of the morally repulsive practices of supposed gods. Sin, like dung, pollutes and degrades and is certainly not worth bathing in. False gods lead to that type of degradation. (Exodus 20:22-25)

The one true almighty God has a perfect and eternal plan established. With light-heartedness, I shall run where God has placed me and continue telling what I have seen. His mercies are new every morning. I have grown and seen the goodness of the Lord. I have seen His righteousness in fresh, new ways for years. I have even seen His judgments. He is altogether awesome. (Matthew 28:8; John 12:48; Acts 13:46; 1 Corinthians 9:24-27; Galatians 2:2; 5:7; Philippians 2:16; Hebrews 12:1-3; 1 Peter 4:4-6; Revelation 7:17; 14:2, 7; 21:1-8; 22:1-3)

One of the primary Christian doctrines is the mystery of godliness. God became manifest in the flesh and named Jesus. He was justified in the Spirit, seen of angels. His doctrine, His gospel, though often misaligned, has been preached to the Gentiles, believed on in the world. He was caught up into glory after His resurrection. How glorious it is to know His Word and have the privilege of fellowshipping with His Spirit. How joyful to know of the Lamb's book of life which is also a doctrine historically taught in most Christian churches. (John 10:10; 17:9; 1 Timothy 3:16; 5:24-25; 6:12, 20-21)

When received, the Scriptures can begin to clarify how to clear rubble from one's garden. Of course if not acted upon, the rubble continues to accumulate and the weeds continue to grow. The written Word of God reveals the historical roots of the Christian faith. They show the way to even dig up deep-rooted, choking roots of bitterness. Accounts of godly men and women are given and illustrate examples that can be followed as we baby-step our way into maturity. Then we are able to walk surefooted with the Lord of lords and King of kings.

> Dr. Everett Ferguson, Professor of Church History, wrote that Irenaeus saw covenants as the way in which God progressively revealed his will to men, as they were ready to receive it. Irenaeus, a man sorting through doctrines in 177 A.D., wrote to counteract Gnostic ideas common in Lyons.[37]

I am content to let God judge the matter. He is the One I trust and follow. As Lord He is well able to give me discernment and I will continue to follow Him according to what He continues to show me in His word. If Iranaeus, my historical example, does not seem to fit the puzzle, I trust the Lord will give wisdom to determine where that puzzle piece actually fits. But covenant includes, as far as I have been able to discern, an excellent way to pull together the puzzle pieces found in Genesis through Revelation. (John 3:3,7; Hebrews 11:6; 1 Peter 1:23)

Theologians do often differ on secondary matters but most seem to strive to stay the course with an accurate compass, the written Word of God. The history of the Church and the history of the Bible comes down to believing God is whom He says He is. He is and always has been well able to direct men, His own creation. He is not a puppeteer, but does work with those who desire to do His will. He gives the needed illumination to know what is of God and what is not. (John 7:17 AMP; Ephesians 4:7-12)

Be aware that principle as used here is not as the principle of equivalence, the principle of relativity, nor is it an accounting principle. It is a basic principle from which truths are derived. It is fundamental to all else. It is the bedrock in construction. It is not a bitter principle when rightly applied. It is a first principle, the very elementary stage of any subject. Though in some areas of principle all may agree, but in detail many split. Man is limited to an indeterminacy principle, which is superseded, and is elementary to the Lord. It is truth to the Lord. His truth is immeasurable. For all that matters to mankind the beginning of all elementary stages of any subject needs to start with Genesis.

> Elohim may be said to express the general idea of greatness and glory. In the name Jehovah, as we shall see more fully, are represented those high moral attributes of God which are displayed only to rational creatures. The name Elohim, however, contains the idea of creative and governing power, of omnipotence and sovereignty. This is clearly indicated by the fact that from Genesis 1:1 to 2:4 the word Elohim alone is used, and that thirty-five times. It is the Elohim who by his mighty power creates the vast universe; who says, and it is done; who brings into being what was not; by whose word the worlds were framed so that things which are seen were not made of the things which do appear (Heb. 11:3). It is this Elohim with whose Greek equivalent Paul confronts the philosophers on Mars' hill saying that He made the world (cosmos) and all things, and by this very fact is constituted possessor and ruler of heaven and earth; whose presence cannot be confined by space; whose power doesn't need man's aid, for through His great will and power and agency all things and nations have their very being.
>
> It is most appropriate that by this name God should reveal Himself—bringing cosmos out of chaos, light out of darkness, habitation out of desolation, and life in His image.[38]

Elohim in making covenant with Abraham, because there is none greater than Elohim, swore by Himself. That was God's guarantee to Abraham. God's Word cannot be changed. His promises are unchangeable, though often conditional.

A conditional promise given is dependent on the receptivity of the receiver. An unconditional promise will come to pass no matter what the receiver may or may not believe, may or may not willingly submit to. Today marriage proposals are dependent on a yes. The sunrise and sunset is not dependent on a receiver. It is a natural law. Natural law operates whether you believe it or not.

Aeronautical Engineers have learned to work with the natural laws of aerodynamics. They know if the engine stops the plane drops. Our willingness to do or not to do does not determine sunrise or sunset. Our will is simply involved in whether we will enjoy or dismiss. Rejoice or complain. Receive or reject. Spiritual principles, indeed spiritual laws, are misunderstood more often than not. Conditional promises are not unconditional. Unconditional promises are not conditional. Making assumptions is foolish when God's word is available to read and study.

Enoch and Noah escaped the coming judgments of their days by walking with God. How were they able to disregard the wickedness continually surrounding them? They met the conditions, or God's stipulations, that were required of them. They walked with God, meaning they habitually fellowshipped with Him. In Enoch's case the supernatural law superseded the natural law. And Enoch was caught away. Elohim initiated covenant with Noah, who found favor as he walked with God. He preached righteousness until the flood came. God's righteousness was more real and powerful to Enoch and Noah than all the evil surrounding them.

The Hebrew word Elohim is a plural noun, according to Finis Dake.[39] The one Elohim then is three persons in total covenant agreement. They are one. *God Elohim said, Let us Father, Son, and Holy Spirit.* I am more inclined to consider we are spirit, have a soul and live in a body along the insights Paul wrote of. We will explore more along that line in a later chapter. (1 Thessalonians 5:23; Genesis 1:26 AMP)

In this way the Amplified Bible shows the plurality of Elohim. It may be said Elohim is not one in number only, but one in unity. He ". . . is not a divided Deity, but three persons in 'one God,' or one Deity."[40] If indeed any can comprehend the magnitude, majesty, and complexity of God, the preceding attempt is as good as any. We know with certainty our God is One. How we explain it will probably be inadequate no matter how hard we try. I have found in my years of study that God indeed is one God. We can all "go figure" on that.

Theologians have written volumes on Theology. My few pages need not be disregarded if they do not fit your preferred doctrine. Consider God is not a divided Deity. Elohim is the name used to define the Trinity by which they represent themselves under obligation of oath to perform certain conditions.[41] Go knowing He is who He says He is. He does what He says He will do. He is all powerful, all knowing, all *and so much more than any of us can imagine*. He is as He describes Himself. Elohim covenanted within Himself to create man in God's own image. It is not uncommon for a person to promise themselves they will do something. God promised—covenanted—even before man was created.

In regard to the first covenant:

> *And God said, Let us make man in our image, after our likeness: and let them have dominion over the fish of the sea, and over the fowl of the air, and over the cattle, and over all the earth, and over every creeping thing that creepeth upon the earth.*
>
> —Genesis 1:26

The stipulations of the first covenant included God's intentions, purposes, and vision for Adam. God covenanted within Himself to create man as one with whom He could fellowship and govern the remaining creation. Understood is the covenant guarantee of the fulfillment of that original intention in spite of hindrances. The mighty, strong, prominent, great, and glorious Elohim guarantees His work. Adam was God's workmanship and the finished work would be perfect. Hindrances may cause a delay but not a cessation of God's plan. God created man and proceeded to make covenant with him.

EDENIC COVENANT

The very first covenant is recorded in Genesis, when God covenanted with Himself to create man and to give him dominion over the remainder of creation. Dominion comes from the Hebrew word *radah* meaning "to rule, tread down.[42] In the first covenant, man was designated a ruler with duties to perform. So God created man and proceeded to make a covenant with him.

> Colossians 1:16 tells us that by Him or in Him were all things created. But creation is the act of the Elohim. Therefore, Christ is in the Elohim or Godhead. Then even in Genesis 1:3 we read that the spirit of the Elohim moved or brooded over the face of the waters. The entire creation animate and inanimate, was, then, not only the work of the Elohim, but the object of a covenant within the Elohim guaranteeing its redemption and perpetuation. It is quite clear that the Elohim is a plurality in unity. So, Dr. Parkhurst continues: "Accordingly Jehovah is at the beginning of creation called Elohim, which implies that the divine persons had sworn when they created. *cf.* Parkhurst, Hebrew Lexicon, See Elohim."[43]

The second covenant spoken of in Genesis was the covenant Elohim made with the sinless man Adam. In the stipulations of the Edenic Covenant, Adam was to be fruitful, multiply, replenish, subdue, have dominion over the fish, the fowl, the cattle, and all the earth. Adam was as a subordinate ruler under God in the Edenic Covenant. (Genesis 1:26 AMP)

STIPULATIONS

Be fruitful. Before Elohim covenanted with Adam he had set in motion a spiritual law that would be effective throughout eternity. God initiated the law of sowing and reaping. "And God said, Let the earth bring forth grass, the herb yielding seed, and the fruit tree yielding fruit after his kind, whose seed is in itself, upon the earth: and it was so," (Genesis 1:11).

The stipulations of the Edenic Covenant included Adam's commission to yield fruit after his kind. The seed of reproduction was within Adam. He was to bring forth children that would be like Adam. Children that would be in the likeness of God and who like Adam, would be blessed. "And God blessed them, and God said unto them, Be fruitful, and multiply, and replenish the earth, and subdue it: and have dominion over the fish of the sea, and over the fowl of the air, and over every living thing that moveth upon the earth," (Genesis 1:28).

The law of sowing and reaping, initiated in the Elohimic Covenant carried into the Edenic covenant and eventually into the Adamic covenant. Being fruitful via sowing and reaping includes much more than can be discussed here. Briefly, however, the principle of sowing and reaping is planting seeds, tending to the area on which the seed has been planted, giving the seed time to grow, and reaping the harvest. Sowing and reaping is a spiritual principle as well as a physical principle.

In the New Testament, Jesus spoke of the word of God as a seed that when planted and cared for would bring forth a bountiful harvest. He also said, "the words that I speak unto you, they are spirit, and they are life. Adam's commission to be fruitful included speaking and acting on God's word, which included naming the things God had created. Adam was to be fruitful and bring forth a bountiful harvest in every area of his life. This commission to be fruitful was given to Adam as well as to all the descendants he would have. (Mark 4:14-20; John 6:63; 1 Corinthians 3:6-9)

Multiply. To multiply means to increase in multiples or to augment.[44] To augment something is to adequately develop it and to cause it to be greater, more numerous, and more intense.[45] Thus Adam was to tend to God's creation so that it would increase and become adequately developed. As Adam increased, his descendants were to take up the assignments of the covenant head and to do their part in causing God's creation to increase and become adequately developed.

Fellowship with God on a daily basis alone facilitates. He is good. Adam was not telling God anything new as they fellowshipped. Adam himself was increasing, multiplying his own talents as he fellowshipped with God. His assignment was manageable, though immense.

Adam was the covenant head of the Edenic covenant. It was with the first Adam God made covenant. The future descendants of Adam were in his loins when Adam was created and commissioned. Thus Adam and Eve's children for all generations were destined to share their assignment and responsibilities. Because of covenant, Adam's decisions and actions affected them. It was God's plan that all the generations following Adam and Eve would, like them, be actively involved in replenishing and subduing the earth. Adam was responsible for bringing forth overcomers like himself, overcomers that would promote adequate development of God's creation. Thus Adam was commissioned to "be fruitful, and multiply, and replenish the earth," (Genesis 1:28).

Replenish. Adam's assignment to *replenish the earth* implies the earth had previously been plenished, filled up. Though the scriptures are not very clear on the issue of the earth being previously plenished, there are hints that this was the case. In the first covenant with man, God alluded to a formerly populated earth. The questions that arise from God's declaration that Adam was to be fruitful, multiply, and replenish the earth and subdue it and have dominion are still baffling. There are, however, some hints as to the cause of the chaos described. (Genesis 1:1-2,28)

Some contend that before Adam was created, Satan's influence was already on the earth. The angels are created beings. Lucifer was one of the most beautiful of God's pre-Adamic creations. Some of God's angels proved themselves faithless to the assignment God had given them, and chief of these disobedient angels was Lucifer. Lucifer is, throughout the scriptures, alternately called the devil, Satan, Prince of this World, Prince of the Air, Serpent, and Dragon. Reverend Finis Jennings Dake said there was an administration of angels over the earth before man was created.[46] When one third of the angels headed by Lucifer were found polluting the earth with their pride and sin, a pre-Noahic flood swept across the earth. Thus *the world was without form and void; and darkness was upon the face of the deep*. (Matthew 4:1; Mark 1:13; John 14:30; Ephesians 2:2; Revelation 12:9; Genesis 1:2; Ezekiel 28:13-17)

Angels are spirits who are created with freedom of choice. They were created to serve. Their service is to God and to man. The angels that have remained faithful to God are "sent forth to minister for them who shall be heirs of salvation," (Hebrews 1:14).

> In the Scriptures, both of the Old Test. and of the New, one of that host of heavenly spirits (angels) that, according alike to Jewish and Christian opinion, angels wait, upon the monarch of the universe, and are sent by him to earth, now to execute his purposes. (Matthew 4:6,11; 28:2; Mark 1:13; Luke 16:22, 22:23; . . . They are subject not only to God but also to Christ (Hebrews 1; 1 Peter 3:22; Ephesians 1:21; Galatians 14:14) who is described as hereafter to return to judgment surrounded by a multitude of them as servants and attendants: Matthew 13:41,49, 16:27, 24:31, 25:31; 2 Thessalonians 1:7; Jude 14. Single angels have the charge of separate elements; as fire, Revelation 14:18; waters, Revelation 16:5, 7:1; John 5.

> In John 1:51(52) angels are employed, by a beautiful image borrowed from Genesis 28:12, to represent the divine power that will aid Jesus in the discharge of his Messianic office, and the signal proofs to appear in his history of a divine superintendence. Certain of the angels have proved faithless to the trust committed to them by God, and have given themselves up to sin, Jude 6; 2 Peter 1:1-4 (Genesis 6:2), and now obey the devil, Matthew 25:41; Revelation 12:7, 1 Corinthians 6:3.[47]

Angels seem to have command of different elements and areas. They tend to be territorial, including the ones who chose to follow the devil. Even before the creation of man the angels were given assignments to perform.

> John tells us that 'the devil sinneth from the beginning' (1 John 3:8), and the Old Testament references to him bear this out. Most of our information, however, comes from the New Testament, where the supremely evil being is referred to as Satan or as 'the devil' (ho diabolos) indifferently, with Beelzebub (or Beelzeboul, or Beezeboul) also employed on occasion (Matthew 10:25, 12:24,27). Other expressions, such as 'the prince of this world' (John 14:30) or 'the prince of the power of the air' (Ephesians 2:2), also occur. He is always depicted as hostile to God, and as working to overthrow the purposes of God.
>
> The witness of the New Testament is clear. Satan is a malignant reality, always hostile to God and to God's people. But he has already been defeated in Christ's life and death and resurrection. And this defeat will become obvious and complete in the end of the age.[48]

Satan's attempted ascendance is spoken of in Isaiah. Lucifer had said in his heart he would ascend and exalt his throne above the stars of God. He wanted to be like the Most High. He has been a bitter loser. He has never and will never come close to the power of God. Since he is a liar, you will never hear that from him. Actually it would be to your advantage to never hear him on any matter. The devil has taken revenge by shaking kingdoms and making the world as a wilderness, destroying cities, and imprisoning people. Isaiah saw the destructive results of Adam's transgression. The covenant with death keeps multitudes in prisons trembling in fear or parading in pride. (1 John 3:8; Isaiah 14:12-18)

Lucifer's thwarted attempt at ascendancy may have transpired before man's creation. Supposedly this was the reason "the earth was without form, and void; and darkness was upon the face of the deep," (Genesis 1:2). The creation of man according to biblical chronology, was about 4000 B.C., but the creation of the universe may have been countless ages earlier.[49] Adam's creation from the dust of the earth gave him legal rights that were verified and empowered in the Edenic covenant. Adam, the subordinate ruler of the Edenic covenant, was to do his part as God's legal representative to replenish the earth. To replenish means *to fill or build up again*, to fill with inspiration or power," "to fill with persons or animals."[50] (Genesis 1:1-2)

Subdue. Adam was to *replenish the earth, and subdue it*. Subdue means to conquer, bring into bondage, to force, to bring into subjection.[51] Adam was to nullify Satan's negative effect on this earth. It was Satan and his influence on the earth that Adam and his descendents were to subdue via the authority vested them in the Edenic covenant. Satan's deceptions were to be disclosed by faith in the truthfulness of God. His destructiveness was to be conquered and replaced with constructiveness.

There was much to be done to fulfill God's command to subdue. Adam had a clear understanding of the stipulations, but understanding the deceptive practices of Satan may have been another matter. Adam was able to rend Satan harmless and ineffective and stand victorious against *the wiles of the devil.* The skills, the authority, the qualification to deal wisely belonged to Adam. He was not to heed the lies of God's enemy. Because of covenant Adam was to hate Satan as God hated him. When insinuations against God were uttered, Adam was to immediately recall and pronounce the truth. He was to subdue the liar in defense of his covenant partner. Adam was to refrain from giving heed to the liar.

As early as 1280 B.C., archaeological finds show it was commonly understood in covenants that covenant partners were forbidden to enter into alliances with others.[52] To disregard the stipulations pronounced by God was to fall from covenant-related fellowship. From that fellowship flowed an abundant supply of all Adam would need. The tree of the knowledge of good and evil in no way ever compared to the best of God. God is good, the creator of good. The liar adulterates everything that is good and scams the gullible with temptations to doubt God. Adam failed to exercise his authority over the devil. Adam and Eve signed over their legal rights to the devil. The devil's corrupted version of good held no comparison to the daily walk Adam had with God. God is good. The devil is evil. (John 10:10; Ephesians 6:11; 1 Timothy 2:14; Genesis 1:28)

Have Dominion. In addition to subduing, Adam was to rule God's creation. He was to guide, with legal authority, in a way directed determined by God. He was to exercise authority submitted to the Creator of all that was good. He was to decide and make declarations about the assignment given him. He was able to name all the animals, which was a major task accomplished. He was to keep in check any non-negotiable rules. Adam was to have dominion.

> The chaos has been effectively restrained, and order prevails; the world is furnished and populated, and mankind has been brought into being to maintain God's created order.[53]

Adam was created to have dominion. He was responsible for maintaining God's order. Dominion is "supreme authority" and "absolute ownership." Adam was created just a little lower than Elohim. (Genesis 1:31-2:1; Psalm 8:3-6)

> *When I view and consider Your heavens, the work of Your fingers, the moon and the stars, which You have ordained and established, what is man that You are mindful of him, and the son of [earthborn] man that You care for him? Yet You have made him but a little lower than God [or heavenly beings], and You have crowned him with glory and honor. You made him to have dominion over the works of Your hands; You have put all things under his feet.*
>
> —Psalm 8:3-6 AMP

Adam was qualified to have dominion of God's creation. The first Adam, the son of God, was certainly qualified. He was the vassal in a covenant with God and was to govern the earth as Elohim's second-in-command. He was to master and rule over all God's creation. He was to have authority and ownership—he was to have dominion. (Luke 3:38)

TYPE OF COVENANT

The Old Testament contains many covenant illustrations. There are numerous examples of covenants between men, and between God and men. Blood covenant examples are numerous and there are covenant examples in which no blood was shed. There was no need for blood to be shed in the Edenic covenant. Adam had been created without sin. Until the day he disobeyed God and ate of the tree of the knowledge of good and evil Adam was sinless. Being sinless, it was possible for Adam to walk in agreement with God. Covenant was possible between a righteous Adam and a righteous God. The Edenic Covenant was the only covenant recorded in the Bible between God and man that had no need for shed blood. *Without the shedding of blood there is no remission of sin.* After Adam's transgression, sin had to be dealt with via a sacrifice to enable man to walk in covenant with God. During the Edenic covenant, however, it was possible for Adam to enjoy an intimate fellowship with God, for he had a semi-equal, bloodless covenant that required only faithfulness. (Hebrews 9:22)

FAITHFULNESS REQUIRED

Faithfulness was essential in this first covenant God made with man, as with all subsequent covenants. Faithfulness to one's covenant partner is a common denominator in secular and biblical covenants. Adam was to faithfully obey the word of His covenant partner. Elohim, likewise, was to faithfully obey the covenant terms.

> *And the LORD God took the man, and put him into the garden of Eden to dress it and to keep it. And the LORD God commanded the man, saying, Of every tree of the garden thou mayest freely eat: But of the tree of the knowledge of good and evil, thou shalt not eat of it: for in the day that thou eatest thereof thou shalt surely die.*
>
> —Genesis 2:15-17

Adam agreed to tend to the garden, guarding and keeping it. He transgressed that covenant when he ate of the tree of the knowledge of good and evil. The penalty for transgression had been clearly stated by God, *thou shalt surely die*. Was death imponderable to Adam? In fellowship time with the Lord, would Adam have heard of the angelic hosts and the probable earlier fall from heaven of Lucifer? Perhaps that would have been a lesson he would learn experientially a little later. That question of fact, Lucifer's fall, has been disputed. (Genesis 2:17; Isaiah 14:12)

PENALTY OF TRANSGRESSION

The transgression of covenant resulted in death, physically and spiritually, for Adam. He immediately died spiritually and eventually he died physically. Reverend Finis Jennings Dake believed the angels were governing the earth before man's creation.[54] This, he contended, gave rhyme and reason for the planting of the trees of life and of the knowledge of good and evil in the Garden of Eden. Those trees were representative of two covenants of which Adam had a choice. One tree was a memorial of the covenant of life; the other tree was a memorial of the covenant of death.

God had clearly declared the consequences of breaking covenant to Adam. By choosing to eat of the tree of the knowledge of good and of evil, Adam handed over the authority God had given Adam to Satan. *Adam knowingly transgressed covenant*, and as Hosea says, *dealt treacherously against God.* (Isaiah 28:15-18; Hosea 6:7 AMP)

Even a fall down a flight of steps can be challenging to comprehend, though one hears of some account. One man fell down some steps and wound up hospitalized. He had been drinking and did not carefully watch where he was going. His recollection was clouded with alcohol and brain damage. His body was impaired, but thankfully not paralyzed. He did not know what happened. He simply knew he could not get around well anymore. He did know he wanted another drink.

That was his request of me when I visited him in the hospital. I did not understand from his report how awful the results of that fall were. The specialists sure knew better than I what he would be dealing with. They could perhaps intellectually have made some skilled guesstimate. But was it possible for them comprehend the moment-by-moment consequences faced for years thereafter by the one who had fallen?

Adam and Eve immediately experienced the bitter fruit of covenant transgression. Though the penalty for breaking covenant was not fully realized, it reverberated throughout Adam's being and through all the generations to come.

EDENIC MEMORIAL NEVER ESTABLISHED

Adam, made in the image of God, of necessity was a spirit being. He was animated, energetic, active, and well-intended for communication with his creator. Like his creator, Adam had a soul. He had decision-making, expression in speech. He lived in a body. With his soul Adam made a decision that caused his spirit to die or to be separated from God. Adam had access to a covenant of life but he chose instead a covenant with death. Adam failed to keep the stipulations. The only semi-equal, bloodless covenant between God and man was not completed. (1 Thessalonians 5:23; Zechariah 12:1)

Having transgressed covenant, Adam's dead spirit began to program his body to die. It took 930 years for Adam to die physically. During those 930 years, Adam's soul was continuously deteriorating. Physical death came earlier for each subsequent generation after Adam because sin became increasingly rampant. Transgression of covenant resulted in death for Adam and his descendants. Abel was slain by his brother Cain. His spirit died immediately. His body and soul learned to die from his spirit and 930 years elapsed before his body succumbed. God had not created Adam to die. Adam disobeyed and rebelled, and consequently had chosen death. (Genesis 5:5)

ADAM'S DESCENDANTS

The covenant God made with Adam affected all of Adam's unborn children, for they were in him when the covenant was originally made with Elohim. Likewise they were in Adam when he transgressed that covenant. Adam had been instructed to multiply and fill the earth and his children in turn inherited that command. The assignment God gave Adam to be fruitful, multiply, replenish, subdue, and have dominion was not withdrawn because of Adam's disobedience. Adam's willing disobedience, however, caused his assignment to become perverted with sin. Adam's children were affected.

The two people who actively make covenant are called the covenant heads. A covenant affects the covenant heads as well as all their unborn children. Descendants reap the consequences of covenant transgressions. The unborn children are considered to be part of the covenant heads when covenant is made. All mankind was nestled in Adam's loins when he transgressed his covenant with Elohim. When that solemn and binding agreement was broken they were immediately and dramatically affected. Because all mankind was in the loins of Adam when he sinned, the consequences of breaking covenant affected Adam and all of his unborn seed. Death, not life, was their inheritance.

COVENANT WITH DEATH

Covenant originated with God. The stipulations given to Adam were no longer binding when Adam made a covenant with death. When Adam transgressed covenant with God, he made an agreement or covenant with Satan. Because of Adam's shifted allegiance, Satan became a partner with Adam and the covenant of death was born, having the very character of death within Adam, Eve, and their forthcoming generations. Cain and Abel were to realize in a traumatic way the awful consequence of the covenant that had been broken.

Authority originally given Adam was transferred to Satan. The covenant with death caused what was Adam's to become Satan's and what was Satan's to become Adam's. Adam had forfeited his kinship to Satan and Satan gave to Adam his own servitude and guilty verdict.

When Adam, by his disobedience, replaced his covenant partner Elohim with Satan, he gave Satan *dominion over the fish of the sea, and over the fowl of the air, and over every living thing that moved upon the earth.* It was then that Satan became the *god of this world.* (John 3:17-18; 2 Corinthians 3:4-8; 4:3-5 AMP; Genesis 1:28; 4:1-9, 13; Hosea 6:7 AMP)

Elohim had sufficient legal reason to annihilate Adam the transgressor. A covenant with God, however, was not just a legal instrument. It was a kinship of love. Satan was not prepared for God's display of love. Angels and men were created and were to follow different rules. They had different legal rights granted by their creator. Because of God's loving kindness, He promised destruction for Satan and a redeemer for Adam. A redeemer that would legitimately recover for Adam's descendants the authority, dominion, and righteousness Satan had gained.

ADAMIC COVENANT

God's love prompted him to promise a deliverer for Adam, and his unborn seed—a deliverer to redeem them from the curse of the broken Edenic covenant.

> By man's deliberate transgression, the Edenic Covenant became null and void. Man was without God and without hope. God gave him a new covenant. This agreement was made with Adam and Eve after the Fall, and before the expulsion from the Garden of Eden. It ushered in the Age of Conscience in place of the Age of Innocence.[55]

Though the scriptures do not clearly give the covenant making steps involved in the Adamic covenant, it does offer us some clues.

CONFERENCE AND CONFRONTATION

When Adam transferred his allegiance from God to Satan, God quickly initiated corrective provisions. God, as the plaintiff in this legal action, called Adam for a conference. Compassionately God called out, *Adam, where are you*? In this way the first step toward making the Adamic covenant was made. Adam and the woman (she was not called Eve until after the pronouncement of the curse) had already realized their mistake and had attempted remedial action. The Bible says that "the eyes of them both were opened, and they knew that they were naked; and they sewed fig leaves together, and made themselves aprons," (Genesis 3:7). They understood clearly now that their choice had separated them from God and had left them without a provider. (Genesis 3:7-9,20)

Their new covenant partner, Satan, was a destroyer, not a provider. Now they were isolated from the source of all that was good. Their walks in the cool of the day with Elohim were over. A dreadful gap replaced the peace and joy they had known as they fellowshipped with their beloved Lord God. Adam and the woman had missed the mark of the high calling of God—they had sinned. The despondency they felt was only the initial wave that swept all mankind. Those waves would intensify in the upcoming generations. (Philippians 3:14)

Adam and the woman were not previously ignorant of good, but evil was something they had not known until they transgressed their covenant with God. Now that their eyes were open to evil, peace was gone. Adam had broken covenant with Elohim. He was no longer there to fellowship with, to advise, to cover them. They vainly sewed fig leaves together to cover their nakedness. Preceding their transgression Adam had been covered with God's righteousness, which was part of God's covenant provision.

Sewing fig leaves together for a covering was motivated by a spiritual, rather than a physical need. Their eyes were opened to the alarming reality of the covenant of death. When their eyes were opened to evil, they gained knowledge of evil and knew they were naked, or separated from God. The knowledge of evil caused them to be blinded to the things of God. *Their eyes were prevented from perceiving and they did not know him as they had before. They had fallen from favor.* Thousands of years later disciples walked along the road to Emmaus and did not know Jesus. Adam immediately feared the voice of the Lord after his transgression. Adam and Eve had followed the voice of a stranger and a price was to be paid. (Luke 24:16; John 10:10; Genesis 3:7)

When Adam heard God's merciful call to him in the garden, *Adam and his wife hid themselves from the presence of the Lord God.* They were afraid. Covenant had been engraved on man's heart at creation.[56] The consequence of transgressing covenant was known to Adam. Hesitance to face the inevitable result of his fall prompted Adam to hide from God. But with God persistently calling, Adam emerged from hiding and hastily presented an inadequate defense. Adam attempted to transfer the blame partially to God and partially to the woman.

For "the man said, the woman whom you gave to be with me, she gave me of the tree, and I ate," (Genesis 3:12). "It was your fault for giving me this woman who tempted me to eat," was what Adam was saying between the lines. This attempt to shift the blame included an insinuation that God's creation, especially of the woman, was less than *good.* Since Adam had realigned his loyalty, he had become one with his new covenant partner and the pride that had been found in Satan was now possessed by Adam. That pride was displayed when he blamed God and the woman for Adam's own blunder.

Adam refused to admit that he was at fault. God had clearly proclaimed that Adam was to have dominion or supreme authority. Adam had failed to take authority over the serpent, thereby he failed in his covenant obligation. He had neglected to exercise his God-given authority. The wiles of the devil used the serpent to tempt the woman. She in turn tempted Adam. Adam had transgressed the Edenic covenant. Pride, Adam's new companion, hampered his repentance. (Genesis 3:8,12)

A companion is a friend in the company of another, a comrade with, a fellow traveler. Satan and pride were one and the same and pride became companion to all men in some fashion when Adam fell. One man said, "if I were truly humble I would be proud of my humility." That is stinking thinking born in the dung-laden nest of pride. Satanic pride began to motivate Adam. He began to assert himself, to argue and struggle against God. The nature of man digressed. Strife replaced the peace that had previously governed Adam. Now Adam was dominated in the covenant with death rather than led in the covenant with life. Dominated by sin he attributed to himself the honor due to God alone. Pride is an arrogant deep-rooted disorder, which can grow to narcissism. By realigning his allegiance Adam's nature had become akin to Satan's. Entering into covenant with Death, Adam had become as one with God's adversary.

> The emphasis placed on pride, and its converse humility, is a distinctive feature of biblical religion, unparalleled in other religious or ethical systems. Rebellious pride, which refuses to depend on God and be subject to Him, but attributes to self the honour due to Him, figures as the very root and essence of sin.
>
> We may say with Aquinas that pride was first revealed when Lucifer attempted to set his throne on high in proud independence of God (Isaiah 14:12-14). The fallen devil (Luke 10:18) instilled the craving to be as gods into Adam and Eve (Genesis 3:5), with the result that man's entire nature was infected with pride through the fall (cf. Romans 1:21-23). 'Haughtiness', gobah, appears as a root cause of atheism in Psalm 10:4.[57]

Like an epidemic, pride passed from generation to generation. Its loud, boastful presence is still universally prominent.

> *The wicked, through the pride of his countenance, will not seek after God: God is not in all his thoughts. His mouth is full of cursing and deceit and fraud: under his tongue is mischief and vanity.*
>
> —Psalm 10:4,7

Thus with mischief and vanity, Adam denied his guilt in the transgression of covenant. Adam's persistent pride served to further widen the gap between himself and God. God was compelled to address the transgression.

The fruit of the trespass was the natural outcome of the sowing and reaping principle God had activated during the creation. Adam had sown seeds of disobedience and rebellion. The harvest reaped was separation from God and the curse that was originally intended for Satan. God was grieved because of Adam's sin but He could not, without compromising His own righteousness, fail to address the issue.

And the Lord God said to the serpent, to the woman, and to Adam, *because thou hast done this*. In this way God began pronouncing his judgment. Covenant transgression to the offenders would be a curse. Adam and the woman previously had access to Jehovah Elohim's protection and provision in their assignment to *subdue and have dominion*. Having joined Satan's camp, however, they had forfeited God's protection and provision and were without defense against Satan's lies. They would seek truth, but the liar would twist as a serpent and crush life more often than not. Bondages would hinder them individually and collectively as their ranks grew and condemnations intensified. The serpent, the woman, and Adam were each actively involved in the transgression, thus they all had a price to pay. (Genesis 1:26; 3:14)

THE SERPENT / SATAN

And the LORD God said unto the serpent, Because thou hast done this, thou art cursed above all cattle, and above every beast of the field; upon thy belly shalt thou go, and dust shalt thou eat all the days of thy life: and I will put enmity between thee and the woman, and between thy seed and her seed; it shall bruise thy head, and thou shalt bruise his heel.

—Genesis 3:14-15

The serpent, having served as the willing vehicle for the temptation, was the first to hear his verdict and was condemned to crawl on his belly forever. The repeated physical crushing of the serpent would be an example of the eventual spiritual crushing of Satan. Because of his part in the trespass, the serpent would forever be a symbol of deceit. Periodically in the forthcoming generations the serpent was worshiped for his deceptiveness.[58] The serpent, Satan's instrument, was condemned to slither in the dust, to be trampled and to become a symbol of humiliation and condemnation.[59] The curse for the serpent contained a warning that eventually and unexpectedly there would be one who would have the authority to permanently render Satan harmless and ineffective. Indirectly the serpent's curse offered a ray of hope to Adam and the woman and to the remainder of God's creation.

Genesis 3:15 is widely acknowledged as a verse that prophecies the coming of Jesus the Christ, who was the only one capable of redeeming man from the covenant of death. The allegiance recently transferred to Satan would again be reversed; God would sovereignly effect reconciliation with Himself.[60] God's promise that the head of the serpent was to be crushed pointed forward to the coming of Messiah and guaranteed victory. This assurance fell upon the ears of God's earliest creatures as a blessed hope of redemption.[61]

THE WOMAN

Unto the woman he said, I will greatly multiply thy sorrow and thy conception; in sorrow thou shalt bring forth children; and thy desire shall be to thy husband, and he shall rule over thee.

—Genesis 3:16

The woman was told childbearing would become painful and sorrowful. It seems God had intended this to be a painless and an encompassing joyful experience. Sin altered that. Lust entered the scene, which resulted in a rapid succession of conceptions. Multiple pregnancies often shortened the lives of women. The pain that accompanied the procedure was often horrendous. That was not God's intention. They had fallen and became so entangled in their sins they often forgot they had even fallen. Adam and the woman had altered God's plan for Man. Things would not again be in focus, as God intended them, until the covenant with death had been annulled. (Isaiah 28:14-18)

Part of the woman's curse was that her desire would be to her husband and that he would rule over her. Her place of helpmate would become rare. Childbearing would be painful. She would too often suffer abuse. Sin caused many men to be as brutal dictators in the marriage relationship. Women were often found guilty of beating and murdering their husbands also. The marriage covenant that God had intended to be equal and peaceful often became instead a stressful, violent, and twisted union.

Adam and the woman entered into a marriage covenant prior to the transgression of the Edenic covenant. Even today, when a man and a woman enter a marriage covenant *the two become one*. God had designed man and woman to function creatively and equally united with love and respect and mutual adherence to God's stipulations. They were to share covenant assignments, goals, and love for God. (Genesis 2:24; Malachi 2:14)

Before sin entered the nature of the woman, her love was first toward God and then toward Adam. Desire and lust replaced love when sin entered their lives. No longer could they know fully a love that was kind and free of envy, jealousy, boastfulness, conceit, pride, rudeness, self-seeking, and resentfulness. The relationship between man and woman would become victim to lustful desire and the exception would be rare. (1 Corinthians 13:4-8 AMP)

> In Hebrew psychology the whole personality was involved in desire. Hence 'desire' could easily become 'covetousness,' leading to 'envy' and 'jealousy,' etc.[62]

The curse of sorrow in childbearing and desire for a husband who would rule was the bitter outcome of disregarding the Edenic covenant stipulations. Covenant had been broken and the curse was the automatic consequence. God completed his declaration to Eve and began speaking to Adam.

ADAM

> *And unto Adam he said, Because thou hast hearkened unto the voice of thy wife, and hast eaten of the tree, of which I commanded thee, saying, Thou shalt not eat of it: cursed is the ground for thy sake; in sorrow shalt thou eat of it all the days of thy life; thorns also and thistles shall it bring forth to thee; and thou shalt eat the herb of the field; in the sweat of thy face shalt thou eat bread, till thou return unto the ground; for out of it wast thou taken: for dust thou art, and unto dust shalt thou return.*
>
> —Genesis 3:17-19

In the Edenic covenant Adam had been commissioned to tend to the soil and claim back the things contaminated by Lucifer's fall before the creation. Adam's sin earned him hard labor among fields filled with thorns and thistles. His work now would be difficult and long. He would wipe muddy sweat off his brow as he toiled to supply food for his family. Each day would be anxious labor for something better—anxious labor that would only end when Adam died. His body would be returned to the dust from which he had been taken. During the creation of man the ground entered into his composition. (Genesis 1:2; 26-29; 3:19)

> *To dust you shall return.* Because the ground entered into the composition of man (*cf.* 2:7), the curse on the ground became a power unto death, working in his very members (*cf.* Nu. 5:16ff.). Death, formerly present in nature in subservience to man, would now terrorize man the covenant-breaker as the wages of his sin.[63]

The Edenic commission included naming *every living creature.* Though he had transgressed the Edenic covenant and was in the process of entering the Adamic covenant, Adam's commission to name *every living creature* did not cease. Remembering God's promise of a redeemer, Adam named his wife *Eve, the mother of all living.* From Eve would come the one who would buy back what had been given away. It was this promise that kept hope alive in every subsequent generation. Everyone, from Adam to Jesus, was encouraged by the promise of one who would provide a solution for the destructive sin nature of man. (Genesis 2:19-20)

LOVING-KINDNESS

God's love for his creation prompted him to go beyond what anyone could have thought possible. Legally, God had no obligation to save man out of the hell each had willingly chosen. But God is so much more than legalities. Law is called in when men push boundaries and choose to steal, kill, destroy what is good. Law is about guidelines but when general rules are broken specific laws are brought out. Breaking general rules at one level often leads to daring the system at another level. Warnings often lead to tickets, tickets add up to court time, and the slide downward continues—as the news around the world testifies. (Romans 1:18-32; 3:19-20)

The entire history of Yahweh's covenantal relationship with Israel can be summarized in terms of *chesed*, which is Hebrew for loving-kindness. It is the one permanent element in the flux of covenantal history. Even the Creation is the result of God's *chesed.*[64] Loving-kindness also contains the meaning of interaction, strength, and steadfastness, as well as love. The word *love* by itself does not adequately define *chesed.* For love, apart from interaction, strength, and steadfastness can become sentimentalized or universalized apart from the covenant. Yet 'strength' or 'steadfastness' suggests only the fulfillment of a legal or other obligation.[65]

Chesed is much more than legality. God's loving-kindness caused him to go beyond what was necessary. His very nature was displayed in covenantal loving-kindness toward Adam and Eve when He promised a redeemer. God's mercy and loving-kindness is spoken of repeatedly throughout the Bible, always with a covenant connotation. Covenant *chesed* implies "the goal and end of all salvation-history."[66]

SACRIFICE

Adam and Eve had attempted, inadequately, to clothe themselves. God, prompted by love, clothed them more adequately. Removing from them their own robes, he placed on them coats of skins. The coats of skins used to clothe Adam and Eve imply an animal sacrifice. The Edenic covenant had not needed shed blood. Now, however, for a covenant to be made between righteous Jehovah Elohim and unrighteous Adam and Eve, their unrighteousness had to be legally dealt with. Thus blood became a necessary requirement in covenant. The penalty for unrighteousness was death. With the death of a substitute, God gave Adam temporary respite from sin. Because of a substitutionary sacrifice, covenant with God was again possible.

This covenant was different from the first covenant in many ways. The Adamic covenant was an unequal, unconditional, and solemn agreement, which was consummated by blood. The Edenic covenant had been a semi-equal, conditional, bloodless, solemn agreement. Even with a sacrifice, because of sin, Adam was incapable of having an equal covenant. But God had unconditionally promised a redeemer. Whether Adam chose to believe God's promise or not, the realization of that promise would come to pass. If, however, Adam and his descendants chose to believe God's promises they would be walking in faith—thereby gaining God's blessings.

The shedding of blood for the remission of sin was necessary for the completion of the Adamic covenant. A sacrifice was required. (Hebrews 9:22)

> The Lord . . . clothed them. This remedy for the obstacle to Adam and Eve's approach to God . . . symbolized God's purpose to restore men to fellowship with Him. Implied in God's provision is an act of animal sacrifice; what is explicit, however, is not the sacrificial mode, but remedial result.[67]

Spiritually, covenant is a garment—a covering and a shield. This truth has been symbolically demonstrated throughout history, as covenant-making universally included giving one's garment to the new covenant partner. This represented giving one's own provisions for the benefit of the covenant partner. Covenant and garments are linked in Ezekiel when God speaks of Israel and says:

Now when I passed by thee, and looked upon thee, behold, thy time was the time of love; and I spread my skirt over thee, and covered thy nakedness: yea, I sware unto thee, and entered into a covenant with thee, saith the Lord GOD, and thou becamest mine.

—Ezekiel 16:8

The Adamic covenant was made, and man's covering provided for, when a substitutionary sacrifice was made. Adam and Eve had doubted God's word and sinned when they ate of the tree of the knowledge of good and evil. Now, because of the Adamic covenant, it was possible for them to regain some of the ground that had been lost by choosing to believe what God said.

"And I will put enmity between thee and the woman, and between thy seed and her seed; it shall bruise thy head, and thou shalt bruise his heel," (Genesis 3:15). The promise of the Adamic covenant and of the Elohimic covenant was the basis of every subsequent covenant that God condescended to make with man. Choosing to believe the Adamic covenant promise of God was the means of salvation. Consequently, from Adam till today, faith in the promised Messiah Jesus has provided salvation.

MARRIAGE COVENANT

And the LORD God caused a deep sleep to fall upon Adam, and he slept: and he took one of his ribs, and closed up the flesh instead thereof; and the rib, which the LORD God had taken from man, made he a woman, and brought her unto the man. And Adam said, This is now bone of my bones, and flesh of my flesh: she shall be called Woman, because she was taken out of Man. Therefore shall a man leave his father and his mother, and shall cleave unto his wife: and they shall be one flesh.

—Genesis 2:21-24

God had covenanted within himself, and with sinless Adam. Adam, following God's example entered into a covenant with the woman God had given him. In regard to the deep sleep that fell upon Adam, *The New Bible Commentary* says, "the deep sleep was not so much an anesthetic for the man as a veil about the woman until she was prepared to be led as a bride to her wedding."[68]

Adam and the woman were joined in marriage according to Jesus. Jesus told the Pharisees that in the beginning man and woman were created to be one in marriage. Then He added *what therefore God hath joined together, let not man put asunder*. (Matthew 19:4-6) The Pharisees had come with questions about divorce. Jesus responded with an answer that made it clear divorce was not God's original plan for man and woman. Rather it was His plan that they be joined in an unbreakable marriage covenant, abandoning all else for each other. They were to cease independent living. Complete commitment to each other was required in this as well as in other covenants. God introduced marriage covenant. Through the prophet Malachi, God scolded Israel for the disregard with which husbands were treating their marriage covenant partners.

> *Yet ye say, Wherefore? Because the LORD hath been witness between thee and the wife of thy youth, against whom thou hast dealt treacherously: yet is she thy companion, and the wife of thy covenant.*
>
> *And did not he make one? Yet had he the residue of the spirit. And wherefore one? That he might seek a godly seed. Therefore take heed to your spirit, and let none deal treacherously against the wife of his youth.*
>
> *For the LORD, the God of Israel, saith that he hateth putting away: for one covereth violence with his garment, saith the*

> *LORD of hosts: therefore take heed to your spirit, that ye deal not treacherously.*
>
> —Malachi 2:14-16

When God created Adam and the woman, He made them as one flesh through the covenant of marriage. The Hebrew word for flesh meant more than just the physical body. Flesh in Genesis 2:24, was in other verses translated tidings, preach, publish, show forth, messenger, or kin.[69] God's covenant with them gave them wholesomeness, wherein their flesh, before the fall, was able to discern what was truthfully good, godly good.

When God made Adam and the woman one flesh, they were in essence made one in thought, intent, and spirit. They were to be single-minded. God had intended for them to walk in total agreement for the two were one, they were in covenant. Adam and the woman were one because God had created in them covenant concepts, covenant principles. Those concepts and principles are still universally prominent, though varied and polluted by the sin issue. "However, where husband and wife abide in the commitment of their marriage vows, all the power of a covenant-keeping God stands behind them and their marriage."[70]

Marriage tradition often involves the bride carrying or wearing on her apparel something old and something new, something borrowed and something blue. As a pastor for nearly ten years, I was an officiate at many weddings. Most brides or families of the brides did not overlook that bit of tradition. It was a bit interesting to me because of my convictions regarding covenant. They usually were unable to give a reason for wearing something old, new, borrowed, or blue. Their reasons verged on superstition more than anything else.

Traditional, biblical, and historical accounts of covenants have withstood the fierce winds of time. Unfortunately, while many of our traditions may be based on some truth, more often than not they are mixed with an excess of folklore with little to no understanding of the commandments of God. As a result, the Word of God becomes of no effect. The truth of the accounts from Genesis through Revelation of covenant became fuel for the devil's advocates. Through the generations the wisdom, knowledge, understanding of the truth contained in the books of the Bible were of little effect. The awfulness of Adam's sin brought into existence the horrors of death. The old truths of Genesis through Malachi were often dismissed by sinful power play by the leaders of Jesus day. (Matthew 15:2-6)

Chapter 3

GIANT STEPS

The first man to walk on the moon spoke of a "giant step for mankind." Undoubtedly, if historical records are accurately maintained through the generations to come, Neil Armstrong's words could be known for hundreds of years. The first man on the earth, according to the Bible view of man, was written about in the Old Testament. For thousands of years his giant step into sin has reverberated throughout the Earth.

To this point we have discussed the principles of covenant from a historical and biblical point of view. As to the accuracy and truth of the historical, only God knows. But He has sworn an oath to the truth of His Word. Where does that leave us? For me the biblical narration of covenant is as "a word fitly spoken, like apples of gold in pictures of silver," (Proverbs 25:11). (Acts 2:30; Hebrews 6:16-18; Numbers 13:32; 14:37; Isaiah 53:1)

THE OLD COVENANT

The Old Covenant is singular and is basically a covenant that at its core has the promise of Jesus. Though the Old Covenant is singular, it is comprised of many covenants. How can that be? The answer will become clearer as we continue this study. But the Adamic, Noahic, Abrahamic, and Davidic covenants are just a handful of those that progressively move the Bible reader toward the singular promise of the Old Covenant. Each covenant narrows the focus of the promise of the former covenant. The Adamic promise included everyone. The Noahic covenant included only his family. The Abrahamic covenant excluded all except Abraham, Isaac, Jacob, and his descendants. The Davidic covenant again narrowed the potential line of the Messiahship to David's descendants. These covenants with God were all continuations of and refinements of the original covenant. Throughout the Bible, we see echoes of what God told Adam in Genesis. God told Noah and his sons to be fruitful and multiply. The memorial of the Noahic covenant was a rainbow.

COVENANT-MAKING STEPS

H. Clay Trumbull lectured at the Summer School of Hebrew. Professor W.R. Harper encouraged Clay to write books on what he had discovered about covenant. The book I read was first printed around 1885. *The Blood Covenant* version I read was printed in 1975 and was the book I referred to frequently as I compiled my study notes. In Clay Trumbull's preface, he said the reception accorded him was greater than his highest anticipation. Scientists and theologians on both sides of the Atlantic were astonished what he reported finding.

> Certainly, the collation of facts comprised in this volume grew out of no preconceived theory on the part of its author. Whatever theory shows itself in their present arrangement is simply that which the facts themselves have seemed to enforce and establish, in their consecutive disclosure.
>
> At the best, my work in this volume is only tentative and suggestive. Its chief value is likely to be in its stimulating of others to fuller and more satisfactory research in the field here brought to notice. Sufficient, however, is certainly shown, to

> indicate that the realm of true biblical theology is as yet by no means thoroughly explored.[71]

It was after several years of considering the topic of covenant in the scriptures that I came across a copy of Trumbull's book. I learned that what I had studied in the scriptures was seen in records around the world. The concept of covenant began with God, was known to the first Adam, was present in the day of the second Adam, and holds true yet today. Sin is a max-polluter, but the scarlet thread still marks the children of God. The scriptures contain the truth, the life, and the records of God that men have transcribed through thousands of years. The writings of Moses and the prophets are still intact and attested to by millions. God Almighty still bears witness in the lives around the world still testifying of His love and amazing grace. (Joshua 2:18)

With covenant being a universal concept, there have evolved some common steps in the covenant-making process:

1. Those steps include the coming together for a conference of the parties who are actively seeking a covenant relationship with each other. They confer until they can reach areas of agreement.
2. Usually there is a step wherein the partners exchange coats. This step includes a pledge that simply says, "Everything I have is yours." The coat symbolizes the nature and assets of the owner. When coats were exchanged as part of the covenant-making process the partners said to each other, "The liabilities you have incurred I will be responsible for. My assets and my very being are at your disposal, draw from them freely as you desire."
3. Covenant making often included an exchange of weapons. This step symbolized and included a pledge of defense. A covenant partner promised to defend his blood brother with his very life if necessary.

Names were frequently exchanged as blood covenants were made. H. Clay Trumbull tells of the covenant custom of exchanging names as it was still actively used in 1852:

> It is related of Tolo, a chief of the Shastika Indians, on the Pacific coast, that when he made a treaty with Col. McKee, an American soldier, in tribal rights, he was anxious for some ceremony of brotherhood that should give binding sacredness to the mutual covenant. After some parleying, he proposed the formal exchange of names and this was agreed to. Thenceforward he desired to be know as 'McKee.' The American colonel was now 'Tolo.' But after a while the Indian found that, as in too many other instances, the authorities making it did not adhere to the terms of the treaty. Then he discarded his new name, 'McKee,' and refused to resume his former name, 'Tolo.' He would not answer to either, and to the day of his death he insisted that his name, his identity, was 'lost.'[72]

5. A sacrifice was frequently offered when blood covenants were made. Usually the sacrifices were small animals, which were then often served in a covenant meal.
6. Usually there was a cut made in each of the covenant partners. This then was the source whereby blood would be drawn and imbibed by various means. Mixing the blood with wine and drinking it was a common way to imbibe the blood of one's covenant partner. With this step complete, the two had become one—for each had the blood of the other within themselves.
7. After the wound had been made and the blood withdrawn the incision was then treated in such a way that an obvious scar remained. The scar served to state to all with whom the two would come in contact that they had a covenant, a commitment

to defend and be responsible for each other. The scar remained a continual reminder, also to each of the two covenant partners that they had a blood brother to whom they had promised to be faithful and from whom they could expect faithfulness.

8. When the terms of the covenant had been agreed upon and written down, it would then be read aloud with a long list of blessings and curses. These were usually read before witnesses. As the blessings were shouted out, the covenant partners would acknowledge that they understood their obedience would cause the blessings of covenant to be a reality in their lives. In acknowledging the covenant terms with its blessings and curses the covenant partners would loudly shout "Amen." Likewise the curses, the just reward of covenant breakers, were shouted and acknowledged with an "Amen." *Amen* is a Hebrew word that means *so be it*. Consequently those responding by saying "Amen" were saying, "I understand the terms of our agreement and knowingly receive the consequence of my actions. By obedience I will receive blessing, by disobedience I will receive curses. So be it."
9. Memorials were usually established. Some of the more frequently practiced means were: (a) inscribing a stone (b) sharing a flock (c) planting a tree or trees. These memorials served as a constant reminder of the covenant that had been made.

Another step commonly included in blood covenanting was sharing of a meal. The meal frequently included the covenant sacrifice plus goblets of wine mixed with blood extracted when the cut of covenant was made. Hebrews, or Israelites, were strictly forbidden to consume blood and instead drank wine as a symbol of covenant blood. After the initial covenant meal, periodically wine and bread would be shared as the participants reviewed the covenant terms. The attributes of the covenant partners, as well as a review of the acts of kindness of the covenant partners, would also be remembered as the covenant was celebrated. (Jeremiah 34:18 AMP)

These ten steps were usually included in making covenant. Bits and pieces of these different steps are sprinkled throughout the Bible. Each covenant we study will include at least some of these steps, though they will not always follow the sequence shown here.

ABRAHAMIC COVENANT

"After these things the word of the LORD came unto Abram in a vision, saying, Fear not, Abram: I am thy shield, and thy exceeding great reward," (Genesis 15:1). Step by step God's covenant with Abraham unfolded. The steps used by God as He condescended to make covenant with Abram began as He sought to confer with Abram. The Lord *said unto Abram*, *the LORD appeared unto Abram*, and *the word of the LORD came unto Abram*. God was beginning the covenant making process with Abram. The two conferred. Certainly this was an unequal covenant. That is without question.

Abram wisely showed himself obedient to God's initial request of him. Faith requires yielding. To yield is to give over, surrender to or relinquish wholeheartedly to the word or presence of another. That is why faith was reckoned to Abraham for righteousness. God is righteous and Abram was yielding to that fact. Righteousness was Abram's because he submitted to the ultimate Initiator of covenant. It is noteworthy that the name "Abram" is used at this point instead of "Abraham," which is explained in step four. (Hebrews 4:9-12; Genesis 12:1,7; 15:1)

Abram knew this was an unequal covenant initiated by God. Why has history and tradition been so befuddled regarding the covenant initiative set in motion? The truth written in Genesis is still true. God is faithful and hastens to perform His word. Even Balaam was smart enough to say, *I cannot go beyond the word of the LORD*. Estranged from God man still prefers to follow ill-advised council. Because of Adam's sin, Cain failed to follow the counsel of the LORD and committed murder. It began with not taking God at His Word. (Genesis 4:7-8; Numbers 22:18; 1 Chronicles 16:15-16; Psalms 105:8-9)

STEP ONE: CONFERENCE

When God initially made contact with Abram, His instructions were to get out of the country he had been residing in and go to a land the Lord would show him. He departed as the Lord had spoken to him. (Genesis 12:1-4)

God continued the covenant-making steps. Because this covenant was an unequal covenant, the steps and stipulations of the covenant was dependent on God's initiative. Righteous God has always been an excellent workman. Thorough series of steps were carefully recorded to the bewilderment of thousands. When the first step was concluded, God made a pledge that summarized the usual second and third steps in covenant-making. God pledged Himself to be Abram's defense and reward.

STEP TWO: WEAPONS

"After these things the word of the LORD came unto Abram in a vision, saying, *Fear not, Abram: I am thy shield, and thy exceeding great reward,*" (Genesis 15:1). When Abram was ninety-nine years old God continued dealing with Abram. (Genesis 17:1)

Typically when making covenant, the second step was an exchange of weapons. God said, *I am your shield.* God was assuring His covenant partner that He would be Abram's protector, defender, and hedge. God was completely committed to keeping the covenant He made with Abram. Because of covenant, anyone that came against Abram came against God, for this arrangement had made the two as one. In condescending to make covenant with Abram, God had bound Himself to fulfill His covenant obligations. God was giving of Himself and Abram was expected to give of Himself. Since God's position and resources were immeasurable and Abram's were severely limited an unequal covenant was necessary. (Genesis 15:1)

STEP THREE: PLEDGING A REWARD

The third step in making the Abrahamic covenant was realized when God profoundly stated "I am *thy exceeding great reward*." With that statement God was saying that conditionally everything He had was Abram's. Without delay Abram reminded his covenant partner he had no children. So the mighty Jehovah, who is more than enough, promised Abram that he would have so many children that they would be innumerable. God was to be a continuous great reward to His new covenant partner. Abram believed the Lord's promise and it was counted to him for righteousness. Throughout Abram's life, God continued to be his recompense, his great reward. (Genesis 15:1,5,6)

STEP FOUR: EXCHANGING NAMES

In the fourth step of making covenant, God said to Abram, "As for me, behold, my covenant is with thee, and thou shalt be a father of many nations. Neither shall thy name any more be called Abram, but thy name shall be Abraham; for a father of many nations have I made thee," (Genesis 17:4-5).

When God gave Abraham a new name it was not just by a random choice that He added the "ah" to Abram so that he became Abraham. And it was not solely that he would have a name that meant *a father of many nations,* although that was definitely part of it. Abram's name was changed because a covenant was being made. In the original Hebrew text, the Old Testament name of God was spelled with all consonants. It was the all-consonant name JHWH that was then translated into Jehovah in the sixteenth century. The original JHWH name is difficult to pronounce in English. The most accurate way of saying YHWH in English is with the breath sound of "ah." (Genesis 17:2-5)

God exchanged names with Abram by adding the breath sound of "ah" so that Abram became Abraham. God in His mercy and loving-kindness did not leave Sarai uninvolved in this step of covenant making. "And God said unto Abraham, as for Sarai thy wife, thou shalt not call her name Sarai, but Sarah shall her name be," (Genesis 17:15).

God had given His name to Abram and Sarai. The exchange was not complete, however, until God took from Abram the "am" and from Sarai the "I" so that God became the *I AM*. Thereafter they each were known by the name of the other. Not only did God refer to Himself as the *I AM,* He also called Himself the *God of Abraham*. Indeed Jehovah was known by His covenant partner's name. Likewise, Abraham and Sarah were known by their covenant names.

Anyone referring to the God of Abraham, to I Am, to Abraham, or to Sarah would remind the hearers that a solemn agreement was in effect. (Exodus 3:14) It was with the name of YHWH or Jehovah that God progressively revealed Himself to His covenant partner Abraham and to Abraham's descendants. The name Jehovah largely replaces Shaddai from Exodus 6 onward, where attention is centered more particularly on Israel as God's covenant people.[73]

God revealed Himself to His covenant partners as Jehovah-*jireh*, the provider; Jehovah-*rapha*, the Lord who heals; Jehovah-*nissi*, Israel's banner; Jehovah-*shalom*, Israel's peace; Jehovah-*tsidkenu*, Israel's righteousness; Jehovah-*m'kaddesh*, the Lord who sanctifies; and Jehovah-*rohi*, the Lord my Shepherd. These compound names of

Jehovah revealed Abraham's provisions made available through covenant. Each time the name of Abraham or Jehovah was spoken, covenant was recalled. What a glorious covenant partner Abraham was given! What an immeasurable blessing to be Abraham's descendant. It was God's bountifulness that made it possible for Abraham to be a blessing to the entire world.

STEP FIVE: ANIMAL SACRIFICE

The fifth step of cutting a covenant with Abraham involved the sacrifice of an animal. God continued speaking to Abraham:

> *And he said unto him, Take me an heifer of three years old, and a she goat of three years old, and a ram of three years old, and a turtledove, and a young pigeon. And he took unto him all these, and divided them in the midst, and laid each piece one against another: but the birds divided he not.*
>
> —Genesis 15:9-10

The sacrifice of an animal testified to the solemnity of blood covenant. Covenant was not to be broken. Obediently, Abraham divided the animals with the understanding that a blood covenant was being made. The oath ritual for which Abram prepared was customary in treaty ratifications. From it derived various idioms for making a covenant, like the Hebrew 'cut a covenant.' The curse conditionally invoked in the oath was symbolized by this slaying and sundering of animals, signifying 'so may it be done to him who breaks this covenant.'[74]

To trespass blood covenant was to give oneself over to death. Both Jehovah and Abraham understood the severity of the penalty of covenant transgression. God spoke of the penalty for breaking covenant when He said:

And the men who transgressed My covenant, who have not kept the terms of the covenant or solemn pledge which they had made before Me, I will make them [like] the [sacrificial] calf which they cut in two and then passed between its separated parts [solemnizing their pledge to Me]—I will make those men the calf!

—Jeremiah 34:18 AMP

This step of the covenant-making process testifies to the desirability of using wisdom when considering covenant. Jehovah wisely pondered before making covenant with Abraham. God had everything to give and everything to lose. Abraham had little to give and everything to gain in this solemn agreement. For in this fifth step in cutting covenant God said, *My covenant will I not break, nor alter the thing that is gone out of my lips*. If God were to break covenant He would become like the sacrificial animal.

Generations later on Golgotha Jesus, motivated by *chesed*, He became like the sacrificial animal in order to rectify the Old Covenant and establish the New Covenant. God had never broken covenant, but man had continuously transgressed covenant. God mercifully took upon Himself our covenant transgressions and He became like the sacrificial animal on our behalf. (John 1:29,36; 1 Peter 1:19; 1 Timothy 3:16; Revelation 5:12; 12:11; Psalm 89:34)

STEPS SIX AND SEVEN: CUT AND TOKEN OF COVENANT

The sixth step in the covenant-making process was fulfilled when Abraham, in obedience to God, subjected himself and his household to circumcision. And it was written,

> *This is my covenant, which ye shall keep, between me and you and thy seed after thee; every man child among you shall be circumcised. And ye shall circumcise the flesh of your foreskin; and it shall be a token of the covenant betwixt me, and you.*
>
> —Genesis 17:10-11

> *Circumcise therefore the foreskin of your heart, and be no more stiffnecked.*
>
> —Deuteronomy 10:16

Because of this cut of covenant, the natural descendants of Abraham are still separated from the majority of the rest of the population of the world. This cut of covenant was a constant reminder to Abraham and his descendants that they had a solemn agreement with Jehovah, an agreement He would not break. Circumcision was a continuous reminder of the promise God had made to Abraham and his descendants.

To Abraham God had promised (1) a great nation (2) blessings (3) a great name (4) radiating blessing and rebounding curse. Abraham was confidant God would perform what He had promised. The manifestation of the Old Covenant promise was Jesus. It was through Jesus, the Mediator of a Better Covenant that all the nations of the world would eventually be blessed. (Jeremiah 1:12)

THE EIGHTH STEP: BLESSINGS AND CURSES

Biblical and secular covenants alike contained a declaration of the advantages of obedience to the terms of the covenant as well as the disadvantages of disobedience to covenant. The Abrahamic covenant was no exception. Though the pronouncement of blessing and curse in this covenant was less flamboyant than in some other covenants, there was nonetheless a definite declaration made that had extensive effects. The blessing was formally declared:

> *And I will make of thee a great nation, and I will bless thee, and make thy name great; and thou shalt be a blessing: And I will bless them that bless thee, and curse him that curseth thee: and in thee shall all families of the earth be blessed.*
>
> —Genesis 12:2-3

Since "bless" means to possess or promote well-being, God was telling Abraham that He would be Abraham's source of well-being and Abraham would in turn be a source of well-being to others. Those who would allow themselves to be a channel of blessing for Abraham would in turn likewise be blessed. Those who chose to be a means of evil towards Abraham in return for evil would receive evil.

This declaration when enacted became another example of the principle of sowing and reaping God had established in the first chapters of Genesis. The curse of the Abrahamic covenant was less obvious than the blessing. To a large extent the curse of the Abrahamic covenant was simply unfulfilled blessing(s). They would choose death over life and bear the iniquity of their own sins. Those who would not receive the promises of God by faith would continue in the curse of the Adamic covenant. (Genesis 3:17-19; Amos 3:2)

STEP NINE: ESTABLISHING MEMORIALS

The memorial established in the Abrahamic covenant is not obvious. Memorials were usually established in one or more of three ways: 1. a stone was set up and inscribed; 2. a flock was shared; 3. trees were planted. In the Abrahamic covenant, a memorial was established when Abraham built an altar unto the Lord. This memorial served as a place of sacrifice. It also served as a reminder of the covenant that had been made between God and Abraham.

In all but four of the Old Testament occurrences of the word "altar," the Hebrew is *mizbeah*, which means "place of sacrifice" (from *zabbah*, "to slaughter for sacrifice"), and one of the remaining cognate *madbah*. While etymologically the term involves slaughter, in usage it was not always so restricted, being applied also to the altar for burning incense.

> The Patriarchs built their own altars and offered their own sacrifices on them without having any recourse to a priesthood. Noah built one after the flood and made burnt offerings on it (Genesis 8:20). Abraham built altars to Yahweh at Shechem, between Bethel and Ai, at Hebron, and at Moriah, where he offered a ram instead of Isaac (Genesis 12:6-8, 13:18, 22:9). Isaac did likewise at Beersheba (Genesis 26:25), Jacob erected altars at Shechem and Bethel (Genesis 33:20, 35:1-7), and Moses erected one at Rephidim after the victory of the Israelites over Amalek (Exodus 17:15). The altars were evidently erected mainly to commemorate some event in which the principal had had dealings with God.[75]

Without doubt Abraham believed in the Lord God. Because Abraham believed God, his believing was counted *to him for righteousness*. Abraham's Covenant would be a means of blessing for the whole world. Without doubt, I believe God is much more inclined to perfect that which concerns us than we can imagine. It is ours to believe what He tells us, His word, rather than all our years of reasoning is able to tell us. I will keep my eyes on Him and trust Him above all else. He alone is worthy to be praised. (Genesis 12:6-8; 13:4,18; Psalm 31:1; 64:10; Proverbs 18:10)

STEP TEN: THE COVENANT MEAL

The Abrahamic covenant meal is illustrated in Genesis chapter eighteen. It was in the plains of Mamre that the Lord appeared to Abraham and shared a meal with his covenant partner.

> *And the LORD appeared unto him in the plains of Mamre: and he sat in the tent door in the heat of the day; And he lift up his eyes and looked, and, lo, three men stood by him: and when he saw them, he ran to meet them from the tent door, and bowed himself toward the ground, And said, My LORD, if now I have found favour in thy sight, pass not away, I pray thee, from thy servant: Let a little water, I pray you, be fetched, and wash your feet, and rest yourselves under the tree: And I will fetch a morsel of bread, and comfort ye your hearts; after that ye shall pass on: for therefore are ye come to your servant. And they said, So do, as thou hast said. And Abraham hastened into the tent unto Sarah, and said, Make ready quickly three measures of fine meal, knead it, and make cakes upon the hearth. And Abraham ran unto the herd, and fetched a calf tender and good, and gave it unto a young man; and he hasted to dress it. And he took butter, and milk, and the calf, which he had dressed, and set it before them; and he stood by them under the tree, and they did eat.*
>
> —Genesis 18:1-8

Though speculative to some, it seems to me the meal confirmed the covenant that had just been made.[76] After the meal the Lord repeated His covenant promise of a son for Abraham. God was reaffirming His commitment to be Abraham's great reward. Though both Abraham and Sarah *were well stricken in age; and it ceased to be with Sarah after the manner of women*, nothing was impossible to Abraham's covenant partner. A son was to be born to Abraham and Sarah. Sarah conceived and gave birth to Isaac when Abraham was 100 years old. God was Abraham's just reward. Abraham and Sarah's longing for a child had been fulfilled. She laughed, and for centuries since then people have rejoiced and laughed at this record of God's great reward. (Genesis 18:11; 21:1-6) God was able and willing to bless His covenant partner. Out of the goodness of God, Abraham and Sarah were blessed.

COVENANT AFFECTS DESCENDANTS

God reaffirmed the Abrahamic covenant with Isaac as He did years later with Isaac's son Jacob, whose name God changed to Israel. Israel's twelve sons were established as a nation in His progressive fulfillment of His covenant with Abraham. As with all blood covenants, not only were the covenant heads affected, but, likewise the descendants of the covenant heads were affected. Generations after the covenant steps were completed with Abraham, the Israelites were suffering at the hands of the Egyptians. God, who had promised Abraham *those that curse you will be cursed*, worked a mighty deliverance for His covenant partners. That miraculous delivery testified of God's covenant keeping faithfulness and power. (Genesis 12:3; 17:21; 32:28)

> *And it came to pass in process of time, that the king of Egypt died: and the children of Israel sighed by reason of the bondage, and they cried, and their cry came up unto God by reason of the bondage. And God heard their groaning, and God remembered his covenant with Abraham, with Isaac, and with Jacob. And God looked upon the children of Israel, and God had respect unto them.*
>
> —Exodus 2:23-25

Because of covenant, God had respect unto the Israelites and summoned Moses to go into Egypt and bring "His" people out. His covenant with Abraham, Isaac, and Jacob was still in effect. Four hundred years had passed since Jacob had entered Egypt with his sons and their families. Because of covenant, God worked a mighty deliverance for Abraham's descendants. Moses heard from the Lord and went to Egypt:

> *Come now therefore, and I will send thee unto Pharaoh, that thou mayest bring forth my people the children of Israel out of Egypt. And Moses said unto God, Who am I, that I should go unto Pharaoh, and that I should bring forth the children of Israel out of Egypt? And he said, Certainly I will be with thee; and this shall be a token unto thee, that I have sent thee: When thou hast brought forth the people out of Egypt, ye shall serve God upon this mountain. And Moses said unto God, Behold, when I come unto the children of Israel, and shall say unto them, The God of your fathers hath sent me unto you; and they shall say to me, What is his name? what shall I say unto them? And God said unto Moses, I AM THAT I AM: and he said, Thus shalt thou say unto the children of Israel, I AM hath sent me unto you. And God said moreover unto Moses, Thus shalt thou say unto the children of Israel, the LORD God of your fathers, the God of Abraham, the God of Isaac, and the God of Jacob, hath sent me unto you: this is my name for ever, and this is my memorial unto all generations. Go, and gather the elders of Israel together, and say unto them, The LORD God of your fathers, the God of Abraham, of Isaac, and of Jacob, appeared unto me, saying, I have surely visited you, and seen that which is done to you in Egypt: And I have said, I will bring you up out of the affliction of Egypt unto the land of the Canaanites, and the Hittites, and the Amorites, and the Perizzites, and the Hivites, and the Jebusites, unto a land flowing with milk and honey.*
>
> —Exodus 3:10-17

The Lord, who generations before had exchanged names with Abram, remembered the covenant agreement and began the deliverance of His people. *I am thy shield, and thy exceeding great reward.* The pledge God had made to Abraham was equally effective for Abraham's descendants. All Abraham's descendants were considered in his loins when covenant was made, consequently the shield and great reward promised to Abraham belonged also to the Israelites, his descendants. The exceedingly powerful *I AM* delivered His covenant partners out of Egypt in spite of all the resistance given them by the Pharaoh and his army. (Genesis 15:1)

ABRAHAM'S DESCENDANTS

Abraham's descendants had become slaves in Egypt. Their bondage was exceedingly harsh. Israel's newborn sons were being murdered in an attempt to slow down the Israelite birthrate. Joseph had been the means whereby God had worked provision for Israel almost 400 years before. But Joseph had been forgotten. He had been sold by his brothers and eventually sold to Potiphar. He had endured through trials and tribulations that cause many to fall. But he held fast to the dream God had given him. Joseph was sent to preserve the descendants of Abraham, Isaac and Jacob by a great deliverance. (Genesis 39:21; Exodus 1:11-17)

Then there was Moses, who after leaving Egypt—kicked out if you will—dwelled in Midian. Israel called to Jehovah for help. God heard them and because of His covenant with Abraham, with Isaac, and with Jacob, He called Moses. Because of covenant Israel petitioned God for aid. Because of covenant God hastened to perform His word on their behalf. He came to their defense. He sent a deliverer. (Exodus 2:24; 3:7-10)

MOSES WAS SUMMONED

God had anticipated Israel's appeal, for He had already been preparing Moses for military service. Moses had been one of the Israelite sons whom the Egyptians had tried to murder. God, however, had a mission for Moses to fulfill and so the Egyptians' attempt to slay him was ineffective.

Moses had been taken into the care of Pharaoh's sister and was raised as her own child. For forty years he was as an Egyptian. With his natural mother having acted as his nurse during his formative years, Moses gained an understanding of Israelite custom in spite of his environment. His Egyptian environment did not nullify his Hebrew heritage. At forty, Moses fled Egypt and went to Midian. There he married Zipporah, the daughter of Jethro, the priest of Midian. After forty years working as a shepherd with Jethro, Moses was drafted into military service by Jehovah.

With his wife and sons, Moses began his journey back to Egypt. (Exodus 4:19-26) Moses was, not unjustifiably, in danger. He had failed to submit himself and his son to the stipulations of the Abrahamic covenant. How could he successfully lead God's covenant people out of Egypt if he was not willing to be obedient to the terms of the covenant himself? Circumcision was a token of the Abrahamic covenant and all Abraham's descendants were to be circumcised. (Genesis 17:9-14)

> This is a difficult passage filled with obscurities. Apparently, Moses neglected to circumcise his son. Circumcision was an action that served as a sign of God's covenant relationship with His people, as designated by God Himself (Gen. 17:10-14). Failure to perform this rite may have been caused by his wife's abhorrence of the practice, or by adhering to the Midianite rites, which called for males to be circumcised at puberty. However, as head of the house, Moses should have performed this rite

> when his son was eight days old. As he is now about to become Israel's deliverer, God is displeased and vicariously uses Zipporah to do what Moses should have done. The meaning of a bloody husband probably refers to Zipporah's indignant feelings about the circumcision just performed.[77]

Obedience to the terms of the Abrahamic covenant caused Moses to be reinstated in the service of the Lord. Moses, joined by his brother, Aaron, went into Egypt and gathered together all the elders of the Israelites. (Exodus 4:30-5:2)

LET MY PEOPLE GO

Repeatedly, Moses, speaking as God directed him to do, asked Pharaoh to *let my people go*. But God's request meant little to Pharaoh. To him, the God of the Israelites was just one of many gods.

The Egyptians worshiped Isis and Amon, who were cow gods; Ra, a sun god; Osiris, a god of the dead; Heka, a frog god; Nechebet, a serpent god; the Nile river; plus many other things were worshipped by the Egyptians.[78] With this array of gods at his beck and call, why should Pharaoh, a god himself, be fearful of the God of the Israelite slaves? He would soon find out why he should fear the God of Abraham, Isaac, and Jacob.

The gods of the Egyptians, like most heathen gods, were believed to have charge of a limited area or element. As chief of their own domain they supposedly often battled other gods to gain or maintain their domain. The God of the Israelites would be no major competition as far as Pharaoh was concerned. Most false gods, however, were then and often even now are, fashioned after some craftsman's perception of some supernatural being. Fallen angels and some demons may have had some actual say over their supposed assigned area and may have been visually perceived on occasion. They may have actually had some spiritual authority over some geographical territories.

Satan himself is able to appear as an angel of light. Thus any number of craftsmen may have fashioned their many idols after some imaginary or actual perception. The fallen angels, even Satan himself, and the demons may have some limited powers, but they were not able to match the one true Almighty God of Abraham, Isaac, and Jacob. (2 Corinthians 11:14)

When Moses began speaking on behalf of Israel's covenant God Jehovah, he said, "Thus saith the LORD God of Israel, Let my people go, that they may hold a feast unto me in the wilderness. And Pharaoh answered and said, Who is the LORD, that I should obey his voice to let Israel go? I know not the LORD, neither will I let Israel go," (Exodus 5:1-2).

With God's extraordinary, supernatural perfection, he began a work then that is still awesome in the sight of millions around the world. With powerful, calculated, and precise action, God would prove Himself as the one true God of Israel. He proved His power and covenant faithfulness to Egypt as well as to all who would hear of the miraculous deliverance of Israel. He proved His power over the Nile, the cow, the sun, the frog, the serpent, over death, and all the gods who were represented. Through plagues the disobedient experienced what Moses pronounced and the obedient experienced God's mercies.

> Egypt, like the rest of the Middle-Eastern cultures, was a land where magic flourished. The belief was that one, through the use of magic, could influence or control the gods. Wise men were those who knew the occultic arts; sorcerers muttered magic formulas and incantations; magicians were the bearers of magic books. Their temporary success shows Satan's power to imitate certain miracles. (See 2 Thessalonians 2:9,10)

> The elders of Israel did not ask for signs, but when they saw them, they believed (4:30-31). Pharaoh asked for a sign (v.9), but when he saw one, he did not believe.
>
> In addition to being called "wonders" (see note on 3:20), God's dealings with Egypt are commonly called His actions: I will smite (7:17; 8:2). This reinforces God's judgment behind them. Many of the plagues are aimed as much at Egypt's nature gods as at the Egyptians themselves. With each plague, God demonstrates that the various Egyptian gods are powerless and judged by Him.[79]

We would all do well to stir ourselves by carefully considering this excellent example of God's delivering power. God has not changed. His power is greater than anything we can comprehend. His covenant loving-kindness is unchanging and His mercy continues forever. (Exodus 5:1-2; Psalm 25:6)

MEMORIAL MEAL

Prior to the final plague, Israel obediently prepared and partook of the memorial covenant meal. (Exodus 12:3-14) Here is the feast, the first Passover, directed by God just prior to Israel's deliverance. God's presence with them protected them for they proved themselves faithful at that time to God's covenant direction. God's judgment dealt with the gods of Egypt.

Those obedient to God's instruction painted their doorposts with the blood of a perfect sacrificial lamb. Because of the blood of the covenant lamb, death passed over the homes of the obedient. This last plague however claimed the lives of the firstborn of all who chose to remain in the folds of the covenant of death rather than in the covenant of promise. Clothed for flight, the Israelites rejoiced while eating the Passover meal.

Moses had repeatedly and boldly proclaimed God's Word to Pharaoh saying, *Let my people go*. Incessant refusal to obey the one true Almighty God brought Egypt to the final and most devastating of all the plagues. (Exodus 12:29-33) Israel's covenant God delivered His people out of Egypt. He had faithfully kept His promise to Abraham. Generations after the Abrahamic covenant was made, God was still proving Himself as Abram's shield and exceeding great reward.

MOSAIC COVENANT

With Moses serving as Israel's leader, God began ratifying the Abrahamic covenant. A ratified covenant is one that is renewed without having been broken. The Mosaic Covenant is an extension of the covenant with Adam that promised redemption from sin. The Mosaic covenant is also a renewal of the covenant with Abraham. The Abrahamic and Adamic covenants were primarily covenants of promise. The Mosaic covenant was a covenant of law.

They all, however, were covenants prompted by love. God's love, which motivated each of the covenants He made with man, was the reason redemption of man was possible. Each covenant having built on the former covenants pointed to the promise of Jesus and the Better Covenant.

CONFERENCE

Because of His covenant with Abraham, God delivered His people out of Egypt. Moses, God's spokesman to Israel, told the Israelites, to obey His voice and keep His covenant. (Exodus 19:4-8) In total agreement the people responded *All that the LORD hath spoken we will do.*

Thus the first step in the making of the Mosaic covenant was completed—the two parties had come together. God then proceeded to give Moses the commandments of the covenant.

COVENANT STIPULATIONS

These commandments, commonly referred to as the Decalogue, related directly to the renewal of the covenant.

> In its form the Decalogue resembles treaties imposed by Hittite kings on their vassals in the 14th-13th centuries. In these the suzerain declares his name and status (cf. vs. 2a) and enumerates his benefits to his vassal (cf. vs. 2b) as a claim to absolute and exclusive obedience (cf. vs. 3) introducing the detailed obligations (cf. vss. 4-17). Heaven and earth and various natural features are called to witness in the Hittite treaties (cf. Deut. 30:19) and adjurations are added as sanctions (cf. Deut. 27:15-26). The covenant formula of the Decalogue seems to reflect this convention of international treaty law at the central shrines of Israel in Palestine; but the apodictic laws themselves, which have no parallel in the Hittite covenants, quite conceivably relate to the early religious community at Kadesh.[80]

Israel, like all the surrounding peoples, understood covenant and its solemnity. The terminology of the entire Old Testament bears witness to that.

In Exodus chapters 21-23, the stipulations of the covenant are given. Those stipulations addressed such things as slaves, homicide, quarrels, theft of animals, compensation for offenses, seduction of virgins, moral and religious laws, the first fruits, the firstborn, duties toward enemies, the Sabbath, feasts, instructions for entry into Canaan, and prohibition of covenants with non-Israelites. As in the Hittite covenants, the vassal Israel was given detailed covenant rules. Israel's covenant obligations were itemized. With exactness Jehovah declared the covenant terms to which Israel was expected to be obedient.

God concluded the stipulations of the Mosaic covenant with an admonishment to refrain from making covenant with the inhabitants of Canaan. (Exodus 23:32-33)

COVENANT SACRIFICE

Most Christians are somewhat familiar with the frequent sacrifices made in the Old Testament. Sacrifices were made according to the direction given to Moses by Jehovah. (Exodus 24:6-8) Especially note the phrases (1) the book of the covenant (2) the blood of the covenant. The book of the covenant was read to the Israelites and sacrificial blood was shed to seal the covenant. The two actions brought the reality of blood covenant to their undeniable attention.

It seems to be a little easier for us to understand the usefulness of reading the covenant aloud. However, the blood of the covenant had a significance that too many currently either do not comprehend or choose to overlook. The sacrifices were a necessary part of this covenant made between a Holy God and an unholy people. The sacrifice was a wake-up call; a solemn reminder of the gravity of life and death and blood covenant. The sacrificial blood, which was sprinkled on the altar, the book of the covenant, and on the people, was a semi-equalizer for unrighteous man and righteous God as they made covenant.

Concerning all the words of the Lord, the Israelites responded by saying, "*all that the LORD hath said will we do, and be obedient,*" (Exodus 24:7). They were willingly submitting themselves to be made like the sacrificial animal should they break the covenant. (Jeremiah 34:18 AMP)

COVENANT MEMORIAL

God called Moses to come up on Mount Sinai where Moses received the detailed instructions for building the tabernacle that would house the covenant. God gave very specific instructions for the construction of the ark that would contain the tablets of the covenant. It was because of covenant that the Israelites could expect God to meet with them and commune with them. God's instruction to Moses on the Mount started with the Ark of the Covenant and ended with Him engraving the tablet of stone that would be housed in that ark. Everything else about the tabernacle prepared them for meeting God in the Holy of Holies where the Ark of the Covenant was kept.

Engraving a stone was one of the three ways typically used when establishing a memorial to covenant. Characteristically, the tablets of the covenant would be deposited in a temple and read periodically as a reminder of the solemn agreement that had been made. A portable tent served as the temple for the Israelites until many years after they were established in the Promised Land. But while Moses was still on the Mount communing with God about the covenant stipulations, the Israelites were already exhibiting unfaithfulness.

ISRAEL'S UNFAITHFULNESS

And the Lord said unto Moses, Go, get thee down; for thy people, which thou broughtest out of the land of Egypt, have corrupted themselves: They have turned aside quickly out of the way which I commanded them: they have made them a molten calf, and have worshipped it, and have sacrificed thereunto, and said, These be thy gods, O Israel, which have brought thee up out of the land of Egypt. And the Lord said unto Moses, I have seen this people, and, behold, it is a stiffnecked people: Now therefore let me alone, that my wrath may wax hot against them, and that I may consume them: and I will make of thee a great nation. And Moses besought the Lord his God, and said, Lord, why doth thy wrath wax hot against thy people, which thou hast brought forth out of the land of Egypt with great power, and with a mighty hand? Wherefore should the Egyptians speak, and say, For mischief did he bring them out, to slay them in the mountains, and to consume them from the face of the earth? Turn from thy fierce wrath, and repent of this evil against thy people. Remember Abraham, Isaac, and Israel, thy servants, to whom thou swarest by thine own self, and saidst unto them, I will multiply your seed as the stars of heaven, and all this land that I have spoken of will I give unto your seed, and they shall inherit it for ever. And the Lord repented of the evil which he thought to do unto his people.

—Exodus 32:7-14

Because of covenant, Moses immediately began to intercede for Israel. God had told Moses, *let me alone, that my wrath may wax hot against them, and that I may consume them: and I will make of thee a great nation*. Israel had transgressed covenant and they legitimately had lost access to the benefits of that covenant. Since Moses had remained obedient, he could legally be the head of another covenant that would have involved his family only. However, blood covenant is more than a legal matter. It is also a matter of love. Moses, who had maintained a right-standing with God because of his obedience, reminded God of His loving-kindness toward Abraham, Isaac, and Israel. (Exodus 32:10)

Moses was qualified to intercede for Israel because of his obedience to covenant. His intercession caused unfaithful Israel to be spared. Though the initial Mosaic covenant had been broken, the Abrahamic covenant was still effective. It was on the basis of the Abrahamic covenant that Moses appealed to God's mercy for Israel.

Throughout the Near East when a covenant was terminated, the tablet on which the agreement had been written was broken. When Moses descended mount Sinai and saw Israel worshiping the golden calf he cast the covenant tablets down and broke them. Since Israel had broken the covenant, the stone tablets on which the covenant had been written must likewise be broken.

> Indeed, the term for canceling a contract in Babylonian legal literature is "to break the tablet" (tuppam hepu). Following the judicial pattern, the renewal of the relationship must be effected by writing new tablets, which explains why new ones had to be written after the sin of the golden calf, and why the ritual Decalogue was repeated in Exodus 34:17-26. Renewal of a covenant with a vassal—after a break in the relationship—by means of writing new tablets is an attested fact in Hittite political life.[81]

The Levites were instructed by God to go through the camp and take vengeance on the covenant transgressors. The transgressors became like the sacrificial beast they had offered to seal their covenant. They were put to death by the swords wielded by the sons of Levi. The Israelites were guilty of breaking a solemn agreement with a righteous God. Covenant was no longer just a matter of ratification, it was now a matter of renewal. (Exodus 32:23-26; Jeremiah 34:18-20)

Israel's unfaithfulness necessitated another covenant. Moses went back to Mount Sinai once more to be with God regarding the primary stipulations for the renewed covenant. We have come to refer to them as the Ten Commandments, and too often today we worship, blaspheme, or apologize for them. Repeatedly, foolishness and the sin of unbelief pervert covenants and promises from God. He remains true to Himself. But His covenant people have often been devoid of good judgment. He has so graciously made His written Word available to us.

Therein we are able to know Him, come to saving knowledge, follow His stipulations, and fellowship with him. He is so glorious and so kind. (Exodus 32:25-29; 34:1-9)

On Mount Sinai, Moses—for the second time—received the covenant stipulations. He also received instruction for building the tabernacle in which the covenant tablets would be deposited. When the tabernacle had been built and the covenant stipulations deposited, Israel began her march to the land God had promised to give them, the land Abraham had claimed for them. (Exodus 33:1-2)

Protected by a cloud by day and a warming fire by night, God lead Israel to the Jordan River. Across the river lay the land promised to Israel. Jehovah had worked miracles on behalf of His covenant people revealing Himself as the almighty and sufficient protector and provider for them. Now they stood on the brink of owning their own land. The land had been promised to them; receiving it, however, required faith and obedience on their part. They would be required to maintain faith in their covenant God and His promise, while faithfully being obedient to Him in order to possess the land promised to them.

The Lord instructed Moses to send twelve men into Canaan to scout the land. For forty days the spies scouted the wilderness of Zin to Rehab to Hamth, into the Negeb, to Hebron, Ahiman, Sheshai, Talmi, and Eshol. They each returned from their scouting with a report. Ten of the twelve spies reported that indeed the land was rich, however, they added their judgment of what was seen. They brought what was recorded as an evil report. (Numbers 13:12-33)

The ten spies' reports discouraged the Israelites and consequently caused unbelief. Their report was contrary to what God had said. God had told Israel that He would drive out the inhabitants of Canaan for them. Israel was choosing to believe what they saw rather than taking by faith what their covenant partner had told them through Moses.

Even in the Hittite covenants, suzerains expected their vassals to trust the suzerain to honor his word in spite of appearances to the contrary. Vassals were also to refrain from murmuring against the suzerain. Should God expect anything less of His vassals? As LORD of Lords and Commander of a heavenly host of angels, He was well able to strengthen them and was even willing to go before them into the Promised Land. They made the mistake of judging God's Word as though its fulfillment was dependent on the strength and power of the cowering, murmuring, unbelieving men in their own camps.

However, two of the twelve spies, Joshua and Caleb, had also seen the fortified walls and the giants in the land. But they were undaunted, for they persisted in believing their covenant partner would defeat those foes as He had defeated the Egyptians. Israel, however, persisted in unbelief and disobedience by choosing to believe the evil report of the ten spies instead of the good report of Joshua and Caleb. (Numbers 14:1-35)

Moses appealed to God to reconsider. He interceded for Israel on behalf of God's *chesed*, His mercy. *Chesed*, an important Hebrew covenant word is often, if not exclusively, translated "mercy" in *The King James Version* of the Bible. God pardoned Israel because of His own covenant loving-kindness and Moses' diligent intercession. (Numbers 14:20) Israel's pardon came after God had conferred with Moses in regard to making covenant with him and his family thus removing the remaining disobedient Israelites from the covenant. (Numbers 14:12)

Being a truly humble man, Moses considered God and Israel above himself. Because of Moses' intercession, the Lord dealt mercifully with Israel by confining punishment to the guilty parties alone. God's covenant would be established with Israel's children. However, the adults guilty of murmuring and complaining would receive the fruit of the seeds of rebellion and unbelief they had planted. They feared men rather than God. They would be punished according to the words they had spoken. They would die in the wilderness. They would not be without covenant benefits, for their descendants would be able to go into the Promised Land because of the promise given so many generations before. Caleb and Joshua, because they stayed strong in faith, would not die in the wilderness as they had spoken boldly that the Lord was able to do as He had said. They would go into the Promised Land. (Numbers 14:12-19)

The Israelites wandered through the wilderness for forty years because of unbelief; they finally came to a position to enter the Promised Land. Unbelief is costly. But Joshua and Caleb and the children of those who had died in the wilderness were ready to enter. Moses himself was denied entry because of disobedience and unbelief at Kadesh. But at the direction of the Lord, Moses gave Israel some final covenant instruction before he died. (Exodus 34:4-8; Numbers 20:7-12; Deuteronomy 3:23-28)

Moses performed a final service for God before Israel crossed the Jordan River. He reviewed the covenant stipulations and promises. Then he instructed Israel to cross the river, enter the Promised Land, and establish a covenant memorial. Great stones were to be set up and covered with plaster and on them Israel was to write the law of the covenant. These stones were to be established as a constant reminder of the covenant between Jehovah and Israel. (Deuteronomy 27:1-8)

BLESSING AND CURSE

Part of the final services Moses was to rend for God included oversight of the pronouncement of the covenant blessing and curse. Moses instructed the entire congregation as to their part in the upcoming performance. Six representatives from six of the tribes of Israel were to stand on Mount Gerizim. From there they would loudly shout the blessing promised to the obedient of the covenant. The remaining six tribes also had representatives, who were to stand on Mount Ebal and loudly pronounce the curse for disobedience to the covenant. The remainder of the congregation was to stand on the grounds around the base of these two mounts and listen to the pronouncements being made.

From their vantage point between the two mounts, the twelve tribes could hear all the blessing and curse being proclaimed. As each blessing and curse was boldly shouted out, the individual members of the tribes would respond with a loud *Amen*. In this way they were saying, *we understand these to be the consequences of disobedience and obedience and we submit ourselves to the fruit of our actions.* (Deuteronomy 27:13-14)

> When God pronounces a curse, it is, firstly a denunciation of sin (Nu. v. 21, 23; Deuteronomy 29:19,20). Secondly, the curse is God's judgment on sin (Nu. v. 22, 24, 27; Isaiah 24:6). And thirdly, the person who is suffering the consequences of sin by the judgment of God is called a curse (Nu. v. 21,27; Jeremiah 29:18).
>
> However, for the Hebrew, just as a word was not a mere sound on the lips but an agent sent forth, so the spoken curse was an active agent for hurt. Behind the word stands the soul that created it. Thus, a word which is backed by no spiritual capacity of accomplishment is a mere 'word of the lip' (2 Kings 18:20 RVMG), but when the soul is powerful the word is clothed in that power (Ecclesiastes 8:4; 1 Chronicles 21:4). The potency of the word is seen in some of our Lord's healing miracles (Matthew 8:8,16; cf. Psalm 107:20), and in His cursing of the barren fig tree (Mark 11:14,20,21).
>
> On the borders of Canaan, Moses set before the people 'life and death,' blessing and the curse. The first national act on entering the land is to set these two in motion: the blessing, which will

> 'overtake' the obedient, and the curse, which will 'overtake' the disobedient. Between these two poles the national life moves. Sometimes the implied reason is the wrath of God (e.g. Isaiah 34:5), but more often it is in order to remove a potential contagion for Israel's sake (Deuteronomy 7:26, 20:17).[82]

By saying "Amen" to the blessing and curse, the Israelites acknowledged that they knew blessing would overtake them if they were obedient and curse would overtake them if they were disobedient. They heard the blessing. They heard the curse and understood as they shouted back that covenant means obedience. All the Israelites knew covenant principles. The declaration was detailed.

Israel was to be blessed by being set high above all the nations of the earth. They would be blessed in the city and in the field. The fruit of their bodies would be blessed, as would the fruit of their ground and the fruit of their cattle and sheep. They would be blessed in their baskets and storehouses. Blessing would be theirs as they came and went. Any enemies that rose against them would be smitten and flee seven ways from the blessed of the Lord. Israel would be blessed in everything they set their hands to in the land the Lord had given them. They would be established as a holy people and all the people of the earth would recognize them as called by the name of the Lord. Because of their covenant relationship with the Lord, all the people of the earth would be afraid of the Israelites. Israel would be rich and lend to many nations while never needing to borrow. Israel was to be the head and not the tail, above and not beneath.

All these blessings were theirs if they would merely hearken to the commandment of the Lord. Obedience would bring blessing. Covenant coupled with obedience gave God a legitimate means to bless His creation. If Israel were disobedient to the covenant, God could not legitimately bless Israel. The disobedient would inherit the just reward of one born of Adam.

The curse of the covenant was declared. The curse included vexation, pestilence, consumption, fever, inflammation, the sword, mildew, the botch, scab, itch, madness, blindness, astonishment of heart, oppression, lack of prosperity, theft, kidnapping, skimpy harvest, captivity, locust, a need to borrow, enemies, hunger, thirst, nakedness, a want of all things, a yoke of iron, maltreatment by nations of fierce countenance, distress, plagues, sicknesses of long continuance, all the diseases of Egypt in addition to all the sicknesses not written in the book, destruction, lack of rest, trembling heart, failing of eyes, sorrow of mind, doubt, and fear. All these would be so grievous that the disobedient would moan everyday throughout the day, *would God it were even, and at even, would God it were morning!* (Deuteronomy 28:15-68; Leviticus 26:1-46).

God had set before Israel life and good, in opposition to death and evil, and blessing that counteracted the curse. What Israel would receive was dependant on her faith, commitment and obedience to her covenant partner. The commandment God gave Israel was not too difficult for her to achieve. As Abraham was blessed and counted righteous because he believed his covenant partner, likewise Abraham's descendants could receive blessing and righteousness from Jehovah by faith. By faith and obedience to the terms of the covenant, Israel could escape the curse that was upon the whole earth and that victimized all its inhabitants. Even the Old Covenant, with all its shortcomings, provided ample provision for whosoever would believe the word of the Lord for nullifying the effects on their lives and nation of a world polluted by sin. Receiving, gaining, and maintaining faith is our part. As Abraham believed, so are covenant partners and descendants to believe the word of the Lord.

Isaiah wrote a song of praise to be sung in the land of Judah. It would be pleasant to hear it sung by them. We can only imagine how it must have sounded. They would sing of the value, the blessings of trusting in the Lord. The song would resound with harp and stringed instruments as the Word of the Lord written by Isaiah was declared. God makes salvation the walls and ramparts of the strong city in the land of Judah. The gates were to be open that the righteous nation may enter, the nation that keeps faith. Context considers that beautiful song was surely joyful, and yet solemnly prophetical. (Isaiah 26:1-21)

God's loving-kindness had made a way for them through His perfectly planned community of covenant. Free of bondages and enjoying God's presence with righteousness predominant. What a giant step for mankind.

Doctrines, folklore, and traditions have often twisted—sometimes in a wily way—the reality of covenant and God's loving-kindness. This does not alter His word and faithfulness, rather it negatively alters the receptivity of His Word and intent. It is for each person *according to their faith*, whether to receive the faith-filled Word that when planted and cared for in good soil brings forth a good harvest. (Matthew 9:29; 13:18; Mark 4; Luke 8)

Chapter 4

PUZZLE PIECES

Every time I read the Bible, more puzzle pieces fall into place. Old questions are answered. Befuddlement is swept away with understanding that had evaded me before. Though I have been born anew, filled with the Holy Spirit, and have read through the scriptures several times, it is still amazing to see the loving-kindness and righteousness of God united and intact throughout the Old and New Testament. God is and always shall be the Creator. Covenant is no exception to all that He has formed. His stipulations, judgments, estimations, and views on all matters are altogether perfect. They are complete and entire, with everything considered a blessing to mankind.

GOD'S ESTIMATION (VIEW) OF COVENANT

In this chapter it should become even clearer that God's view of covenant must not be ignored. It cannot be replaced by any one doctrine. Doctrine, which means teaching, when scripturally sound is firmly based upon the rightly divided word of God. All of God's doctrines intended for His covenant people are part of the everlasting covenant of which Jesus Himself is the mediator. The study of covenant helps pull Bible verses together like pieces of a puzzle. Scripture is clarified. Doctrines of men and doctrines of demons are exposed in the bright light of God's holy scriptures and His better covenant. The rightly divided word of the new covenant is worth studying far over and above any other book ever written. (2 Timothy 2:15 NKJV; Acts 17:10-12)

Each one of us has a call upon our lives in the body of believers. Wherever our individual struggles lie, a heart discernment of God's will, His Spirit, and His covenant can make each of us more savvy in our walk with Him. God's doctrines are to be held onto, when rightly divided. No doctrine will pass God's righteous judgment. He alone is worthy, able, and willing to determine what is right. The reason—He is the only righteous judge. His Word and His Spirit gives all anyone will ever need to walk in habitual fellowship with Him. If Enoch and Noah were able to walk (habitually fellowship) with God, even before Abraham, how much more is the truly born again better covenant believer able to walk with Him?

Every book in the holy scriptures contains a picture of the ultimate, better, and everlasting covenant. It also contains puzzle pieces of other types of covenants, which ultimately show the universal concept of covenant as pointed out in the first chapter. The book of Joshua contains several puzzle pieces helpful in putting together the picture our Lord has painted.

JOSHUA

God instructed Israel about what was expected as they went into Canaan. Even while Moses was still with them, Jehovah gave directions, so that all of the Israelites understood what they were to do when they went into their promised land. The land was theirs. They needed only to maintain a close relationship with their covenant partner and to walk in obedience to Him and they would possess the land. God compassionately reminded them that though they had been small in size, He had redeemed them out of slavery in Egypt. Because of His love for them He instructed them regarding the land He had promised Abraham. (Deuteronomy 7:1-26; 8:1)

Forty years before Joshua led Israel into their promised land, Moses sent twelve men from the wilderness of Paran into the land of Canaan to spy out the land. An evil report given by ten of those spies encouraged unbelief in the adult Israelites. The result was fear, which seems to accompany rebellion as sour accompanies a lemon. Because of fear and unbelief all the adults who had been delivered out of Egypt died during Israel's 40-year wandering through the wilderness. It would be interesting to know if they were still murmuring and complaining when they died. They had not exercised faith in their covenant partner, Jehovah.

Now the next generation was ready to go in and take possession of the land God had promised Abraham centuries before. Joshua and Caleb were the only ones of the adult generation that came out of Egypt, who had the privilege of going into Canaan. They had maintained faith in Jehovah their covenant God. Joshua and Caleb were leading the new generation into Canaan because they had dared to believe what God had said. Abraham's blessings belonged to them.

Entry into the Promised Land began with another sign from God. It fit into the puzzle. It was a sign, which emphasized the covenant. The Levites, bearing the Ark of the Covenant of the Lord, stepped into the Jordan River as Jehovah had directed. "The priests that bare the ark of the covenant of the LORD stood firm on dry ground in the midst of the Jordan, and all the Israelites passed over on dry ground, until all the people were passed clean over Jordan," (Joshua 3:17).

The people of Canaan trembled as the covenant partners of Jehovah began their entry. Previously Joshua had sent two men to spy the land. During their expedition was discovered Rahab hid them from her king's men. Israel crossed the Jordan following the Levites who carried the ark of the covenant. Joshua set up 12 stones according to the number of the tribes of the children of Israel (Jacob) as a reminder *the Lord is mighty*.

The kings of the Amorites and all the kings of the Canaanites trembled at the news. Then came the battle of Jericho. The priests carried the ark of the covenant, the ark of the Lord, around the city once each day for seven days. The walls of the city came tumbling down but Rahab and her family were saved.

Israel trespassed, sinned when they battled the Amorites at Ai. They had transgressed covenant and took *some accursed thing and placed it among their own stuff*. After God's correction, Joshua's intercession and Achan's punishment at the valley of Achor Israel was able to be victorious at Ai. The kings of the land who hoped to devise a plan that would defeat the invaders. Failure to stop the Israelites would certainly mean death. The Gibeonite king, one of the chief members of the conference, realized a victorious encounter would call for more than force. So he separated himself from the rest of the kings who were still deliberating. Neither Ai nor Jericho had been able to escape the Israelites. Jericho had fallen.

The power of Israel's God was seen and the strategy of the Israelite camp was bringing fear throughout the land. The Gibeonites realized they would have to devise a more effective plan, for mere brawn would not be sufficient. They had been allied with all the kings west of the Jordan. A scheme was needed that would allow Gibeon to join the Israelites in an attempt to save their lives. They left their alliance with the other kings and set a plan in motion. Gibeon desired a covenant with Israel, a treaty, a league. Perhaps they had heard of Rahab. They may have been encouraged to develop a plan fashioned after her example. (Joshua 9:1-4)

RAHAB

Rahab was living in Jericho when she became aware of Israel's instructions to destroy all the natives. None of the Hittites, Amorites, Canaanites, Perizzites, Hivites, or Jebusites would be allowed to live. Jericho would be confronted and destroyed—all except for Rahab and her family. She was wise enough to realize the Israelites, though large in number, were not altogether an inescapable foe. As a vassal she might be able to escape.

Like the other inhabitants of Canaan, Rahab had heard of Israel's deliverance from the mighty power of Egypt. Jehovah's presence with Israel was conspicuous. Who could miss that flame at night and that cloud by day? Jehovah had provided for His covenant partners. As they wandered around for forty years God miraculously furnished them with water, food, shelter, and clothing. Now the natives of Canaan understood that God was giving Israel land to become established in. For the present inhabitants of the land, that meant death. But Rahab knew the fine art of survival.

Rahab understood that Israel's power was actually that of their faithful covenant God. All in her land had heard of the mighty power of Israel's Jehovah with whom they had a blood covenant. Fearing Israel's God and certain the Israelites would be successful in taking Jericho, Rahab negotiated with the spies and made an agreement—a covenant—with them. Did she know the significance of the scarlet ribbon? She chose to make their God her God if the spies representing Israel would consent that she and her family could live. (Deuteronomy 20:10-18; Joshua 24:14-15; Hebrews 11:31)

The spies assured her that she and her family would remain safe while the rest of Jericho was destroyed. Rahab's successful deliverance for herself and her family when the walls of Jericho fell surely offered a ray of hope for the Gibeonites. (Joshua 2:8-14; 6:21-25) Because of the solemn agreement she made with the spies, Rahab survived.

Then came the city of Ai—and the first bump on the road to victory for the people of Israel. At first, Ai was temporarily successful in battle against Israel because one of the Israelites transgressed covenant. (Joshua 7:11-13)

> The sin of one member of the community was held to be that of the whole people. Israel was now a nation, and the sin of the individual was the sin of the nation until the nation repudiated its expiation was made.[83]

Israel repented and dealt with the transgressor as God directed and then they again saw victory. They were able to continue toward fulfilling what God had promised. The Promised Land was theirs.

Gibeon, considering all that had happened at Jericho and at Ai, decided it was wise to appeal to Israel for a *beriyth*. If Gibeon could cut a *beriyth* with Israel, they would become allies rather than foes. A treaty seemed to be their only hope. Following Rahab's example, Gibeon sought a covenant with Israel. The trickery of the Gibeonites began to take form. (Joshua 9:3-6)

GIBEON

The Gibeonites devised a scheme that would hopefully save their city. They gathered props and rehearsed their parts like actors preparing for the stage. By falsely representing themselves they hoped to confer with Joshua about cutting a covenant. Costumed with old, torn clothes and carrying props of dry, moldy food, the Gibeonites went to Israel, who was camped at Gilgal, pretending to be ambassadors from a far country.

Jehovah had told Israel the cities from afar desiring peace were to be treated differently from the inhabitants of the Promised Land, which included the Gibeonites. The inhabitants were to receive only death, while those from far away were qualified to enter into a covenant of peace with Israel. To enter into a covenant with Israel was to enter into a covenant indirectly with Jehovah. Ai and Jericho demonstrated that the area's gods, to whom the Gibeonites had for centuries sacrificed their children, were powerless before Jehovah. Thus Gibeon set their gods behind them as they initiated their plans to confer with the Israelites about making a covenant—a covenant that would enable them to make Jehovah their God. (Deuteronomy 20:10-11, 15-16; Joshua 9:3-6)

Israel's God was different from any of the gods of the natives of Canaan. This Jehovah had condescended to make covenant with Abraham several generations ago. All the surrounding countries had heard of His faithfulness to covenant as He led Israel out of Egypt. They had watched as this Almighty God had separated the waters so the Israelites could escape Pharaoh's army. They knew the Egyptians had been drowned in the very place where the Israelites had passed over on dry land. Moses' song of deliverance may have echoed throughout the land and actually been heard by the inhabitants of the area. The grapevine communication system may have reverberated the song. Yet however it happened, somehow the Gibeonites knew how—because of covenant—Jehovah had delivered and provided for Israel. They also knew Egypt's power had been no match for Israel. Jehovah was awesome in power. Again Jehovah had parted the waters for Israel as they crossed the Jordan to come into Canaan as He had parted the waters when they left Egypt. Trouble was on the way.

Now with fear and trembling, the Gibeonites approached Israel for a treaty of submission, a covenant, a league. League in those verses is translated from the Hebrew word *beriyth* (ber-eeth'), which is translated "covenant" more than 300 times in the Old Testament from Genesis through Malachi. (Exodus 15:1-19; Joshua 9:6,7,11,15,16)

DELIBERATION

Beriyth was not something one entered into light-heartedly. A covenant was a solemn agreement that demanded serious deliberation. A blood covenant was more than just a lifelong commitment, though it certainly was that. The agreement made would affect the lives of the descendants of the covenant heads. On their part, the Gibeonites would willingly hand over all they had to the Israelites. They would commit themselves to defend and to serve the Israelites. They would obligate themselves to totally obey their covenant partners. A full commitment to covenant would be required. Thus they typically would swear that, "All I have is yours and I will defend you with my very life if necessary."

Though it sounded like total bondage, covenant in reality, would be a liberating contract for Gibeon. For in a covenant with Israel, the Gibeonites would be recipients as well as donors. They would live and not die as fellow benefactors in Israel's covenant with God.

If a covenant could be arranged, Israel would be committed to defend Gibeon. Because of covenant, the Gibeonites could expect their needs to be met by their covenant partners, within specified limits. In addition, Israel's covenant with God would, with some restrictions, be extended to themselves. Gibeon sought a covenant relationship with Israel knowing that a blood covenant bond would grant them possession of Israel's assets. Gibeon would have an avenue to Jehovah if a covenant with Israel could be arranged.

Covenants were nothing new to the Gibeonites, nor to the Israelites. Gibeon as well as Israel had a common heritage in Noah and in Adam to whom God had revealed the sanctity of blood covenant. All the generations since Adam had made covenants, Gibeon was no exception. Though each society had a variety of covenants, they each knew blood covenant to be the most solemn and binding agreement possible. Being well acquainted with covenant, the Gibeonites cautiously approached Israel for a conference.

CONFERENCE

Pretending to be from afar, Gibeon's representatives approached Israel. They followed the script they had rehearsed and wearing old, torn garments and carrying dry, moldy food they approached Israel. They began what could be considered today as an award-winning act that earned the confidence of the Israelites. Israel and Gibeon conferred and as a prize for their winning performance, an agreement was made and the steps to establish it were taken.

A COVENANT WAS MADE

One of the steps taken to finalize the agreement was to share a covenant meal. The Bible says that the Israelites partook of their food and " . . . asked not counsel at the mouth of the LORD," (Joshua 9:14). The deceivers began to relax when the Israelites did not consult the LORD about making this covenant.

Relieved, the Gibeonites knew that even if the Israelites found they had been deceived, safety was relatively sure. A *beriyth* had been made and Jehovah had been called on to witness the oath. God's righteousness would judge the transgressed. The Gibeonites and the Israelites knew severe penalties would be the just reward for the one who dared to transgress covenant.

DECEPTION DISCOVERED

Within three days after the league, or covenant, was made, the deception of the Gibeonites was discovered. Joshua and the Israelites were justifiably angry. Joshua had a difficult time convincing Israel the covenant could not be broken simply because deception had been the catalyst. Since the oath had been taken, Israel was obligated to covenant faithfulness. Joshua made the assembly understand that because they had sworn by the Lord God of Israel they could not harm their covenant partners the Gibeonites. Israel was compelled to fulfill her agreement. The covenant was effective though deception was used to initiate it and Israel had not approached Jehovah for counsel when they consented to covenant. (Joshua 9:16-20)

When confronted about their deceptiveness, Gibeon acknowledged their fraudulence. In their defense they pleaded guilty and admitted knowing that all the inhabitants of Canaan were to have been destroyed. They also knew that the lives of the residents from afar would be spared if they were willing to make an unequal covenant with Israel. (Joshua 9:24-27)

Gibeon's unequal suzerain-vassal covenant provided for her safe-keeping. But the newly formed covenant between Israel and Gibeon was soon tested.

> The defection of the Gibeonites at this stage helped Joshua to drive a wedge still further into the central part of Canaan: this, and the possibility that he might use the resources of the great city Gibeon to intensify his attack against the whole land, explains the urgency with which the five kings of the Amorites now moved against Gibeon.[84]

The remaining kings of the area had counted on the aid of Gibeon. When the news of the covenant between Israel and Gibeon reached King Adonizedek, he was filled with fear. (Joshua 10:1-2) Adonizedek, king of Jerusalem, knew that Gibeon's allegiance with Israel and her strategic location would make it nearly impossible for the remaining Canaanites to win over Israel. Gibeon was located in the central part of

Canaan. Their alliance with Israel meant Joshua had gained valuable military assets for the conquest of Canaan.[85]

Gibeon was a great city with many mighty men. With Gibeon in league with Israel, an already formidable host, the kings of the Amorites felt hope of survival was dashed. Adonizedek had good reason to fear when Gibeon made peace with Israel. He was not only fearful, he was angry. With those two spirits motivating him, Adonizedek sent messengers to the kings of the surrounding areas. His call for a united effort against Gibeon brought several other area kings with armed forces ready to fight.

TESTING OF ISRAEL'S COMMITMENT

Covenant faithfulness is required of the Lord. Gibeon, though its men were mighty, was not so foolish as to overestimate their ability. Without Israel's help, the battle would be lost to the kings arrayed against them. The mighty kings from Jerusalem, Hebron, Jarmuth, Lachish, and Eglon had an allegiance. United, these kings had in their service the greatest warriors the land had to offer. These were the sons of those whose very appearance had frightened the previous generation of Israelites who died in the wilderness. But there was another generation arrayed against the armies of the kings. (Numbers 13:28-33; 14:9, 31, 33)

Gibeon called on their covenant partner whose God had shown Himself faithful throughout the area east of the Nile. They were grateful for their covenant with Israel. With confidence due a covenant partner, an appeal was sent to Joshua. They sent a reminder that because of covenant, Israel was expected to defend Gibeon with their very lives. Israel, true to their God who had witnessed their oath and expected covenant faithfulness, went forth to defend their vassals. Knowing God established and honored covenant, they confidently traveled in the will of, and therefore in the strength of, their God. (Joshua 10:6-8; Psalm 89:34)

With faith in their covenant partner Jehovah, Israel went to the defense of their covenant partner Gibeon. It was during this battle that Joshua exercised great faith in Jehovah. Israel's mighty men of valor needed more daylight to pursue and battle in the mountainous area east and west of Gibeon.

> *Then Joshua spoke to the Lord in the day when the Lord delivered up the Amorites before the children of Israel, and he said in the sight of Israel: "Sun, stand still over Gibeon; and Moon, in the Valley of Aijalon." So the sun stood still, and the moon stopped, till the people had revenge upon their enemies.*
>
> *Is this not written in the Book of Jasher? So the sun stood still in the midst of heaven, and did not hasten to go down for about a whole day. And there has been no day like that, before it or after it, that the Lord heeded the voice of a man; for the Lord fought for Israel.*
>
> —Joshua 10:12-14 NKJV

Joshua and Caleb were men of faith. Again Israel had supernatural help from the Lord of hosts. God honored Joshua's faith and another puzzle piece was placed aright into God's marvelous plan. Almighty God showed Himself faithful and strong on the behalf of His people.

Joshua proved himself faithful to covenant before God and in sight of the Israelites and the Gibeonites. Still today as believers read these verses they are encouraged in their own walk with the Lord of lords and the King of kings. We are to walk aright with God. He has not changed. He is faithful and we are to be faithful. (Joshua 10:6-14)

The Lord fought alongside Israel as they defended their covenant partners, the Gibeonites. Israel rejoiced that their God had again proven Himself faithful to covenant. Stopping the sun and moon at

Joshua's word was another miracle that confirmed God kept His promises. God was establishing His covenant faithfulness. He was showing Himself strong to His people. They were discovering for themselves that He would not break His covenant or alter the promises that He had made.

Israel and Gibeon had made a national treaty or covenant. A national covenant involved all the population of the areas represented by the covenant heads. The covenant between Israel and Gibeon was like the Hittite suzerain-vassal covenants. In addition to covenants that affected entire nations there were also covenants that involved individuals and their descendants. One such covenant was the one made between David and Jonathan.[86]

DAVID AND JONATHAN

Often detail is lacking in the relaying of information. Biblical detail is not always available for men to "figure out" what is meant. But as Pat Harrison repeatedly says, "How I love the Holy Ghost." His teaching relayed to the heart supernaturally belies (shows to be untrue) anything that is not of God. But for one like David who was a man after God's own heart there is given insight for His people to know what is of the One True Almighty God and what is not true.

If any author were to pen details of all major events in the history of creation we would not have a Bible we could carry to church. Semi-trucks would be needed even if only a more detailed version of Genesis were written, bound in a book to be carried about. But the process of making covenant was something familiar with that age and a lot of detail was not needed. Jonathan and David made a covenant. In chapter one the concept and steps of covenant were shown to be historically and internationally practiced and at least partially understood.

Covenant love was indicative of a highly esteemed, respectful, and honorable appreciation for a friend wherein they became as brothers. A phrase that is somewhat familiar today applied to them. They became blood brothers. Jonathan gave David his princely robe, his garments, his sword, his bow, and his girdle. By doing so, Jonathan was acknowledging the God-given authority of succession to the God-appointed future king of Israel. Jonathan was also showing his own life was bound up with the life of David.[87] As blood brothers, Jonathan was committed to defend David. It is honorable of Jonathan that his defense of David was excellent while at the same time he was able to continue honoring his father Saul. David honored Saul referring to him as God's anointed. (Proverbs 18:24; 1 Samuel 18:1-4, 12; 20:16-18)

David had been in the fields tending the sheep when Samuel had sent for him. Anointed at God's direction, the Spirit of the Lord came upon David. He was known to Saul's servants as one who was a skillful player on a harp; and yet a mighty valiant man. He was a man of war, and prudent in matters. He was a comely person and the Lord was with him. David was summoned to serve Saul. David served with music and was able to cause Saul to be refreshed after having been harassed by an evil spirit. (1 Samuel 16:16-18)

David had not only ministered to Saul with music, but was also his armor bearer. Saul and Jonathan saw David's heroic confrontation with Goliath. Jonathan, the son of King Saul, seems to have recognized David's call from God. Jonathan could have easily fallen in with his father and harbored anger and bitterness. Instead he committed himself to a covenant with David. The solemn agreement between David and Jonathan had some inherent difficulties. In giving David his royal robe, his armor, his sword and his bow and his belt, Jonathan was giving his authority of succession to his father's throne to David.[88]

Saul's love for David turned to hate because Saul realized the Lord was with David. Saul stumbled at God's Word, but David maintained integrity honoring the Lord with his faith. Saul realized the Lord was no longer with him as had been evident when Saul was first anointed king of Israel. Envy, hate, and fear continually set Saul against David. Saul's hate and constant conspiring against David, understandably, put Jonathan in a precarious situation. As Malcolm Smith, a speaker and author on the subject of covenant said, "though Jonathan was of the family of Saul, he was not like Saul."[89]

We will explore this statement further in a later chapter of this book. Around 1977, someone at a Bible study gave me a series of tapes by Malcolm Smith. His teachings on covenant triggered my interest in the subject. Later, in 1984, Malcolm graciously granted me permission to refer to what he taught. I found that his example of David, Jonathan, and Mephibosheth excellently illustrated the better covenant spiritual truths. The usage here is primarily based on my own studies but full recognition is given to Malcolm Smith for his inspiration in the series of tapes I heard back in 1977.

Unlike Saul, Jonathan had a heart turned toward God. Because of Jonathan's love for the Lord and because of his understanding of covenant, Jonathan and his armor bearer took a stand against the Philistine garrison at Michmash. With faith in the God of Abraham, Isaac, and Jacob, Jonathan went into the garrison of the uncircumcised Philistines. By using the term *uncircumcised*, it seems Jonathan was saying, "the Philistines are not in a covenant with the Lord, but we are. We have the evidence of the covenant with God even in our flesh. We are circumcised. Therefore with assurance of aid from our covenant partner, we can go into the camp of the Philistines knowing victory is ours." (See 1 Samuel 13:23-14:15.)

Because of his understanding of covenant, Jonathan drew strength from Jehovah and won over the Philistines. David also understood covenant. Like Jonathan, David had an encounter with the Philistines. For days the Philistines' champion Goliath had been intimidating Israel.

When David heard Goliath's charges and intimidating threats, he did not consider the size of the man who had been speaking fearsome words against the army of Israel. All David knew was that Israel's army was blindly disregarding their covenant Partner and fearfully heeding the voice of a giant.

David knew the covenant provisions of God included victory—even over such a man. Victory was a small task in comparison to Moses facing all of Egypt's soldiers. Vain self-promotions and boastful proclamations shouted by a towering man like Goliath did not deter David. Instead, David was even more determined than when he faced dangers while shepherding.

Though he was just a young man, David had a faith in God that has awed believers for more than three thousands years. He made decisions according to the authority granted by His covenant God. His remarkable victories began in the sheep fields when he fought a lion and a bear. The challenge from Goliath was seen by David as another opportunity to defeat a destroyer an enemy of God. The *uncircumcised* giant threatening the *armies of the living God* would not be any more successful than the lion and bear David had already defeated. The faith David was displaying encouraged Saul to say, "Go, and the LORD be with thee." (1 Samuel 17:26, 33, 36-37)

With five smooth stones, a shepherd's bag, and faith in the God of his fathers, David prepared to meet Goliath with his sling in hand. His covenant partner had promised to be his shield and reward. Abraham's promise was for his descendant David that day as he hurried toward Goliath. The promises were intended for David's brothers, Saul, and the rest of the Israelite army, but they allowed fear to choke their faith. God's promises are yes and amen. They had passed on an opportunity to believe God was faithful to covenant. David won a victory that Saul and his army could have won.

The Philistine's ridicule did not deter David. He boldly shouted in faith as he ran toward the enemy:

> *"You come to me with a sword, with a spear, and with a javelin. But I come to you in the name of the Lord of hosts, the God of the armies of Israel, whom you have defied. This day the Lord will deliver you into my hand, and I will strike you and take your head from you. And this day I will give the carcasses of the camp of the Philistines to the birds of the air and the wild beasts of the earth, that all the earth may know that there is a God in Israel. Then all this assembly shall know that the Lord does not save with sword and spear; for the battle* is *the* LORD's*, and He will give you into our hands."*
>
> —1 Samuel 17:45-47 NKJV

David knew the battle was the Lord's. He knew God's grace and strength to overcome the bear and the lion as he guarded his father's sheep. The Philistine's ridicule only increased David's faith in Jehovah, his Covenant God. David had prevailed.

Within covenant relationship, use of the name of one's covenant partner is expected. Respectful expectation is still part of godly support, a good connection between two who are moving together. In marriage, it is godly wisdom to be equally joined together. The last name of husband and wife usually become the same when they are married. In today's marriages, a wife has legal right to bear her husband's name unless she determines to do otherwise.

David confidently faced Goliath in the name of the Lord. The name used by David is the Hebrew word JHWH, translated Jehovah in the Old Testament of the *King James Version* of the Bible. Don't let the difference befuddle you. JHWH, Jehovah, LORD are the same and will be explained more thoroughly later.

David certainly was not confused. He knew where his strength came from. God's covenant relationship with Israel was broadcast as David confronted Israel's enemy. Dispersing his faith in YHWH's name through the valley and into the hills, David ran toward the enemy of God's covenant people. David's victory again broadcast Jehovah, Israel's shield. David had clearly shown he understood the immeasurable magnitude of Israel's covenant with Jehovah. God's host was there for David. Victory was Israel's because one among them was anointed and took the lead as a man after God's own heart. (1 Samuel 4:4, Psalm 83:18)

As David received accelerated recognition, he and Jonathan cut a covenant with each other. Understanding clearly the advantages and disadvantages of covenant they became as blood brothers. Each willingly committed to the stipulations of their covenant. Their lives became intertwined. They ceased to live independently. By faith and covenant they committed themselves to the defense of the other. They swore to defend each other and aid each other even in the face of death. With an undying, unselfish, God-kind of covenant love, a wholesome bond between Jonathan and David was established.

Though Jonathan loved David, Jonathan's father Saul hated David. Saul was jealous of David's victories in battle. But the blood brothers remained faithful to their covenant with each other and their covenant with the God of their fathers. Fearful and unfaithful, Saul was as a thorn in the flesh to both David and Jonathan. (1 Samuel 18:28-29; 19:1)

Saul demanded his family assist him as he actively sought to kill David. He argued that they should kill David before David could kill them. Saul was stumbling with a load of jealousy, pride, bitterness, and assumptions. He would not allow Jonathan or David to help him. Instead his lies became progressively worse, like fiery darts aimed at David. When David reminded Jonathan of their covenant, he called it *a covenant of the Lord*. God bore witness when they entered into their covenant, which followed the example of God's covenant with Abraham and Moses. Jonathan remained loyal to David in spite of Saul's entreaty, his command that David be killed. Jonathan repeatedly defended David until the day he died. He had remained helpful to Saul even in their last battle on Mount Gilboa. Jonathan honored his father. He faithfully honored the LORD by keeping covenant with David. (1 Samuel 20:8)

When David heard of Jonathan's and Saul's death, the Bible says he "... mourned, and wept, and fasted until evening ... because they were fallen by the sword," (2 Samuel 1:12). He mourned for Jonathan because they were blood brothers and David loved Jonathan as his own soul. He mourned for Saul because David loved the Lord, and Saul was God's anointed servant. David and Jonathan had remained faithful to God and to each other. And both, in spite of Saul, remained faithful to Saul. David and Jonathan understood covenant.

MEPHIBOSHETH

David never forgot his covenant partner, Jonathan. After David was established as king, he sought for any descendants of Jonathan that he might *show him kindness for Jonathan's sake*. David and Jonathan were the covenant heads, and the covenant they made involved their unborn children. Loving-kindness and covenant faithfulness[90] was David's heart for Jonathan's son, Mephibosheth. (2 Samuel 9:1-13)

Mephibosheth, lame since he was five years old, had been raised in LoDebar. He was handicapped and an orphan dependent on the servants of Saul. It is probable that the servants would have told Mephibosheth that David was an opponent to be feared. Saul had told his family and servants that David was out to destroy them. The servants may have even said David would try to kill Mephibosheth so that Saul's throne would not return to a descendent of Saul. He may have feared for his own life.

The effects of that type of indoctrination probably did not cease with Saul's death. Mephibosheth, as a member of Saul's family, surely heard that David was determined to kill him. It is speculation on my part, but Mephibosheth may have planned to kill David, as this was not uncommon retaliatory behavior under similar circumstances. But the physical handicap he suffered would have hampered plans of vengeance. The scripture does not spell out details. What may have been bitterness and anger toward David was not given space. But we do know the emotional weight of grief often entangles family members who can be susceptible to the tricks of the devil when the Lord's comfort is rejected. (2 Samuel 9)

Mephibosheth's physical handicap probably had less effect on him than the emotional handicap caused by Saul's lies. The hate, which probably resulted from those lies, could have borne weed seed and bad fruit, likely leaving Mephiboseth imprisoned and bound with roots of bitterness. Each day he probably struggled against physical and emotional handicaps to even get his body out of bed.

My mother's body was 100 percent paralyzed on her left side. Though I helped as much as I could, she struggled even to see. The paralysis affected both her eyes. Conspicuously handicapped to people around her, even she probably did not know all the internal damage done. The left side of each of her eyes was completely blind. Mephibosheth had been living in LoDebar for over twenty years crippled. The challenges he faced could not have been fully realized, no matter how many people tried to help him.

I can imagine Jonathan's covenant descendant, Mephibosheth, getting up one morning. Struggling to move, his hair most likely disheveled and his clothes crumpled, he probably splashed water on his face to refresh himself. He may have even been imagining what it would be like to be reestablished in the palace and in the kingdom his grandfather Saul had reigned over. There surely would have been a lot more help for him if he could occupy the throne. While hiding in LoDebar things may have been tough. Mephibosheth most likely fought depression over what might have been. Bitterness is as a deep root capable of choking even good intentions.

Meanwhile, David had inquired and learned that Jonathan had a son. He sent troops to bring him to the palace that David might show him covenant kindness. Perhaps they arrived as Mephibosheth was struggling to prepare for the day. David's troops approaching would surely have been alarming. Ignorant of the covenant his father had made, he probably assumed David's troops were hunting to kill him. Taking him dead or alive remained to be seen. The reward would probably be the same to those hunting him. Mephibosheth's reaction to the troops would probably have been a disturbing mixture of feelings.

As with those who initially hear the news of the Lord of hosts today, often there is a mixture stirring in the heart. Self-justification and pride melt away little by little as the goodness of the Lord shows forth. Then they find themselves in a valley of decision. Mephibosheth may have had a little hope that everything might be OK. The mix in his own heart probably included anger—because in his estimation he should be the one living in the palace instead of in LoDebar. And fear would be there too, because the one he had hated and perhaps even planned vengeance against definitely had the upper hand and had proven to be strong. He must have thought as he was being ushered into the presence of David by the king's men that he would be facing certain death. That likely seemed the just reward for having spent an entire life running and possibly planning to kill David—and for simply being one of the descendants of Saul.

When brought into the presence of David *he fell on his face, and did reverence*.[91] He probably had difficulty believing the good news David spoke to him. David assured him there was no need to fear. Then David told Mephibosheth that for Jonathan's sake, David intended to show kindness to him. Indeed, David promised restoration and provisions. Mephibosheth began to see things differently because now he knew there had been a covenant made between his father, Jonathan, and King David when Jonathan was prince and David was barely more than a shepherd. Having traveled through hate, rebellion, and fear, Mephibosheth faced a decision.

Pausing with feelings of unworthiness he muttered, "What is thy servant, that thou shouldest look upon such a dead dog as I am?" (2 Samuel 9:8). David's loving-kindness presented a choice. As many others in a valley of decision, Mephibosheth had a choice to make. He could stay in the palace, fellowship with David, and eat at David's table, or return to LoDebar. Would he enter in or would he choose to return to his own place his old ways? (2 Samuel 9:6,8; Joel 3:14)

Believers in the Lord Jesus Christ before being born again are a lot like Mephibosheth was before he entered David's presence. They come into the light of the presence of the Lord. Having heard the gospel, some retreat into the darkness of LoDebar. Some prefer the darkness and refuse the light and deliverance of the Lord. But many, many do enter into a new way of life. Mephibosheth chose to remain in Jerusalem and eat at the king's table. He became like one of the king's sons.

> Mephibosheth would be like one of the king's sons. In all of this David was a type of our Lord who redeems, restores, and returns us to our Father's table in peace.[92]

God is good and His provision is waiting to be received, but many prefer a comfort zone that is filled with old and even evil things. The covenant David made with Jonathan affected Mephibosheth who was only one generation removed from the covenant heads. Mephibosheth was affected because he was in the loins of the covenant head Jonathan when the covenant was made. He was benefited because David, a man after God's own heart, honored God with covenant faithfulness.

Another biblical example of descendants and the duration of covenant began with the heads of the covenant between Joshua and Gibeon. Joshua's agreement with Gibeon affected their descendants even 430 years after their covenant was made.

THE DESCENDANTS OF GIBEON

For three years Israel had suffered a famine because Saul had sought the extermination of the Gibeonites. As leader of Israel, he broke covenant with the Gibeonites and all of Israel was suffering as a result of this unfaithfulness to their covenant partner. Even 430 years after God had witnessed the making of the solemn agreement between Joshua and Gibeon, the covenant was still in effect. But Saul had systematically and zealously slaughtered the Gibeonites. The zeal that motivated him was not of God and his action did nothing to help the Israelites as he had erroneously thought it would. Saul's misdirected zeal was costly for Israel. The curse pronounced centuries before for disobedience to their covenant was still effective as was the price of restoration.

> After the victories at Jericho and Ai at the very beginning of Joshua's conquest of Canaan, the Gibeonites tricked Joshua into making a covenant with them, ensuring they would never be harmed by Israel. In exchange for this protection, they would perform menial work for Israel. (Joshua 9) They are also called Hivites in Joshua 9:7.[93]

Joshua and the king of Gibeon were the covenant heads of the solemn agreement made 430 years earlier. Joshua had sworn to the Gibeonites by the Lord God of Israel that Israel would not harm them, but Israel breached that promise.

Saul had caused great harm to Israel's covenant partners and consequently to his own nation. The price of Saul's transgression had to be paid. Israel and Gibeon knew breaking covenant meant wrath would consequently fall on the transgressors. Israel was suffering for their transgression. Famine was a curse frequently pronounced as covenants were initiated so that those entering into covenant would be informed of the consequence if they were disobedient. King David sought the Lord about the cause of the famine. The Lord answered, "It is because of Saul and his bloodthirsty house, because he killed the Gibeonites." Saul the king, the head of the nation Israel, had broken covenant. God told David the cause of the curse and the Gibeonites told him the cost of restoration. The descendants of the transgressor Saul would pay the price of redemption to the transgressed Gibeonites. (2 Samuel 21:1-7)

When Israel had honored their covenant with Gibeon hundreds of years earlier and went to their defense, God gave them a monumental victory. But now when Israel chose to transgress God could not bless them. Israel suffered a curse caused by breaking an oath sworn to Gibeon in the name of the Lord. David understood covenant and he understood the extent of the transgression. Obediently he delivered to the Gibeonites what they requested. Seven sons of Saul were hanged for Saul's violation of covenant. The exception was Mephibosheth, the descendant of Jonathan—David's own covenant partner. Again David had shown kindness to the descendant of his covenant partner.

When the price was paid the rain fell, and the land was refreshed. ". . . For God was entreated for the land." The Gibeonites had suffered a massacre at the hand of Saul but were avenged by David. God had clearly not forgotten and David was mindful of their covenant. Israel knew the instruction of the Lord in regard to keeping their vows. He had clearly told them that it would be better not to vow, than to vow and not pay. To make a vow, a covenant or a solemn pledge and not keep it was to cause destruction to one's person and belongings. One who was obedient to covenant received blessings and one who was disobedient received a curse; this was typical scripturally, as well as secularly. (2 Samuel 21:5-6,14)

Even the Hittites regularly included this in their own covenants. A curse that was upon Israel in the form of a famine was not because God randomly chose to cause a shortage of food. Rather Israel under the leadership of a misdirected national leader transgressed covenant, thus they were removed from fellowship with the covenant God. Because they had chosen to be transgressors, they were reaping the reward of the transgressor, and there was a famine in the land.

God is faithful. He is altogether righteous and faithfully keeps His word. His covenant faithfulness is eternal. He never breaks his word. Moses, the prophets, and the apostles all bear witness—God is faithful to covenant. He expects faithfulness from those that enter into covenant. He supplies all we need to do all He tells us to do. He is our strength and song and He has become our salvation. Jesus is the mediator. (Romans 12:2; 1 Timothy 2:5; 1 Corinthians 1:25-31; Hebrews 12:24; Exodus 15:1-2; Psalm 28:7-8; 118:14-29; Isaiah 12:1-3)

Covenant faithfulness is a twenty-four hour a day, seven-day a week, lifelong necessity for those whom God has joined together. He is our strength. He is true. (John 15:1-27) How is that lifelong faithfulness possible in covenant relationships? How can He expect us to keep our word, our covenant with Him and with others? How? By being a doer of God's Word. The wisdom to remain faithful is attainable.

With all His goodness available in covenant relationship it is glorious to walk with Him. In walking with Him, He gives strength, insight, and wisdom into the mysteries of Christ within—more than enough to excel. All questions who, what, when, where, plus more is contained in Genesis through Revelation. We can abide and live according to His covenant stipulations. (Romans 12:18; 14:8; James 1:5; Ephesians 6:3; Galatians 5:25; Psalm 145:18)

Gibeon called on their covenant partners for help. When Israel decided to honor their covenant agreement and to fight against the five kings who came against Gibeon, God strengthened them and gave them victory. They kept their word and God blessed them. With great covenant grace and mercies God is able to minister to all. *His mercies are new every morning*. With His written Word and ever-present help of the Holy Spirit, all we need is made available to us.

When Mephibosheth decided to walk in obedience to covenant, he was blessed. God has established covenant and He respects those who are faithful to covenant. He strengthened and enabled those faithful to covenant in the Old Testament. We are privileged and tremendously blessed to live in a better covenant. The decision is ours. Will we live in the New Commandment love and walk in faith that pleases God and does not frustrate the grace of God with unbelief? The choice is ours. Indeed, whose report will you believe? (Isaiah 53:1)

God is good. Harshness is not the issue. It is all about the kindness of God, which David had shown to Mephibosheth for Jonathan's sake. It is about Almighty God who is altogether righteous and holy. His ways are revealed to the humble little by little, but are hidden from the proud. His is a perfect plan in process. Many are physically blind, some partially so. But spiritual blindness is all about choice. Whose God will you serve? As for me and my house we will serve the LORD.

Chapter 5

RESPECT

Placement of puzzle pieces is easier when assembled in a well-lit room. In dim light or darkness a puzzle can be impossible to assemble. The light itself is a key to seeing the partnering of the reference picture and the pile of pieces lying on a tabletop. Supposed contradictions in the Bible can be like these puzzle pieces. A person without adequate reference or adequate light will have problems.

The matter of respect involves a collection of puzzle pieces intended for a portion of the puzzle. The reference writings of the New Covenant are valuable. To disregard the Old Covenant and only consider the New Covenant is as foolish as disregarding the New and considering only the Old. They are both to be considered by believers with the help of the Holy Spirit. God's perfect plan of salvation is clearly shown in both the Old and the New. The New Covenant is understandable when the old is made new, as explained by the Lord Jesus Christ. Multitudes comprehended and were made new as expounded in the gospels, epistles, and revelation. Without the Old Testament, writers of the New Testament would have had much less to write about in their explanation of the Better Covenant.

Israel's sole claim to covenant with God has puzzled most who have even a hint of comprehension. The place of the Gentiles in God's Word can be puzzling. Favoritism often causes bitterness. Doctrinal differences can be puzzling. New believers ponder which Bible to read.

Rabbis, church elders, and ministers likewise puzzle over many Bible precepts. Both the Old and New Covenants are a source of confusion for many. Hopefully we can bring some clarity to the forefront and allow the light to shine on God's point of view.

GOD—NO RESPECTOR OF PERSONS

Cornelius. The way of God's blood covenant and the way of respect is a marvelous and admirable mystery. Jesus himself said he is the way, the truth, and the life. Present tense is still the way it is. He is and ever shall be. Jesus, the Word made flesh, said, *God is no respecter of persons* spoken through Peter when he ministered to Cornelius and his household. (John 1:14; Acts 10)

During His last three years ministering, Jesus lived and spoke the way, the truth, and the life of God—fulfilling all that had been written by Moses and the prophets. The gospel, however, had not been shown forth into all the earth yet. Such a marvelous mystery had come to pass so that even the apostles had not fully understood the extent of what the Lord had told them or of what they had studied since they were children. Though perhaps it was simply the time had not arrived yet for Cornelius to be the first in the better covenant to hear it said, "God is no respecter of persons." (Acts 10:34; John 14:6; Mark 16:15)

He had the Lord's attention and an angel was sent to minister. Obediently Cornelius summoned two of his trusted servants and a soldier to accompany them.[94] They were all sent to Joppa to find Peter and urge him to return with them to Caesarea. (Acts 10:1-5; Hebrews 1:7, 13-14; 2 Corinthians 3:1-6)

> Cornelius, (was) a member of the class referred to by Luke as 'God-fearers,' who attached themselves to the spiritual and

monotheistic Jewish worship in the synagogues without becoming converts to Judaism. . . . [95]

Though not a Jew, Cornelius believed in Jehovah Elohim, worshipped in the synagogue, studied the teachings of the Old Testament and practiced Jewish customs. "His devout character was manifested by his liberal alms to the people and his regular prayers to God."[96] As a Roman centurion, he was a military officer who commanded from fifty to one hundred men. He was not an Israelite and had no natural birthright to expect any of the covenant benefits available to the Israelites. However, God had graciously provided for the inclusion of such *strangers* into a limited covenant involvement with himself even in the Old Covenant. (Numbers 15:14-16)

Cornelius' devotion to God paved the way for the introduction of the good news to the Gentiles. In his day, a Gentile was a non-Jew or one who was not of the Jewish faith. Later, the term Gentile included non-Christians. For the first time the good news, the gospel of Christ, was available even to the non-Jew. The good news was the better covenant of Jesus; it was the New Testament; it was the finished redemptive work of the promised Messiah. Now that good news would finally be made available throughout the world.

Abraham had been promised his seed would be a blessing to all the families of the earth. Jesus was the narrow passage of the hourglass promise of redemption. Now the grains of covenant blessing, privilege, and even stipulations would pour through Jesus to all who would believe, including the Gentiles. Christianity would no longer be limited to the Jews as it had been previously. Since Jesus' death the good news of salvation through Him had been exclusively Jewish. Cornelius would be one of the first to see the end of that exclusion. His step of faith was about to bring incalculable benefits to himself, to his entire household, as well as to the entire Gentile population. The hourglass effect was continuing.

The topmost part of the hourglass included all men beginning in Genesis. As time passed, the channel through which the promises would come narrowed. Jesus, the narrowest passageway of that hourglass, became the grace through faith passageway for all men who would see and enter into the kingdom of God through Him. The lower compartment of the hourglass was available to all men. They would need, however, to come in faith to Jesus, the narrow passageway into the final stage of the hourglass. Cornelius would be one of the first of all the nations; that would be blessed because of the obedience of the Lord Jesus Christ. (Galatians 3:7-9, 29; John 3:3-21)

Peter. Having sent for Peter, Cornelius began to prepare for his arrival. Peter, still unaware of God's intent, was in Joppa. He had gone upon the flat roof of his residence to pray. The roofs in Peter's day were extensions of one's house, where, in the cool of the evening, men would frequently go to pray. Peter was still on the roof in prayer when he had a vision in which God revealed a door was opened which Peter had not yet understood.[97] (Acts 10:9-16)

Jewish law forbade the eating of certain animals and birds. Peter had always been obedient to the Jewish law. Instruction to eat the unclean animals he saw being lowered from heaven in his vision was completely alien to him. Three times God repeated his instruction not to call common or unclean what God had cleansed. For the first time Peter perceived the worldwide significance of God's cleansing by the shed blood of the Lord Jesus Christ. The importance of the better covenant was just beginning to be realized. (Acts 10:1-48; Leviticus 11)

> The apostle understood the significance of the vision given to him on the rooftop. He realized that the distinction between clean and unclean foods had an application to human beings, and that, contrary to Jewish belief, no people were to be thought

of as unclean in the sight of God. God shows no partiality to any one people.[98]

The new covenant was available to all; thus it was a better covenant. Everyone could receive cleansing by grace through faith in Jesus, the mediator of the Better Covenant. Having received this revolutionary news, Peter contemplated its significance while below Cornelius' men approached the house where Peter was staying. (Acts 10:17-23)

Respecting the Jewish tradition, Cornelius' men waited outside the gate for Peter. They were aware of the many Jewish laws that curtailed their involvement with the Gentiles, but as Roman soldiers they could have entered without waiting. From the gate they called out and inquired for Peter. Peter came from the rooftop to find out what they wanted.

THE GENTILES

Remembering that God had cleansed the formerly unclean, Peter invited the Gentiles into his host's house. The men told Peter of Cornelius' angelic visitation. After hearing the details of God's instruction to Cornelius Peter made plans for the trip to Joppa.

The next morning some fellow Christians from Joppa joined Peter as he began his journey to Caesarea. For three days they traveled thirty-five miles along the coast of the Great Sea on their way to bear witness of God's abundant grace and perfect plan of salvation.

During Peter's preparation and travel time Cornelius used his time wisely. While continuing in prayer, he worked to arrange for Peter's visit. In faith he invited his family and close friends to join them as they waited for their visitors. Anticipating good news, Cornelius wanted all those he loved to be there when Peter arrived. Because Cornelius was an influential man, there were many who responded to his call. Anyone who has ever entertained a large group for several days knows the time and effort that goes into preparation. Surely there would have been foods prepared, serving vessels readied, and sleeping arrangements made. In addition there certainly would have been time spent by Cornelius relating to his guests the vision he had seen and of the joyful expectation that arose within him in regard to Peter's visit. When Peter arrived Cornelius and his guests were prepared to hear the good news. (Acts 10:24-43)

Peter began telling the good news of the better covenant that had been made available to all men. The blessings of God were no longer limited to only the believing Jew but now they were attainable by whosoever would believe. Cornelius, his household and his guests gladly believed all that Peter said. Then a marvel was experienced when the Gentiles heard the word preached.

> *While Peter yet spake these words, the Holy Ghost fell on all them which heard the word. And they of the circumcision which believed were astonished, as many as came with Peter, because that on the Gentiles also was poured out the gift of the Holy Ghost.*
>
> —Acts 10:44-45

Peter's venture into the home of a Gentile to tell of Jesus' work, death, and resurrection for the salvation of all who would believe caused some problems. When many heard what had happened, all types of questions were asked. The Christian community was initially Jewish and they believed Gentile inclusion was to be avoided. They were astonished that God would pour out His precious gift of the Holy Spirit to cleanse and benefit the Gentiles.

God's revelation of the provision of cleansing for the Gentiles caused waves throughout the Jewish community. The Jews were familiar with the Old Testament passages in which God was declared to be no respecter of persons, but they had assumed those passages applied only to the Jewish community. Because of Peter's bold obedience to God, the Jews' limited vision of God's plan of salvation was being stretched, even shaken. They began to perceive that indeed God is no respecter of persons. (2 Samuel 14:14; Romans 2:6-12; Ephesians 2:11, 6:9; Colossians 3:25; 1 Peter 1:17)

Saul/Paul. The journey on the road to Damascus became a life-changing confrontation for Saul. A devout follower of the Old Covenant, Saul came near his destination when suddenly a blinding light appeared. The Lord himself intercepted Saul's ride. Having followed his own understanding gleaned from years of studies, this puzzle piece did not fit into the picture Saul had drawn from the Old Covenant. Suddenly he was confronted by the Lord, who called, *Saul. Saul, why are you persecuting Me*? The persecution was being taken personally.

Saul intended to continue and believed he was doing God's will. God knew otherwise. The puzzle piece given to Saul when he held Stephen's coat remained in his own concept of correct placement. That day the light of the Lord caused blindness when loving-kindness brought Saul to the realization of his own misplaced mission. He had been in a very dark place when trying to manage the problem of the Christians.

Saul was later called Paul. A man of intellectual aptness dealt with his *Damascus Road* conundrum with a simple question, *who are You, Lord*? The answer contained an allusion his mind could not handle. However, within Paul's question was the answer to the question he was asking, *You, Lord*. The puzzle given him, the picture shown him was a matter to be received from the Lord alone. *I am Jesus, whom you are persecuting*. Jesus, the mediator of a better covenant, was a mystery Paul had yet to grasp. He had zealously, religiously been there when Stephen was stoned. As a religious man zealously persecuting followers of the Lord, it had nonetheless been hard for him to resist the pricking of his conscience as he watched Stephen die. James wrote that any man who seemed to be religious but whose heart was deceived was a man whose religion was vain and worthless.

Paul began an even more zealous walk following the Lord Jesus Christ and began to hand out puzzles pieces to millions of believers. The puzzle had come together for him and he faithfully shared insights given him by the Holy Spirit. His epistles still stir the hearts of believers in their own walk with the Lord. (Acts 9:1-20; 13:9, 13,16, 43-50; 17:2-4; 22:1-15; James 1:26-27; Romans 1:16)

More than 2000 years later, Paul's contributions to the New Testament are encouraging the same faith he had tried to destroy as Saul. In his epistle to the Romans he wrote, "there is no respect of persons with God." Saul, respected by many because of his zealous works, was conspicuously missing *the mark of the high calling of God.* The Lord had no respect for Saul because of his zeal, his religion, his works. However, his sudden supernatural change of heart placed him in a new and very spacious sphere. One in which the Lord would bless him and give revelation light into *the mystery of Christ within.*

Old things passed away for Paul on the *road to Damascus*. He was made new. The light was turned onto the Old where he had so diligently camped and studied. The New came alive to him when the light was turned on for him. (Mark 4:11; Romans 11:25; 16:25; Matthew 13:52; 2 Corinthians 5:17; 2 Peter 1:9)

Many of the believers, including some of the apostles, had trouble believing God's loving-kindness could have been extended to Paul. That God had even shown any mercy to Paul seemed impossible. The Christians of Paul's day had seen the Lord's resurrection and innumerable miracles, but Paul's salvation was especially challenging for them to believe. Remembering his persecutions caused fear. Faith would have to be reinforced to believe the Lord would extend His saving grace to Paul.

Sometime later Paul wrote *there is no respect of persons, no partiality, with God.* (Romans 2:11; 2 Timothy 2:15-16) But there are also verses that say he had respect for Israel, for Abel, and others. Where do these puzzle pieces fit? Reading the Bible without consideration of context can cause the puzzle itself to remain unfinished. Focusing on one verse to establish a doctrine is dangerous. That can be an easy way to fall into error. To attempt to rightly divide this portion of scripture we must consider covenant concepts, which can help clarify this supposed contradiction.

GOD—A RESPECTOR OF PERSONS

When all is considered in the scriptures, the answer to what may have otherwise been perceived as a contradiction is explained. When the Holy Spirit of God dwells within He helps any who truly desire to do God's will to know what is of God and what is not. The Holy Spirit is a teacher without comparison in excellence. (John 7:17 AMP)

ABEL

With accounts of the commandment of the Lord told by Adam and Eve, their sons Cain and Abel made decisions about their offerings unto the Lord. (Genesis 2:15-17; 4:4-7)

> . . . Concerning the nature and meanings of different sacrifices, this narrative shows Abel lovingly and trustfully reaching out toward God with substitute blood, in order to be in covenant oneness with God; while Cain merely proffers a gift from his earthly possessions.[99]

It was only on a covenant basis that God could interact with man. Cain and Abel were no exceptions. These two brothers shared the same heritage and environment. They had both heard a first hand report of the creation and the original covenants. Likewise they both shared a common dilemma—sin had caused them to be separated from God. The Adamic covenant promise was available to them. However, faith and obedience were mandatory to activate the covenant promise in their own lives.

To be obedient to covenant they must bring a sacrifice before God, a sacrifice that provided for the remission of sin and reinstatement of fellowship with God. The Scriptures indicate God introduced sacrifice to Adam and Eve as He made the first blood covenant, the Adamic covenant. Adam and Eve would have instructed their children so that Cain and Abel were aware of the blood sacrifice requirement. Abel's sacrifice was in obedience to God's covenant stipulations while Cain's was not. By faith in God's covenant promise and obedience to the covenant terms, Abel had God's respect. Cain could just as easily have had God's respect by ruling over sin and rebellion and offering a sacrifice that was pleasing to God. (Genesis 1:26; 2:7-8; 15-17; 3:15-19; 4:1-5; 15:9-10; Hebrews 9:22; 11:4; 12:24)

The Lord spoke through Moses and told the Israelites, "If thou wilt diligently hearken to the voice of the Lord thy God, and wilt do that which is right in his sight, and wilt give ear to his commandments, and keep all his statutes, I will put none of these diseases upon thee, which I have brought upon the Egyptians: for I am the LORD that healeth thee," (Exodus 15:26). The covenant is seen clearly in the context of this verse. Yehovah (Yahweh-Ropheka/Rapha) the covenant God of Abraham, Isaac, and Jacob again spoke to His people declaring His attributes and covenant intent to them.[100] In his own valley of decision, Cain chose to rebel and when sin was at the door he did not rule over it, but rather killed his brother. (Exodus 15:26; Joel 2:14)

The Garden of Eden was not so far removed from Cain and Abel that Cain would have been ignorant of God's covenant promise to

Adam. Covenant principles were recently demonstrated for Adam and Eve. Surely they would have told their sons. God was not randomly touching one and not the other. He had introduced and activated covenant. The hourglass was filled with time like grains of sand, which would begin sifting through the top into the bottom. From Adam's transgression to the coming of the one promised, time like sand passed through the ages. It still puzzles me how that simple device, an hourglass, can be accurate in measuring time. It would be aggravating to wear on a watchband but convenient near the stove when boiling eggs.

God had introduced covenant and some covenant principles in Genesis that would continue to be functional as long as there was a heaven and earth. From the beginning to the very end, the Alpha and Omega, we are to have respect unto Him and His covenant. No hourglass or Big Ben can measure the Alpha and Omega. But God has made a way for us to understand and therefore to trust His Word. His timing is much more perfect than any man's invention can compare to. (Genesis 3:15; Exodus 3:15; Psalms 74:20; 119:6,15, 117; Isaiah 17:7-8; Matthew 5:18; 16:19; 18:18; 24:35; Rev 20:9, 11; 21:1)

One of those principles was the law of sowing and reaping. Seeds of obedience and faith reaped righteousness and blessing while seeds of disobedience reaped fear, sin, and curses. (Genesis 1:11-12)

> Abel's sacrifice (Gen. 4:4) was acceptable, because he was righteous (1 John 3:12), and because it was offered in faith (Hebrews 11:4). On the entrance of Sin, it seems, God had ordained such sacrifice. It appears to have been a sort of primeval picture of the Atoning Death of Christ.[101]

Though God does not respect anyone because of works' as we often understand works. He does not respect mental aptitude or physique. He does respect those obedient to covenant, those who honor Him and call upon Him as their covenant God because of the Lord Jesus Christ.

ISRAEL

God had respect for the descendents of Abraham. Because of covenant, God performed miraculous works of deliverance. His respect for them prompted Him to repeatedly display His mighty power on their behalf. Though Israel understood covenant, they did not completely realize the ability, power, and might of their covenant partner. The plagues that were brought upon Egypt displayed God's superiority over the gods of the Egyptians. With the deliverance of Israel out of Egypt, God clearly showed His respect for Israel and lack of respect for Egypt. God is exonerated from contradiction because of faith and covenant. What one does in and of himself apart from God will not earn respect from Jehovah.

Paul said it well when he wrote that salvation is not of works. Otherwise we would be inclined to boast of our works. God is a respecter of persons but not in a random manner. He carefully chose to make covenant and clearly made known the stipulations, which included a simplified version known as the Ten Commandments. Carved on tablets of stone those precious words were carried in the Ark of the Covenant. Breaking covenant was a serious matter. Honoring Jehovah and keeping covenant was to be expected. Indeed it was the way in which Israel had God's respect as opposed to other nations.

However up and down waywardness often caused them to fall. The privilege of calling on the Lord in time of unfavorable consequences was sometimes a last resort for them. Falling at the hands of oppressors, a few faithful would call on the Lord. At those times they usually abandoned songs like Frank Sinatra sang, *I Did It My Way*. Repentant they called on the God of Abraham, Isaac and Jacob. (Ephesians 2:9; Hebrews 9:22; Genesis 15:9-10; 17:7; Exodus 2:23-25; 74:20; Lev 26:44; 2 Samuel 14:14; 12-13, 18-21; Psalm 74:)

From Adam, Noah, Abraham, and Moses covenant principles abounded. Without fellowship with the Lord and insights from His Spirit, godly covenant principles were perverted in nations around the world.

Perversions like arillodes, which pulled sap from the good seed planted even before man was created. What is an arillode? According to *Webster's New World College Dictionary Fourth Edition* an aril is "an additional covering that forms on certain seeds after fertilization, developing from the stalk of the ovule." An arillode is "a false aril, developing from an opening in the covering of the ovule instead of from its stalk."

Nations around the world like the Hittites knew to make covenants. Like arillodes, they used covenants, including blood covenants, sapping strength a lot from people. Like Satan, people perverted God's Word, God's covenants, and used covenants in their own way, sapping from the branch. With few exceptions, attention was diverted from the Lord God Almighty who initiated covenant. Accordance of rights was given to falsity. Through God's covenants with Abraham and Moses, privileges were available which astounded all who observed. The nations around them knew covenant principles but the gods by which they swore were always faltering. Israel terrified the kings of Canaan Land. Joshua foolishly did not consult the Lord when he made a covenant with the Gibeonites. They came with lies knowing their gods were no match for Israel's God.

It seems appropriate for the parable of the Sower to be considered in Joshua's covenant with the Gibeonites. For the Word spoken by the Lord tells of plant development both fruitfully and futilely. God began telling Adam of orderly conduct. From Genesis through Revelation covenant principles were made known. Recently a very successful man said good business concepts are based on biblical principles.

It is possible to care for plants without having any kind of degree. But too often plants are neglected. Sometimes weed seeds are dropped from the mouths of birds flying overhead or blown by the wind to grow up as weeds in someone's garden that is well tended. In the Synoptic Gospels' parable of the Sower, the wisdom for planting is given. Having lived on a farm I know that parable has wisdom physically and spiritually. Good seeds planted for food can be easily lost to birds or rodents if planted by the wayside. Shallow roots develop when seed is planted in rocky, root-laden soil or otherwise unfavorable soil and can be easily pulled up. Good seed can be thrown into thorny bushes and be choked above and below the ground. If weeds grow and aren't pulled out, they can sap the nutrients and moisture needed by good seed. Good seed will yield vegetables or fruit when sown on good ground and cared for. Some plant, some water, but God gives the increase. Covenant principles lacking root, choked by thorns, or sapped by false arils is not God's intent. It is His desire all are saved but not all will be. God is a respecter of those who are doers of the word and not hearers only. Plant good seed, tend to the garden and enjoy the fresh produce. Trust God for increase. (Mark 4:1-20; 1 Corinthians 3:6-7)

God respects covenant faithfulness, diligence, and durability. It is possible to bring forth good fruit and seed with an above-average return of thirty to one hundred percent. I remember one man said as he prayed he asked God for seed to sow and bread to eat. God is the one who gives increase.

After reminiscing about the marvelous works of Jehovah, a psalmist appealed to Jehovah for aid against wickedness. He called on God to *have respect to the covenant; for the dark places of the earth are full of the haunts of cruelty.* God's intention is abundant life. There is a thief that steals, kills, and destroys. He messes with the lives of anyone who believes the lies of the thief. All need to respect God. (Genesis 3:1-24; 1 Chronicles 15:29-16:1-2; Psalm 74:16-23; Mark 4:1-20; John 10:10)

The book of 2 Kings shows the respect the Lord gives because of His covenant with Abraham, Isaac, and Jacob. The prophecies of Elisha were fulfilled and Syria, Israel's oppressor, was turned back and Israel was given relief[102] and time to repent because of the Lord's covenant mercies. (2 Kings 13:15-19; 23; Leviticus 26; Revelation 2:20)

DAVID

Concept of God's respect for the faithful was understood by Moses, and likewise by David and Solomon. David's understanding and the vastness of covenant are reflected in his writings. He knew that God respects covenant and desires that we do likewise. David recognized the blessings available to those who respected the Word of God's covenant. When we respect covenant we gain God's respect. (Psalms 25:10-14; 119:5-6; 14-16)

David rejoiced in the way of God's testimonies and meditated in His precepts and delighted himself in the Lord's statues and determined not to forget His word. David was speaking with covenant terminology. It seems obvious that David's heart felt respect for the covenant words of God and therefore gained God's respect for him. Walking in covenant relationship with God, David became great and was established and his kingdom exalted. (2 Samuel 5:10-12; 7:16; Psalm 89:28, 34-37)

More than 900 years after the Davidic covenant was made, Jesus was born. Jesus the promised one, David's seed, indeed endures forever and his throne is established. Jesus' obedience to covenant was one of the things that qualified him to establish a kingdom wherein his throne would endure. Many of David's descendants were unfaithful to covenant, but God remained faithful to the Davidic covenant and preserved the redemptive seed (Jesus) promised in the Adamic, Abrahamic, and Davidic covenants.

Israel's multiple transgressions caused plague that surrounding nations knew were the result of Israel's covenant transgressions. God told Jeremiah to go to the house of the king of Judah. The king was told to do, carry out, and execute God's orders. The king of Judah was to submit to the King of kings and *carry out judgment and righteousness and deliver the spoiled out of the hand of the oppressor. He was to do no wrong, no violence to strangers, the fatherless or to the widows*. Jeremiah continued relaying the word of the Lord of the covenant, *"if you will not hear and do the word given 'I swear by myself, saith the LORD' this house shall become desolate.*" The disobedient, and unrepentant not having God's respect, were overtaken by a multitude of curses. (Leviticus 26; Deuteronomy 28; Jeremiah 22:1-9)

SOLOMON

Like his father David, Solomon understood respect was due the obedient. Confidently, Solomon approached God in prayer after finishing the monumental task of building the tabernacle and placing the Ark of the Covenant in the most Holy Place. His prayer began with a reminder of the task he had completed for the Lord and of the covenant God had made with David. As Solomon continued in his prayer, he reminded God of the Abrahamic and Mosaic covenants of which the Davidic covenant was an extension. He rehearsed Israel's deliverance out of Egypt. (1 Kings 8:6, 22-23; 26,28)

Solomon had appealed to God for respect because of his covenant relationship. That covenant relationship enabled Solomon to boldly approach Jehovah in prayer. Solomon is still remembered for the supernatural wisdom displayed in his early years as King of Israel. But he loved women of the nations the Lord had forbidden intimacy with. Because of those women Solomon stumbled. Their covenants witnessed by their gods was essentially their personal covenant with Death. God had forbidden interaction with them even at the national level.

Solomon's fall into worship of the gods of his women, wives, and concubines, split the strong nation David had built. The Lord told Solomon, because he had done this the kingdom would be torn from Solomon's descendants. But for David's sake, a small portion, the tribe of Judah would remain. The Ark of the Covenant remained in Judah's tribe. Solomon had led the nation into the dark world of false gods. The wisdom of God remained with the Lord. Solomon became dependent on his own resources. He had broken covenant and his descendents would pay the price. (1 Kings 9:2-7; 11:11)

God is no respecter of persons and men like Solomon are no exception. Yet God had respect for men like Abel as opposed to Cain, Israel over Egypt, and David over Saul. Understanding covenant clarifies many of what otherwise may seem like biblical discrepancies.

RESOLUTION

Practical covenant knowledge is the Bible element that resolves what may be perceived as contradiction. When God says He is no respecter of persons, He means what He says. At the same time, He respected Abel, Israel, and David with an active, heartfelt loving-kindness. They were faithful in covenant with God because of His covenant mercy and their desire to do His will.

Covenant stipulations are the reconciling elements. Adherence and obedience is the outcome of faith. In the Hittite covenants a suzerain was a lord to whom faithfulness was required. The vassal was expected to believe what the suzerain said in spite of the way things looked. Indeed, faith in one's covenant partner and his word gained respect even for the vassal in a Hittite covenant. Much more so God's respect is there for all when faith is exercised. He is the Lord of lords, the King of kings who authored covenant. Outside of faith in Him, man messes up everything. Faith in the covenant of God and in the God of the covenant gains His respect. Therein is the walk of faith seen in the accounts written in the New Testament. (Hebrews 11:1-31)

The New Testament book of Hebrews uses the word covenant and covenant-related terms frequently. The writer states that, "without faith it is impossible to please God. Those that come to God of necessity must believe that He is, and that He rewards those who diligently seek Him," (Hebrews 11:6). Faith has been associated with fortune in the minds of a lot of people. Good fortune subscribed to unpredictable circumstances the senses can code into whatever receptor is available. Misfortune is attributed to ignorance.

God looks for those He can respect. *Without faith it is not possible to please God.* Desiring to do God's will is necessary for keen insight and good judgment in all matters of life. To hold fast, stick with the Old and New Testament. His covenant principles are the only way to keep from falling. The world is shaking with the consequences of unbelief in the God of the Lord Jesus Christ. He is always and shall be forever the mediator of a better covenant and the only safe harbor in a world gone mad with false teachings. (John 3:17-21; 7:17)

When someone works for a reliable and prosperous company, he has faith that his check will be waiting for him at the end of his work-week. The employee had an agreement with his employer about the salary he would earn for a week's work. The employee, trusting that the employer is reputable, takes his check to the bank to deposit it. He is confident that the check will be legal tender. After depositing the check he may stop on his way home to pay a bill. With faith in his employer's ability to back the check just deposited, he writes a personal check. Thus every person who has ever received a check has exercised some faith. Faith in the one issuing the check allows the holder to confidently approach the bank teller. God is faithful. He expects faithfulness from His covenant partners. (John 7:17; Hebrews 11:6)

It is in this way that a person with a personal relationship with Jesus can have much more faith in God's legal tender—the written Word of the Lord regarding His covenant promises, provisions, and stipulations. Of necessity, faith must be in both God and the overall principles and the specific stipulations of His covenant. For a Christian to walk in faith he must *believe that God is and that he is faithful to reward those that diligently seek Him.* He must also believe His Word is settled in heaven. (Hebrews 11:6)

To walk in faith is to habitually fellowship with the Lord. Just the privilege of habitual fellowship with the God of the covenant is rewarding. Perhaps that is part of the meaning of the Lord's statement, "I am come that they might have life, and that they might have it more abundantly," (John 10:10). The law of faith is part of the everlasting covenant of God. The good news includes an accurate telling of the better covenant, which includes accuracy in all God's doctrines. (Hebrews 11:6; Psalm 119:89; John 10:10; Romans 3:4-13, 27-31)

Enoch walked with God. Noah walked with God and found favor with Him. "Walked with God" means they habitually fellowshipped with Him. With the accounts of their walk, how is it that they were part of the Old Testament believers that longed to see our day? They were part of those who paint a picture of the completed work that would not appear for thousands of years. Enoch saw it because of faithful fellowship with God. Noah built an ark. Enoch was caught away in a type of ascension made clearer in the New Testament writings.

Perhaps Enoch and Noah longed to see the outcome of stone-dead hearts miraculously changed by the power of God. Perhaps they wanted to see the power of God made available to all true believers. The indwelling Holy Spirit would empower believers. Is that what they longed for? Could they have seen a glimpse of the better covenant?

Old Testament muralists from Genesis through Malachi painted an exquisite work seen only by those who sought the Lord. That mural would be unveiled a little at a time and spiritually perceived. Finally the day came when the blessings of Abraham and redemption from the curse was ready to be unveiled. Much of what they saw spiritually in their daily fellowship with God would have been impossible to pen without the help of their faith in God. The indefinite details were limited to mortal men even though anointed. The very life of God in the limitations unregenerate man had was nonetheless awesome.

The promises of the Redeemer may have allowed Enoch and Noah to figuratively fast-forward to the moment when Jesus told the parable of the lost son. The prodigal son left his father and brother and proceeded to waste his portion of the inheritance. He returned home when he began to perish with hunger. When the father saw him coming compassion came forth for his wayward, foolish, selfish son. His son that was dead was alive again. A celebration was in order. It was good news. Provision was made and a best robe, a ring, and shoes were put on him.

Old Testament believers longed to see our days. They longed to see their Redeemer, the Lord Jesus Christ. They had known anointing according to the gifts and calling of God. Elijah and Elisha and many faithful besides them had seen monumental feats. But to walk with God as we can was not possible for the Old Testament believer. (Hebrews 11:40)

The New Testament phrase "new creation" was elusive for them. They could only see a portion of the mural set before them. By faith they saw brief glimpses of the day when the Messiah would come. They understood the best was still to come. They knew what the Lord said. They repeated God and said, "Thus saith the Lord". The shepherd David prophetically wrote in Psalm 23 of Jesus. In the Gospel of John, Jesus Himself said, "I am the good shepherd".

> Verily, verily, I say unto you, He that entereth not by the door into the sheepfold, but climbeth up some other way, the same is a thief and a robber. But he that entereth in by the door is the shepherd of the sheep. To him the porter openeth; and the sheep hear his voice: and he calleth his own sheep by name, and leadeth them out. And when he putteth forth his own sheep, he goeth before them, and the sheep follow him: for they know his voice. And a stranger will they not follow, but will flee from him: for they know not the voice of strangers. This parable spake Jesus unto them: but they understood not what things they

> were which he spake unto them. Then said Jesus unto them again, Verily, verily, I say unto you, I am the door of the sheep. All that ever came before me are thieves and robbers: but the sheep did not hear them. I am the door: by me if any man enter in, he shall be saved, and shall go in and out, and find pasture. The thief cometh not, but for to steal, and to kill, and to destroy: I am come that they might have life, and that they might have it more abundantly. I am the good shepherd: the good shepherd giveth his life for the sheep. But he that is an hireling, and not the shepherd, whose own the sheep are not, seeth the wolf coming, and leaveth the sheep, and fleeth: and the wolf catcheth them, and scattereth the sheep. The hireling fleeth, because he is an hireling, and careth not for the sheep. I am the good shepherd, and know my sheep, and am known of mine. As the Father knoweth me, even so know I the Father: and I lay down my life for the sheep. And other sheep I have, which are not of this fold: them also I must bring, and they shall hear my voice; and there shall be one fold, and one shepherd. Therefore doth my Father love me, because I lay down my life, that I might take it again. No man taketh it from me, but I lay it down of myself. I have power to lay it down, and I have power to take it again. This commandment have I received of my Father. John 1:1-18

What Abraham was promised, Moses saw in the law given and enforced. What Samuel saw as a Judge, David saw as a King; What the Prophets saw in visions and dreams Jesus knew personally as the promised Messiah. What of certainty in the New Covenant. God is no respecter of persons. (Luke 15:11-32; John 3:3, 7, 16-21; 10:1-18; Acts 10 & 11; 1 Corinthians 12:31; 13:1,13; Galatians 3; Hebrews 11:5; Jude 1:14; Deuteronomy 28; Joshua 47:6,11)

Chapter 6

THE NEW

Enoch, Noah, Moses, and the Prophets, among others, longed to see our days. The covenants had God-given stipulations and shadows of things to come; visions and dreams recorded for future generations to read that portrayed a beautiful mural depicting God's plan. Out of necessity, the handwritten account of a God-inspired vision or dream is relatively brief. Consider Enoch, whose exceptionally long life is contained within just a few written verses. But how blessed are those few verses to believers! Those priceless verses are indeed blessed with the very life of God, which in the heart of a believer bears witness of the truth. As a wind blowing through the trees, the Holy Spirit of God is moving upon people around the world.

There are reports from all around the world of the marvelous things that are happening still today. The good news that Jesus is not merely an excellent teacher or prophet is going forth. He is indeed Lord of lords and King of kings. Qualified King, Redeemer, Savior of whosoever will believe. Jesus came that we *"might have life, and . . . have it more abundantly,"* (John 10:10). Obedience to the better covenant commandment still enables whosoever believes. (Matthew 13:16-17; Luke 15:11-32; John 3:3, 7, 15-16; 12:46; 16-21; 10:10; 1 Corinthians 12:31; 13:1,13; Galatians 3; 1 Peter 1:18-25; 2:24; 1 John 2:20,27; Joshua 47:6, 11; Deuteronomy 28)

THE LAW OF FAITH

The Law of Faith in the New Covenant is based on the entirety of the holy commandment. Summarized by Jesus, the first and greatest commandment in the law of Moses is to love the Lord God with all one's heart with all one's soul and with one's mind. He said the second commandment is like the first; love your neighbor as you love yourself. (Matthew 22:35-41) Granted a lot of people do not seem to love themselves. Perhaps that has a lot to do with the disregard of the law and the love for the Lord. Faith works by love. That topic alone could easily fill another book. But suffice it to say that faith and love are essential elements of the New Covenant. (Galatians 5:5-6)

All the statutes, commandments, and precepts of the Bible can build faith for the believer who is willing to be a doer of the Word and not just a hearer of the Word. Being a doer of the Word involves doing what *the rightly divided word of truth* says to do. Partial understanding of covenant will not equip us for avoiding life's hazards. The Word of truth indeed sets free if it is known—with certainty, with clarity, and in its proper setting. When we know God's Word from reading, studying, application, and consultation with the Author, we will surely *rightly divide the word of truth.* The believer who keeps the *law of faith* joyfully alive in their heart is well able to overcome the challenges of this world. (Romans 1:2; 3:27; 7:12; 2 Timothy 2:15; 3:15-16; 2 Peter 2:21; 3:2; Revelation 12:11; Numbers 14:44)

The *law of faith* is part of the New Covenant. Though the word covenant is not used as frequently in the New Testament as it is in the Old Testament, it is present enough that it cannot be justifiably dismissed. It has been a long-term debate with Bible scholars about what to do with the dispensational and covenant theologies. Can the two theologies be seen as harmonious if the chaff is blown away from the seeds within the two teachings?

I will not linger on this game of "hot potato." What I do know is that covenant is the one of the two that has helped me stay balanced in some very strong winds. Together, let you and I, and whoever will hear, commit to let the Word of the Lord decide which is the way to go. When adversity hits, face it with faith in God and His Word. Cooperate with the high priest of your confession of faith. The law of faith is yours in the name of the Lord Jesus Christ. Fight the thief who steals, kills, and destroys. Take the law of faith, the shield of faith, and fight the good fight of faith. Neglecting this truth quickly turns to danger. Truth repeated from heart to heart cannot be overstated. (John 10:10; 1 Timothy 6:10-12; Hebrews 3:1; 4:14; 10:23) Even under the Old Covenant, Moses and the Prophets saw the power of faith *and* the benefits of law. Why not keep that in mind as the better covenant is considered? (Romans 3:27; Hebrews 11)

THE BETTER COVENANT

The Old Covenant was good. It provided blessings that included favor with man and God, prosperity, protection, and health. Since the creation of Adam, God provided salvation and hope via covenant. The Old Covenant was the vehicle for faith that delivered men from adversity. But the New Covenant is better. (Hebrews 7:21-22; Hebrews 8:6-8)

Though the Old Covenant contained a multitude of benefits, the mortal participants retained their sinful natures. Because of Adam's transgressions, each person was born in sin. Some, like Abraham, believed God and it was counted to them for righteousness. But their righteousness was not that of a recreated being. It was a righteousness gained by looking in faith toward God who had promised a messiah. God's Old Covenant word was their assurance, their title deed, that the messiah was a fact not yet fully revealed in their hearts. Though they were able to gain righteousness by faith, they were unable to be born again.

It was not until the blood of Jesus was shed that it became possible to become a new creation. The ability to change one's own nature was lacking to sinful man. Changing a sinful nature to a sinless nature was a work that could only be accomplished by Jesus, the mediator of the better covenant. The miraculous transformation of the new birth was possible only after the completion of the better covenant. When in Christ, believers become new; old things are passed away. (Hebrews 11:1 AMP)

The author of Hebrews wrote, "without faith it is impossible to please [God]." He goes on to boldly declare, "for he who comes to God must believe that He is, and that He is a rewarder of those who diligently seek Him," (Hebrews 11:6 NKJV). The latter *diligently seek* is often disregarded. It is an impoverishing shame to discount portions of scripture, which do not fit comfortably into some doctrine or tradition. Hear, read, and consider His Word. Make adjustments where needed and continue on your walk with Him. God does indeed reward those that *diligently seek* him. All the men and women listed in Hebrews' hall of faith pleased God and obtained a good report because of faith. They, however, without us could not be made perfect. Because the blood of the perfect Lamb of God had not been shed and the better covenant had not yet been made, the men of the Old Testament could not be made perfect. They could not be born again until the Covenant was completed. (2 Corinthians 5:17; Hebrews 11:6)

> The biblical idea of perfection is of a state of ideal wholeness or completion, in which any disabilities, shortcomings, or defects that may have existed before have been eliminated or left behind.
>
> The Bible also speaks of God's perfecting of His covenant relation with man. This is the perfecting of men through Christ with which the writer to the Hebrews deals. "The perfecting of men refers to their covenant condition . . . To perfect . . . is to

> put the People into the true covenant relation of worshippers of the Lord, to bring them into His full fellowship' (A. B. Davidson, Hebrews, p. 208). God did this by replacing the old covenant, priesthood, tabernacle, and sacrifices by something better. The 'old covenant' in Hebrews means the Mosaic system for establishing living fellowship between God and His people; but, says the writer, it could never 'perfect' them in this relationship, for it could not give full assurance of the remission of all sins (Hebrews 7:18, 9:9, 10:1-4). Under the new covenant, however, on the ground of Christ's single sacrifice of Himself, believers receive God's assurance that He will remember their sins no more (10:11-18). Thus they are 'perfected for ever' (verse 14). This perfection of fellowship with God is something that Old Testament saints did not know on earth (11:40)—though, through Christ, they enjoy it now, in the heavenly Jerusalem (12:23 f.).[103]

One reason the New Covenant is better is because by faith in the word of God whosoever will do so can become new. John explained the perfection available by faith. As many as received him, to them He gave power to become the sons of God. How? By believing on his name. By believing on his name it is possible to be born, again. Not of the will of the flesh nor of the will of men, but of God. Of God people come into a better covenant. He did not disregard one group and receive another. All are welcome if they will believe. (John 1:12-16; Romans 1:16-17; 10:9-13)

COVENANT STEPS

Covenant steps like those used in the Adamic, Abrahamic, and Mosaic covenants are in the New Covenant also. The church has been put to a disadvantage by unpleasantness among theologians. With little discussion one tends to promote what the other denounces with little consideration of scriptural evidence presented. The word covenant is used thirteen times in Hebrews alone. Six other times it is mentioned in other books of the New Testament. Several of that total of nineteen times it is used in direct reference to the Old Covenant and brings the Old into the New.

God has not forgotten covenant, neither with Israel nor with the better covenant mediator. Jesus is man's link to God. Jesus the mediator bore our sins in the New Covenant. Risen, He represents those willing to accept Him as their Lord. It seems from my research through the years one reason covenant may not have been mentioned more often in the New Testament may have something to do with Rome's political intrigue, and Caesar-god worship. But whatever the reason, the number of times the word covenant is used makes the subject worth studying. In comparison the number of times dispensation is employed indicates the burden of theological proof lies more in the camp of the dispensationalists than the covenant theologians. My analytic search for the steps taken to make the better covenant are presented in opposition to the infrequent covenant details preached in most churches today.

CONFERENCE

The covenant conference is witnessed and recorded in the gospel of John and the book of Genesis. In Genesis, God was recorded saying, "Let us make man in our image," (Genesis 1:26). John wrote in chapter one verse one, "In the beginning was the Word, and the Word was with God, and the Word was God." John later stated, "the Word was made flesh, and dwelt among us. . . ." This gospel is different than the Synoptic Gospels written by Matthew, Mark, and Luke. It seems John determined to emphasis the Christ, the signs and wonders, the glory of God, and the Holy Spirit of God, which was to come. (John 1:1-14; 14:15-26)

Three times in the first verse of John's gospel, "Word" is capitalized which is significant. It is the very name of the Lord. "Word" in the Greek version was *logos,* which regards the orderly linking and knitting in connected arrangement, according to the definition for *logos* in *The Complete Wordstudy New Testament.* The Lord has excellently arranged, orderly linked, and knitted His perfect plan of salvation. The promise of the Old Covenant was to be fulfilled. By the time John wrote his gospel the New Covenant had been completed. By grace through faith in His Word we are privileged to take part in the best plan ever developed. His Word is there for us to see what the better covenant is about and how we are to appropriate its benefits, see and enter into His Kingdom. (John 3:3-7,16-21; Revelation 19:13)

Elohim, the triune God, had agreed within Himself to create man in his own image. Jesus, as God in the flesh (1 Timothy 3:16), was born as seen in John 1:14. God in the flesh came to reaffirm the Elohimic Covenant made even before man was created. In the flesh as a man, Jesus made the better covenant as our representative. Because he was born of the flesh, as we are, he could legitimately represent us and make an equal covenant for us. Because he was God in the flesh, he could legitimately represent us. God (Father, Son, and Holy Spirit) had said, "Let us make man in our image, after our likeness." God had already covenanted before man was created. They already conferred. The better covenant was already planned before Jesus was born. God in the flesh came to dwell among us and bear our sins. (1 Timothy 3:16; John 1:1, 2, 14; 1 Peter 2:24)

EXCHANGE OF ROBE AND PLEDGE

When He prayed shortly before Judas betrayed Him, Jesus said, "Father, the hour has come. Glorify Your Son, that Your Son also may glorify You," (John 17:1 NKJV). Jesus' definition of eternal life in that prayer is so refreshingly stated. Eternal life is that people may know the only true God, and Jesus Christ, whom His Father had sent to do what no one else could do. (John 17:1-7; Revelation 5:6; 7:17; 14:10; 19:9; 22:1-3)

Jesus had exchanged robes with His father. They each pledged everything they had to the other. Jesus, having been born of flesh, did not think it robbery to be equal with God. They were making an equal blood covenant, a solemn irreversible agreement. Jesus made no showiness as He ministered. Rather He ministered as a servant like no one had ever been able to do before Him. When one is truly born of God he is to let this mind be in him, which was in Christ Jesus. We are to love and serve others as He did. He humbled himself, made himself of no reputation, took the form of a servant, yet did not think it robbery to be equal with God. (Philippians 2:5-8)

As Elohim, the entire universe had been at his disposal within covenant limitations. That, however, was before his incarnation, before becoming God in the flesh and dwelling among men. Few people can imagine God as poor. Before his incarnation he was not poor. During his incarnation he was relatively poor. Relatively speaking is important to keep in mind. He humbled himself and became like man. In his pre and post incarnation incomprehensible riches and influence were his. But as a man and as an Israelite, Jesus lived in obedience to the Old Covenant.

Jesus, as a man and God in the flesh, was as rich as it was possible to be for anyone walking in obedience to the Old Covenant. According to the Mosaic covenant, Jesus was blessed when he came and went, and blessed at everything to which he set his hand. He was blessed with abundance in all that a physical man needed. Even that, however, was not as abundant as the riches at his disposal before he was born of flesh. (Deuteronomy 28:6,8; 2 Corinthians 8:9)

The man Christ Jesus exchanged a pledge with his covenant partner. He gave himself as a man to God his Heavenly Father and pledged everything he had to God. In return, God clothed Jesus with robes of glory and righteousness. By exchanging robes, the two had completed one of the covenant steps—symbolizing a pledge each to the other of all that each had. Jesus, a man, and His Father God were finishing the steps of the most remarkable blood covenant ever made. It would have even more than a universal impact. (Philippians 1:2-11)

Because Jesus was sinless and righteous, He represented us. The Messiah, Christ Jesus the Lamb of God bore our sins. Before the cross He was mocked, spit upon, stripped, and then they placed on Him a scarlet robe and a crown of thorns. He became poor that we might become rich. In His great love for us, He bore our sins. (Matthew 27:28-31; John 19:5)

JESUS DEFENDS HIS COVENANT PARTNER

Jesus had traveled from Cana of Galilee to Jerusalem to celebrate the Passover. The memorial meal was celebrated every year in remembrance of the Covenant that had been made centuries before. Israel's deliverance from Egypt because of covenant was a somber event. Passover was to be kept a feast to the Lord. Jesus, in obedience to the law, traveled approximately seventy miles from Cana of Galilee to take part in the festivities. Families and friends, who formed a type of family unit, shared chores and expenses as they prepared to offer a sacrificial animal at the temple in Jerusalem. The sacrificial animal provided meat for the Passover meal in homes and shelters throughout the area. The streets were crowded with people from the entire Roman Empire. Jerusalem was a walled city with a three and half mile circumference and there were probably around 25,000 people compacted within those walls.[104]

Many of the people, like Jesus, were tired after their long trips, but out of necessity they hurried to make arrangements for the Passover. They usually rented a room from one of the residents or they set up tents outside the city walls. Some of the group would unpack or purchase the bitter herbs needed to prepare the meat. They would measure and mix the ingredients for the unleavened bread, and then begin baking it. There was a need for a flawless animal for sacrifice. Some brought their sacrifices with them. Some bought their sacrifices in the surrounding fields where shepherds tended their flocks in anticipation of the Passover market.[105] The court of the Gentiles was also an option where a sacrificial animal could be purchased.

Jerusalem was preparing for the Passover when Jesus came into the temple and found intrusive money-changers and merchants. The Lord came in with others from His own family and friends and possibly with their own sacrificial animals. However, many came without their sacrifices and would buy when they arrived. People needed their money exchanged. The Lord's covenant partner's house had been intended as a house of prayer, but instead was being used as a house of merchandise. It had been written, *the zeal of your house has eaten me up*. (John 2:13-17)

The court of the Gentiles had been ordained by God as the area of the temple available to Jewish converts. This was as far as the Gentiles could go. They could not go into the court of Israel.[106] It was in the court of the Gentiles that the money changers and the animal marketeers did their business. The sacrificial animal business had defiled the temple and reduced it to a place of demeaning profiteering.

Jesus was appalled at the way God had been scorned. The court of the Gentiles designed for prayer and rejoicing, had been turned into a cheap market place. Angered, Jesus fashioned a scourge of small cords and came to his covenant partner's defense. The zealous defense of God's temple on that Passover day angered the Sanhedrin and started the scheming that eventually cost Jesus his life.[107] Jesus had pledged to defend his Covenant partner with his very life if necessary.

JESUS TAKES HIS COVENANT PARTNER'S NAME

Names were exchanged, as another covenant step was completed. Jesus received the name of his covenant partner when he referred to himself as I AM. (John 8:58-59) We've studied about how I AM was one of the names of God that was the direct result of his covenant with Abraham. When Jesus referred to Himself as "I AM," those opposing Jesus understood that he was claiming that he had been co-existent with God before Abraham even existed. That claim was possible only if Jesus was who he said he was.

Jesus was confirming a covenant that had come to pass before man was created. Because the Jews understood Jesus' claim to be a declaration of preexistence coupled with covenant connotations, they picked up stones and tried to kill him. In their estimation, His claim was blasphemous. No one had the right to call himself by the name *I AM* except one who was actively involved in a covenant relationship with God.[108]

The attempt to stone Jesus proves the people understood he was claiming a covenant relationship with God. The Jews already had a covenant relationship with God through Abraham. Jesus' claim was that he was greater than Abraham and that the covenant he was making was greater than the Abrahamic covenant. His claim seemed outrageous. They could not comprehend how it could be possible for this man Jesus to do more than Abraham had done.

COVENANT SACRIFICE

The sacrifice is probably the easiest covenant-making step to identify in the better covenant. Jesus was the sacrifice of the New Covenant. He was oppressed but did not defend Himself. Isaiah said he was *brought as a lamb to the slaughter*. Seven hundred years before Jesus was born, Isaiah prophesied concerning Israel's redeemer. The sacrifice of the blood covenant was the Lamb of God Himself who purposed to take away the sin of the world. Who would believe the report written by Moses and the prophets? (John 1:36; Revelation 22:3; Genesis 3:15; Isaiah 53:1,7)

Israel had been waiting for Him. They speculated about how he would come. Most of them believed he would be a gallant soldier and earthly king like David. Few anticipated that he would come as Isaiah had prophesied, a lamb for the slaughter. After John the Baptist had baptized Jesus in the Jordan River, he said of Jesus, "Behold the Lamb of God, which takes away the sin of the world." Jesus had come to make a better covenant. The better covenant was to have a perfect sacrifice. (1 John 1:29)

The Epistle to the Hebrews says more about the New Covenant than all of the other New Testament books combined. The reason may be found in the historical accounts of covenants. The Hittite covenants, which lend evidence to validate giving to Caesar what belonged to Caesar, may have included obedience to Roman law regarding matters of blood covenants. Obedience to the Caesars and laws of the Roman suzerain probably included refraining from covenanting.

Covenants were strictly regulated and suzerains typically did not permit their vassals to make any other covenants. Suzerains along with their allies would deal quickly and usually with cruel severity with anyone daring to break covenant. Ancient history gives accounts of the curses rebellion and disobedience would bring to vassals. Was Rome any different? (Joshua 7:11-15; Judges 2:1, 20-23; 1 Samuel 11:1-2; 2 Kings 17:35-38; 18:11-12)

In the Epistle to the Hebrews it says, "Behold, I have come—in the volume of the book it is written of Me—to do Your will, O God," (Hebrews 10:7 NKJV). The sacrifice of the better covenant had been prophesied and Jesus the Lamb was examined and prepared for the final sacrifice. The everlasting covenant was the means whereby the will of

God would be fulfilled. Because of Jesus, we can be sanctified, set apart from sin, and set apart unto God—sanctified through the offering of the body of Jesus Christ once and for all. (Hebrews 10:4-10; 1 Peter 2:24; Psalm 40:7)

As a Lamb, Jesus purposely came to offer Himself as the sacrifice of a better, solemn, and unbreakable blood covenant. The Cross, anchored on Calvary, was the altar for that sacrifice. (1 Peter 2:24; Revelation 5:6; 7:17; 14:10; 19:9; 22:1-3)

THE CUT OF THE NEW COVENANT

The cut of the New Covenant was completed when Jesus was nailed to the cross. His hands and feet were scarred with large iron spikes. Those nail-scarred hands have been, for thousands of years, a constant reminder of the work Jesus did and the blood covenant he made.

Nailed to the cross, Jesus bore more than the wounds of the nails needed to fasten him there. He had been scourged with the flagellum, sometimes called a cat-of-nine-tails. The flagellum was a whip made of nine leather strips with small pieces of metal or bone tied to them. This whip was forcefully applied, and then slowly drawn across the back. Without mercy, this cruelty was repeated up to forty times.

As a result, Jesus had nearly been beaten to death before he was forced to carry the crossbar of his cross to Calvary. At Calvary his hands were nailed to the crossbar. It was then lifted and dropped into position on the upright post of the cross. When the cross was dropped into place, the jarring motion caused his bones to be painfully dislocated. Finally his feet were nailed to the post. Prophetically speaking of that day Isaiah said, "his visage was so marred more than any man, and his form more than the sons of men," (Isaiah 52:14). In the Psalms, David perceiving Jesus' death wrote, "I am poured out like water. My bones are out of joint. My heart is like wax, melted in the midst of my bowels. My strength is dried like a potsherd. My tongue cleaves to my jaws. I am brought into the dust of death. Dogs have compassed me. The wicked have surrounded me. They pierced my hands and my feet. They part my garments among them, and cast lots for my cloak," (Psalm 22:16-18).

It is beyond me to fully comprehend Jesus' love. He personally bore our sins. The horror of sin is as incomprehensible as the goodness of God's love. For our sins the Lord's back was lacerated. His joints were dislocated. His wrists and feet were punctured with nails. His head was bruised and swollen from the crown of thorns and the beatings. His face would also have been swollen and bloodied where his beard had been pulled out. Jesus was hardly recognizable even to those who dearly loved him. That was the sin of the world, the sin of Adam, the sin of all men and women. It was sin—yours and mine—for which He died. A better covenant sacrifice made by a sinless man was the necessary element needed for activating a better covenant, which would break the power of death.

> *When Jesus therefore had received the vinegar, he said, It is finished: and he bowed his head, and gave up the ghost.*
>
> —John 19:30

> *Jesus, when he had cried again with a loud voice, yielded up the ghost. And, behold, the veil of the temple was rent in twain from the top to the bottom; and the earth did quake, and the rocks rent; And the graves were opened; and many bodies of the saints which slept arose, And came out of the graves after his resurrection, and went into the holy city, and appeared unto many. Now when the centurion, and they that were with him, watching Jesus, saw the earthquake, and those things that were done, they feared greatly, saying, Truly this was the Son of God.*
>
> —Matthew 27:50-54

Jesus cried with a loud voice "*it is finished.*" Finished is the English translators choice for the Greek word *teleo*. It means the goal reached, the completion, conclusion of one, and the beginning of a new order of things. Jesus cried with a loud voice "*teleo*" to which the Roman centurion said, "Truly this was the Son of God." It was typical for the commander of an army to shout *teleo* with a loud voice when victory was won. *Teleo* is to make complete or to accomplish a goal. Jesus did much more than was required of Him. He fulfilled and finished His assignment, and did so perfectly. He destroyed the yoke of bondage and brought victory to its destined goal. He executed and carried out His assignment.[109]

Why did he bother? Love. He was motivated by a love that man would never be able to comprehend. Believers have some appreciation for His love and have learned through Him to love Him in return. Seldom, however, is a group of Christians wholeheartedly in total love with Him. Jesus' love is still a marvel to consider. The Triune Godhead had such a compelling love that even *before* Adam's initial sin, provision was made for man's redemption. The physical pain Jesus suffered at the Cross was a light affliction compared to the glory that was set before him. (Hebrews 12:2)

He died to provide a covenant whereby men could have hearts made capable of, and desirous of, intimate fellowship with God. By his death Jesus became the way for men to become new creations. Jesus suffered a multitude of injuries at his death yet when he rose from the dead three days later the injuries were all healed. Though the wounds were all healed, the cut of covenant was fixed in such a way that it would always be obvious.

At dusk on the day Jesus was resurrected from the dead, two of his disciples were on their way to Emmaus, discussing what had happened at the tomb. They did not recognize Jesus when he joined them. The late hour, their dulled eyes, and Jesus' health kept them from perceiving that the resurrected Jesus was walking with them. Jesus had appeared to the disciples *in a different form.* When they saw Him last, just three days ago, He was marred beyond recognition and His wrists and feet pierced. The person with them now was healthy, but uninformed about what had happened. How could this person not have heard of the mighty works the Lord had done? How could he not know of the crucifixion.

Christ Jesus had suffered and entered into his glory. His good health belied what he had endured and they were oblivious. Though they may have had some faith, they certainly lacked joyful expectation of seeing the resurrected and healed Christ Jesus, their Master and Teacher.

Meanwhile, stories of Jesus' resurrection sifted back to Thomas. He reasoned away hope and faith. He probably thought of a thousand reasons why he should not believe what was said. Though he may have wanted to believe, he had difficulty when Mary Magdalene told of her visit to the sepulcher. She claimed when she arrived at the tomb it was still dark. Supposedly as she drew nearer she saw the massive stone at the entrance to the tomb was rolled away.

Since the day Jesus had cast seven demons out of Mary, she had been scrupulously trustworthy. The fact that Joanna and Mary the mother of James had been with her lent even greater credibility to Mary Magdalene's story. But it was still too difficult to believe Jesus was alive. Jesus alive and well was too incredible for Thomas to allow himself to accept. Surely he at least hoped it was true. He must have wanted to believe.

The other disciples hadn't believed Mary's report either. All those who had so dearly loved Jesus had been under tremendous stress those last few days. Perhaps they were distraught and getting delirious, Thomas reasoned. Peter and John had run to the tomb. They testified the stone had indeed been rolled away. (Mark 16:1-20; Luke 24:10-35; John 20:4,11-28)

It is possible that, considering the reports, Thomas may have remembered what Jesus had said just three days before. When they celebrated Passover, Jesus had mentioned the blood of the New Testament. But though they said He was alive, unless Thomas saw the cut of covenant he would not believe. (John 20:24-25)

To believe that Jesus had cut covenant with God as Abraham had cut covenant with him would not have been so hard to believe before the crucifixion. Jesus was an impressive man. Unbeknownst to those following Him, Jesus had taken steps to make covenant. The covenant-making process had been halted with his crucifixion. But the disciples saw Him as triumphant King. They had failed to see Him as a Lamb to the slaughter.

Timothy explained away the good news that Jesus was alive. Eight days later, Thomas was with the other disciples when Jesus suddenly stood in their midst—despite the doors being shut. He repeated what they had heard from him so many times, "Peace." The sound of His voice alone was worth following. With agape love, the Lord allowed Thomas to thrust his finger into the holes in his hands and side. Thomas must have been trembling when he said, "My Lord and my God." (John 20:26-28)

Having seen the cuts of covenant, Thomas could believe. All the crucifixion wounds were healed except the ones that would remain throughout eternity as a reminder of the better covenant. The covenant cuts in Jesus' hands, feet, and side were fixed in such a way that they would always bear witness of his covenant relationship with God. As believers received Jesus as their Lord and Savior, those cuts would be a continuous reminder of what had been accomplished on their behalf.

With faith, Thomas uttered a possessive salutation to Jesus when he said, "my Lord and my God." That same expression of kinship is used today as Christians speak of Jesus. It is not uncommon to hear Christians speak reverently of "my Jesus," "my Lord," "my Savior," "my God."

With varying degrees of enthusiasm, they speak of the head of the better covenant they have received and known personally. The nail-scarred hands of Jesus are still verifying the better covenant to believers. Those nail marks testify of their everlasting better covenant. (John 20:28)

BLESSING AND CURSE

Jesus, God in the flesh, loved and prized the world. One day, a man named Nicodemus came to inquire of the Lord. As a man, Jesus answered the questions asked of him and pronounced the blessing and curse of the New Covenant with simplicity. His answer is still cherished by millions, as it provides insight into the purpose of God.

But though Nicodemus was a man of the Pharisees a ruler of the Jews, he was not able to understand the words of the Lord or the supernatural ability and power of God. He was puzzled by what Jesus said. Jesus demonstrated God's love in three ways: (1) the words He spoke, (2) the works he did, and (3) the miracles He performed. His words and works baffled those following Him. The disciples at least were close enough that they could ask questions. What Jesus was doing did not fit preconceived ideas about the Messiah. But at least Nicodemus was willing to inquire of the Lord.

He came by night to ask of the Rabbi Jesus an explanation of the things being taught and done. In His great love, the Lord gave Nicodemus a lengthy answer. Jesus answered him the way He often spoke to people. Rather than answer the question that was troubling the mind, the Lord addressed what was on the heart. Thereby Nicodemus gained a clue the truth hidden in his heart, which was a mystery to his mind. But the clue was still like a ping-pong ball bouncing off the ceiling. *How can a man be born again*? (John 3:3,7; 1 Peter 1:23)

The statement "*you must be born again*" was a puzzle in itself. Now bewildered, Nicodemus asked another question. "*How can this be*?"

and Jesus answered with a question of His own. "*Art thou a master of Israel, and you do not know these things*?" Even the earthly things were not being grasped, how much more incomprehensible were the heavenly things the Lord could have given Nicodemus?

How tragic that after the better covenant has been preached all over the world, error still persists and many still do not comprehend being born again. Leaning on one's own understanding, whether ignorant or educated, causes problems. To trust in the Lord with all your heart when your head is filled with formulas that do not fit takes faith. Faith in God favors listening to the voice of the heart and moves with trust in the Lord. The law of faith remains intact. Genesis through Revelation and from ever on it shall remain intact. God will never change. Believers are to avoid being tossed to and fro with every wind of doctrine. Faith works and it is essential. (John 3:1-17; Ephesians 4:14; Proverbs 3:5)

New Covenant blessing and curse is clearly stated. Everlasting life. Everlasting death. The prized sixteenth verse in chapter three of John's gospel states the blessing is eternal, everlasting life, while the curse is death and destruction. In verses eighteen through twenty, the curse and blessing are explained a little more. The one who believes on Jesus is not condemned but the one who does not believe is condemned already. The covenant of death was activated when Adam ate of the forbidden fruit and brought death to all who were in him when he transgressed covenant. Jesus activated a better covenant, as ultimately righteous judgment for sin was laid on Him. Belief in Him kept believers free of the penalty of condemnation. (John 3:18-21)

Whosoever believes in Jesus will not perish nor be condemned. That is the blessing of the New Covenant. Whosoever does not believe in Jesus has already been condemned. The Lord has given a beautiful synopsis. Everyone was included as Jesus announced the blessing and curse of the better covenant being made. Many were called, few chosen. Who are the chosen? The chosen are those who respond and follow when they hear the Lord's call. Whosoever receives must follow the stipulations.

Believe. Believe what? Believe the New Covenant stipulations contained in the gospels, the epistles, Revelation. Believers enter the Kingdom of God and are given a heart capable of understanding. New believers can grow strong by applying themselves to the guidelines within the Word of God.

Blessing was excluded from those who would not believe in Jesus. For this reason, those who have chosen to believe that Jesus means what he says have proceeded to repeat the declaration of the blessing and curse of the New Covenant wherever they can. These ministers of the New Covenant, motivated by the Holy Spirit of God, desire that all men know the blessing and the redemption provided through Jesus. God in his immeasurable love has provided the way for all to be saved out of their misguided allegiance to the head of the covenant with death—Satan. Because of involvement in the covenant with death, men have changed the truth of God into a lie, and worshipped and served the creature more than the Creator, who is blessed forever. (John 3:16-21; Romans 1:16-32; 2:1-11)

Because God is blessed, the man that puts his confidence in God is likewise blessed. The truth of God's covenant Word conveys blessing. It is via the truth of God's Word that the blessing of the new birth is conveyed to man. By being born again through Jesus, the new covenant believers receive the very nature of God. They enter into covenant with Him. They become one in a blood covenant so that the regenerated man's spirit is reunited in fellowship with God, from whom he had previously been separated. Because of God's work the recreated man is in a position to be blessed.

The covenant with death was annulled and its effects rendered ineffective to those who put their confidence in Jesus. He actively annulled the covenant with death and delivered those who feared death and were in bondage because of fear. Primarily the blessing of the New Covenant is redemption from the effects of sin and it's condemnation. The blessing includes (1) a new spirit; (2) the indwelling of the Holy Spirit; (3) authority to use the name of Jesus; (4) continuous fellowship with Jehovah; (5) all the blessing of the Abrahamic and Mosaic covenants; and (6) eternal life. (Matthew 5:44; Luke 6:28; John 3:3, 16-20; Hebrews 2:15; Isaiah 28:14-18)

Because Satan is cursed, the man that puts his confidence in Satan is likewise cursed. Deception is Satan's primary weapon in the continuous spiritual warfare that surrounds men. Deceptions are primarily anything that deletes or alters the truth of God's covenant Word. Satan has already been judged. All who are in bondage to him share the judgment against him. The curse is basically the just reward of one who chooses to remain in the covenant with death rather than enter into the covenant of life. Faith is the key. (Matthew 25:41; John 10:10)

Jesus made the covenant of life, which annulled the covenant of death and the curse that had dominion over men who, like Adam, gave Satan the right to reign in their lives. Anyone since Adam who agreed with God by faith was able to withstand the wiles of the devil. Even though they were unable to be born again, Abraham's faith and Moses' law indicated a way of escape was available. Jesus, implementing a better covenant, declared, *he that believes not is condemned already.* The covenant with death was the means whereby unbelief brought condemnation. Satan has already been condemned and misplaced covenant allegiance causes condemnation for man. But Jesus did not come to condemn, but to provide a way out of the condemnation. (John 3:18; Hebrews 11)

Though there is no curse in the New Covenant, there are innumerable curses outside the New Covenant. There is no condemnation for them which are in Christ Jesus. But walk in the flesh and reap condemnation. It is possible to be filled with pride and fall into the condemnation of the devil. Therein lies the curse. Jesus shed His blood and made a way of escape for those in bondage to sin. The curse is the result of failing to submit oneself to the better covenant stipulations. (Romans 8:1; Ephesians 6:11; Galatians 3:13; James 4:7; 1 Peter 5:6-9; Genesis 2:17, 3:10; Deuteronomy 28:15-68)

Using lies to deceive and trick, Satan holds his subjects in bondage until the day there is no more hope of salvation. Hope for salvation ceases for the unbelievers at the time of physical death. The first death will be followed by a second, when they will be united for all eternity in the lake of fire with Satan, who so skillfully deceived them. Freedom from the power of death can only be received by faith in the Lord Jesus Christ. Believe and you will be saved. Personal involvement is required. Each person is individually responsible for receiving redemption from condemnation. All will make their own decision. Death is the last enemy to be put under foot. Each believer awaits the return of the Lord of lords and King of kings. (John 10:10; 1 Corinthians 15:26; Revelation 19:20, 20:10,14-15; 21:8)

Every individual true believer is a vassal to the Sovereign Lord Jesus Christ. He came that we might have abundant life. A deceived unbeliever is a vassal to the Thief, the defeated accuser who by his wiles steals, kills, and destroys. (John 10:10) Thousands called of God have made appeals for a commitment to the only covenant of life through the only mediator of a better covenant—the Lord Jesus Christ. The covenant of life says there is only one way to God and that is through Jesus. The covenant of death says there are many ways to God.

Like an occupying army believers need to be alert to the wiles of the devil. We overcome lies that would hamper our walk with the Lord. We are to occupy until He comes again. (Matthew 28:8; Romans 8:37; 1 Corinthians 9:24-26; Ephesians 6:10-20; Galatians 2:2; 5:7; Philippians 2:16; Hebrews 12:1; 1 Peter 2:7-17; 4:4)

The covenant with death offers countless options while demanding, or at least convincing its adherents to not get involved with the narrow-minded Christian view. The liar, Satan, contends the Christian God is only one of many gods. With ill-advised recklessness, adherents in covenant with death follow their father the devil. Doing what is right in their own sight, they remain in bondage in their covenant with death. Each person chooses the covenant he will be actively involved in—the covenant of life or the covenant of death. God has set before us life and death, blessing and cursing. Then He compassionately advises us to choose life so that we can live. (Deuteronomy 30:19-20; Joshua 24:15)

The blessing of the New Covenant is salvation in Jesus; the curse is the condemnation that comes from unbelief, which gives the wily devil freedom to move in spite of the truth declared. Jesus is the truth. His Word is truth. And so with profound power and wisdom, Jesus declared the blessing and curse of the New Covenant. Only a fool says in his heart there is no God. Jesus is well able to keep that which is committed unto Him. Believers run strong in the Lord and in the power of His might. (John 10:10; Psalm 14:1; 53:1; 92:6; Luke 12:20)

COVENANT MEMORIALS

Memorials could be established in one of three ways. In the New Covenant all three ways were used. A stone was inscribed, a flock shared, and trees were planted as the better covenant memorial was established. Those memorials still testify of the magnificence of the New Covenant made two thousand years ago. The New Covenant is still affecting the descendants of the covenant head. A multitude of Christians around the world are living memorials of the covenant of life.

Though Jesus had no physical descendants, He had a multitude of spiritual offspring. His spiritual offspring are those who have truly been born again by the Spirit of God. They are called Christians. Though they initially were called Christians or soldiers of Christ[110] derogatorily, the title remained for the spiritual seed of Jesus the Christ. But the term Christian is too broadly and inaccurately used today. It is often used to include almost everyone who has ever gone to church.

One man thought he was a Christian because he was born in the United States of America. He used faulty reasoning to conclude that because he was born in a Christian country, he was a Christian. Faulty reasoning may have opened a few doors for him in this life, but they will not open the doors of heaven for him. A Christian is one who is born again, as Jesus instructed Nicodemus; those who regularly confess Jesus as their Lord and who believe in their hearts that he died for them, was raised from the dead, and now sits in heavenly places with God. These Christians were, and continue to be, the living memorials of the better covenant. (John 3:3; Romans 10:9-10; 1 Peter 4:16; Isaiah 53:10-11 AMP)

ENGRAVEN STONE

One way a memorial could be established was to engrave a stone and set it in a prominent place. The stone engraved in the New Covenant is the heart of the Christian. The heart of the Christian is his regenerated spirit. Obviously, this is not a physical heart that's being spoken of.

> The Hebrews thought in terms of subjective experience rather than objective. . . . It was essentially the whole man, with all his attributes physical, intellectual, and psychological, of which the Hebrew thought and spoke, and the heart was conceived of as the governing center for all of these. It is the heart which makes a man what he is (Proverbs 16:23, 23:7), and governs all his actions (Proverbs 4:23).[111]

The "heart" as used in the New Testament is similarly the governing center of a person. The New Testament speaks of a person as a spirit, a soul, and a body. The heart is made flesh or otherwise stated; the spirit, is born again. The soul, the emotional and reasoning part of a person, deciphers messages primarily by the five senses, and must be renewed by the Word of God after the spirit is recreated. With the spirit's regeneration and the soul's renewal the body is brought into obedience to the dictates of the regenerated person's spirit and mind.

A major difference between one who is born again and one who is not should be evident to all. When the spirit is born again, the soul is renewed and the body disciplined. The regenerated man is to be led by his spirit, not by his senses—sometimes called his flesh. The body (the flesh) fights the dictates of the born again spirit and the renewed soul. Jesus put it so beautifully when discovering the disciples asleep after he had admonished them to pray. (Matthew 26:36-41; Romans 7:18-8:2; 1 Thessalonians 5:23; 3 John 2; Hebrews 4:12)

It was the heart (spirit) of the new man that Jeremiah was speaking of prophetically when he said, of the covenant to be made, that the Lord would write his law on the hearts of His people. The hearts God writes (engraves) his covenant on had previously been hearts of stone. (Jeremiah 31:33; Ezekiel 11:19; 18:31; 30:26-27; 38:26; 2 Corinthians 3:2-6)

SHARED FLOCK

Another way to establish a covenant memorial was to share a flock. Jesus frequently referred to his disciples as sheep and to himself as a shepherd. Jesus and his covenant partner share a flock that will be a continuous reminder of the agreement they have made. Each time they see their flock growing, they remember the unbreakable covenant they have made. In anticipation of the growth of his flock Jesus prayed, not only for the disciples that were with him then, but also for those that would believe in him because of their testimony. (Matthew 26:31-32; Mark 14:27-28; John 10:1-16,27-30; 17:6-10,20)

PLANTING OF TREES

Another way of establishing a covenant memorial was to plant trees. Christians were prophetically referred to in Isaiah as trees. When Jesus took the disciples aside to encourage and instruct them just before he was betrayed by Judas, he referred to Himself as the vine and his disciples as the branches of that vine. With covenant terminology, he emphasized the necessity of maintaining intimate fellowship with him. They must, he said, *abide in the vine*—for a covenant alliance demands fellowship, which is closer than a natural relationship. Because of covenant a Christian becomes one with his covenant partner—the covenant head of the better covenant. Aware of the emptiness offered by the alternative covenant with death, Jesus instructed that as grafted branches believers were to abide in him. (Isaiah 61:3,8; John 15:4-5)

In the epistle to the Romans, reference is made to the memorial of the better covenant. Restating Jesus' instruction to remain *abiding in the vine*, the author spoke of Christians as branches of an olive tree. Israel, with whom the Mosaic covenant had been made, transgressed covenant by persisting in unbelief. Consequently, the Gentiles were grafted into the vine to replace the natural, but unfruitful, branches that were pruned away. (John 15:3; Romans 11:17-22, 27-28)

The first covenant's promise of a redeemer was fulfilled in Jesus. Both the Old Covenant and the better covenant required the faith of its participants.

> The difference between the branches broken off and the branches grafted in consists in the presence of faith. Unbelief meant rejection. Faith meant acceptance.[112]

The natural and grafted branches that abide in the vine are living memorials to the better covenant. The palm tree is like the uncompromisingly righteous who flourish, are long-lived, stately, upright, useful, stable, durable, and incorruptible and will bring forth fruit even in old age. That is true for any believer that abides in the vine, the Rock of our salvation. (Psalm 92 AMP)

MEMORIAL MEAL

Another covenant-making step fulfilled by the better covenant was the memorial meal enacted in the New Testament. The memorial meal was shared by Jesus with His disciples and has been repeated by Christians since he introduced it. The New Covenant memorial meal is frequently referred to as communion. Christians review the covenant—with its promises and its provisions—as they take communion. It was for the purpose of taking part in the memorial meal of the Old Covenant that Jesus and his disciples prepared for the Passover. Jesus explained communion to his disciples while celebrating Passover. Passover was the Old Covenant memorial meal; communion was the New Covenant memorial meal.

Jesus, the Word of God made flesh, said, "take and eat my body." Covenant terminology was used as Jesus appealed to the disciples to read, meditate, and obey the covenant word of God. Jesus was speaking of God's word, which is spirit and life, when he spoke to the disciples at the Passover meal. His declaration was not strange to them, for they understood covenant and covenant terminology. They were not startled when *the Christ, the Son of the living God* employed covenant terminology at this covenant (Passover) meal. The disciples were not startled for they were familiar with the Old Covenant promises of a messiah who would come to make an everlasting covenant. (Genesis

3:15; 17:7; Isaiah 28:15-18; Jeremiah 31:31-34; Matthew 16:16; 26:26-28; John 1:14; 6:36)

Almost a year before this final Passover feast with Jesus, the disciples had been with him as he taught in the synagogue in Capernaum. It was then he had referred to himself as the bread of life. He had used covenant terminology then also as he said, *He that eats my flesh and drinks my blood, dwells in me, and I in him.* This offended many of his disciples and many of them left. They were not yet able to distinguish between the physical and the spiritual.[113] But from the terms Jesus was using they were aware he was speaking of covenant. Six hundred years before Jesus was born there was a great interest in covenant. That interest continued through the years between the testaments.[114] (John 6:51,56)

> The NT, or New Covenant, was the term used by the church for the new body of Christian literature appended to the Old Covenant. The primary source for this interpretation in the literature itself is to be found in passages describing the Lord's Supper as the "new covenant" (1 Corinthians 11:25) or covenant in Christ's blood (Mark 14:24; cf. Matthew 26:28; a reference to Exodus 14:8). The new covenant in Christ is the referred to also both by Paul (2 Corinthians 3:6) and by the author of Hebrews (e.g. 7:1-22; 8:1-13). Yet since in NT times 'covenant' had come to mean almost exclusively obedience to the Jewish law. One can observe that New Testament writers were not comfortable with the term, except to point out that the covenant in Christ was not of law but of faith or of the Spirit.[115]

They knew Jesus was speaking of covenant, eating of His flesh was offensive partly because they had difficulty with abstracts. Surely, if He were truly the Messiah, He would not change the Old Covenant. But there was another reason to seriously consider what Jesus was saying.

Roman law forbade making covenant under penalty of death. All those under Roman jurisdiction were to hail Caesar alone as lord. Loyalty was to be solely due to him.

> This view is expressed by G. E. Mendenhall. He writes: "The surprising infrequency of references to covenant in the NT raises great difficulties, even though it is understandable. The covenant for Judaism meant the Mosaic law and for the Roman Empire a covenant meant an illegal secret society. This two-sided conflict made it nearly impossible for early Christianity to use the term meaningfully" *(The Interpreter's Dictionary of the Bible,* 1962, s.v. "Covenant," p. 722). Note that even the covenant meaning of the Lord's Supper ("new covenant in my blood"— 1 Corinthians 11:25) is not found in the post-NT literature (such as *Thdache,* 9, 10, 14), presumably because of the same Roman *hetaeriae* (n. 22) legislation.[116]

If Jesus' followers did anything other than proclaim Jesus a passive 'religious' leader, they would all be in jeopardy. Whether in danger from Jewish leaders, Roman commanders, or God Himself, the early disciples were presented with the possibility of incurring hazards they chose not to deal with. Jesus' bold teaching and preaching of kingdoms, kingship, and covenant tested the loyalty of His followers. But Jesus had come equipped to make a better covenant. Though his followers deserted him, he would accomplish this step of the better covenant. Neither Jewish law, Roman law, nor fickle (wavering) follower law would deter the Lord from finishing what he came to do.

With twelve of his more loyal disciples, Jesus shared the first communion meal as a memorial of the better covenant. The communion meal replaced the memorial meal of the Old Covenant. As the disciples ate unleavened bread and drank wine with Jesus, they were agreeing they were one together with their covenant head who was actively making a solemn agreement as their legal representative.

Paul admonished the church at Corinth to consider what Jesus had accomplished when they celebrated the New Covenant meal. All who are involved in the better covenant are required to judge themselves regularly. The measure for judging must be the New Covenant Word of God and the indwelling Holy Spirit of God. To celebrate the covenant of life by taking communion, one must set aside all involvement with the covenant of death. To attempt to take part in both covenants at the same time is to live precariously. Such double-mindedness results in insecurity and instability.

Communion has, since Jesus introduced it to his disciples, regularly been part of worship services throughout the world. Communion time remains a time to meditate on the splendor of the better covenant. (1 Corinthians 11:23-31)

THE NEW COVENANT – A BOND OF LOVE

Blood covenants were the most solemn of all agreements. They were more than legal matters—they were bonds of love. When the blood covenant process was complete, an unbreakable union was made that demanded uncompromising commitment. Partial commitment in blood covenants was unsatisfactory. "No man, having put his hand to the plow, and looking back, is fit for the kingdom of God," (Luke 9:62).

Jesus had completed the steps in making a better covenant. With his work finished, he ascended and sat down with His covenant partner to intercede for us as His covenant descendants and representatives. (2 Corinthians 3:6; 5:19-21; Hebrews 10:12-29)

Love covers a multitude of sins. Though no love compares to His, we, with the help of the Holy Ghost, can learn to walk more sure-footedly in what He commanded. God is always faithful to covenant. If there are doctrines and theories that differ about any subject, let God's love prevail. Agape love allows one to study the scriptures and patiently wait on the Lord for clarity on any subject. Sound prayer principles and maintaining a desire to do His will brings illumination to know what is of God and what is not of Him.

Love is the New Covenant commandment—through Him we can love those of like precious faith. And refrain from warring with one another. How glorious is our God when by grace through faith we are made new! By the precious blood I have been made new, and made fit as a vessel of honor. The Word of the Lord and the infilling of the Holy Spirit has helped me renew my mind. I have stayed in faith and have learned more and more about not leaning on my own understanding. (John 7:17 AMP; 2 Corinthians 8:16-24; 13:1-13; James 1:1-27; 2:8-24; 4:1-3; 5:20; 1 Peter 4:8; Proverbs 3:5; 13:2)

The rightly divided word of God is like medicine to the wounded. It is freedom to the bound. It is fresh air, joy, light, life, truth, right and pure. For me, the study of covenant has been a move into an area with a continual supply of fresh air. I have rejoiced daily as I read the scriptures and see how the pieces fit together. Seeing the Word of the Lord and growing to understand blood covenant has been a source of light, purity, and truth. Through eyes developed to see covenant links in Bible verses has been remarkably valuable and has helped me understand more clearly the placement of such phrases as "the first and last Adam."

Chapter 7

ADAM, THE FIRST & THE LAST

The phrase "first Adam and second (last) Adam" is easier to understand in the context of covenant. It seems either the first or second Adam could have made a covenant with God. Adam's transgression disqualified him. Christ Jesus succeeded because, though he was tempted as the first Adam, He was not seduced. (Luke 3:38; John 8:34; Romans 5:14)

Problems can exist without one being aware there is even a problem. Death is commonly associated with the word cancer. Fear runs rampant when that report is given. There are exceptions. Some Christians have learned how to use the sword of the Spirit and the shield of faith. But cancer is a fear monger because of the power of the covenant with death. Cancer is only one destructive problem, which can remain undetected for a long time.

Disobedience and rebellion are destroyers of spirits and are as cancers to the soul and body. The first Adam caused sin to enter the world and its cancerous effects left him and his descendants struggling to pay the price of disobedience. He was not deceived. He disobeyed God's command. He had entered into a covenant with death and with hell. (Genesis 3; Isaiah 53:1)

Death entered when sin entered. The first man fell. The man Adam, the son of God, was the reason death reigned even over those who had not sinned as Adam did. His fall was to the detriment of all ever to be born after the first Adam.

There is a terrible price to pay for sin. It enslaves and the devil is an unmerciful taskmaster. Worse than any slave-driver ever known, Satan horsewhipped his servants. Satan snared, bound, and harassed them because of the covenant with death.

THE FIRST ADAM—A LIVING SOUL

The first Adam was *a living soul*, the son of God. He was a blessed soul in daily fellowship with his Heavenly Father. Adam came to know the goodness of the Lord God. Adam, when tempted, let God's goodness take second place. Adam was righteous, a living soul, and the son of God, but he pondered over words when tempted. Not using his God-given authority, Adam's hesitation proved fatal. Once tempted, Adam was hooked. A fatal end was the consequence of his disobedience. Sin is a prelude to a hellish end. He and his descendants paid a terrible price. (Luke 3:38; 1 Thessalonians 5:23; Genesis 3:15; Isaiah 28:15,18)

The first man Adam was created to have dominion, absolute ownership, and authority over the earth—submitting only to His Creator. He was created to be second in command to God. He was a living soul. Adam was given the job of subduing the earth, tilling the soil, and ruling. He had dominion. Adam was positioned for tactical reasons. Obviously there was an enemy. The tempter, who was unknown to Adam, apparently was watching.

Adam was instructed to name and to tend God's creation. God is spirit, and has a soul and a body. Man, created in God's image, likewise is a spirit, has a soul, and lives in a body. He was a living soul, for God had breathed into Adam's nostrils the breath of life. As a living soul, Adam was able to fellowship with God. However, Adam never ate of the tree of life. Though called the son of God by Luke, Adam was a living soul who foolishly decided to follow the deceiver. Joseph's lineage was followed back to the son of Adam, which was the son of God. (Luke 3:38)

A man's soul was living for the first time, because the breath of life was given him. He dwelt in a flesh designed by God. Daily fellowship with God did not automatically give him victory. It did not prevent Adam from turning from the covenant stipulations he was given. Receiving covenant stipulations, instructions, and a command, Adam failed to accomplish what he was created for.

The job he had been commissioned to do was left unfinished. God's command was broken. The covenant was broken. Adam had transgressed and disobeyed. Instead of providing a solution, Adam presented a problem by eating of the tree in the midst of the garden. His sin caused all his seed to be born in sin. As head of the covenant with God, Adam's seed within him was likewise affected when Adam chose to disobey. They would be born under the penalty of Adam's sin. Continuous misconduct and disgraceful disgruntlement would be written wherever they dwelt. Also would be recorded their version of what had happened on that fateful day in the garden.

Every person is a spirit, has a soul, and lives in a body. Adam became separated from God, who is a Holy Spirit. Adam was a living soul but aligned himself with the covenant of death, when he could have eaten of the tree of life. His soul became disgruntled, his body died eventually. He continued breathing. He still had breath in his body. He still had a soul. His spirit was separated, out of fellowship with God. His soul began a progressive decline as he adapted his lifestyle to harmonize with the one who authored the death covenant.

Adam's living soul died for lack of fellowship with God. His intellect and emotions ran rampant. His children, with a few exceptions, followed suit. Knowing what God had said, Adam chose to disobey his Lord when Eve gave him the fruit. It seems Adam's sin came from disobediently following the woman's voice rather than following God's voice. He ate of the tree God told him not to eat of.

Adam's spirit could have remained obediently aligned with the will of God. Woman took of the fruit and ate of it. Adam was with her and could have countered the voice of the serpent. He had the authority to do so. Adam, Eve, and their seed could have been spared. Adam could have, should have, heeded the Lord God's voice instead. However, new creation, Holy Spirit hindsight is thousands of times better than living soul foresight. Adam could have disallowed what the woman had done. (Luke 21:8; John 7:47; 10:3-5,16; Romans 7:11; 1 Corinthians 6:9; 15:33; Galatians 6:7; 1 Timothy 2:14; 2 Timothy 3:13; Genesis 2:9; 3:17, 22-24; Proverbs 3:18; 11:30; 13:12-14; 15:4; Revelation 2:7; 22:2, 14)

Because of Adam's covenant transgression his spirit died immediately. Repetition with variation is a good design principle. Thus I repeat, yes Adam was a spirit, for he was made fully after his creator, the triune God. The life of God was not fully, vitally alive in Adam. Simply defined, death is separation from life. Righteousness and unrighteous cannot abide together; they are all together contradictory. For this reason, Adam tried to hide himself and his sin from God. He was no longer able to conduct himself as he had done before. He had followed *the voice of a stranger*. The manifold blessings missed when he did not choose to continue would eat away at him. Everything would be eroded. Neither Adam nor his descendants would have the privilege of habitual fellowship with God, as he had previously known, unless they found grace in the eyes of the Lord. Noah found grace in the eyes of the Lord. He was just and perfect (mature) in his generation at a time when the earth was corrupt and filled with violence. (Genesis 6:8-11)

The first Adam had the unique distinction of being created rather than born. He had the distinct opportunity to eternally walk with God. The thief used trickery to deceive the man (Adam) through the woman. She saw the tree was good and pleasant to the eyes. Listening to the wrong voice, she took of the fruit and her knowledge of what was good became perverted. She told Adam the tree was good for food, pleasant to the eyes. The tree, she said, was desired to make one wise as she gave the fruit to her husband. In truth, only God is good.

Their guilt and their slave driver god of darkness immediately hit them with condemnation—they were naked and were ashamed. Who told them? The devil. He began immediately to bring condemnation. He became their constant accuser. They began to walk on in darkness.

Adam and Eve tried to defend themselves with excuses while denying their guilt. They did not take responsibility for their disobedience. "The woman is the cause." "No, it was the serpent." "No, it was. . . . " Judgment came quickly. (1 Thessalonians 5:23; Leviticus 16:8, 10, 26; Deuteronomy 32:17) After each offered excuse, God proclaimed His judgment. Perhaps the serpent offered no excuse because he no longer had a leg to stand on. Not one of the three was exempt. The voice of a stranger caused loss of righteousness. They had sinned. It is not at all wise to waste time trying to distract the righteous God of all the earth. Their fallacy and incorrect reasoning was not persuasive. God is inclined to get to the heart of the matter. Hearts can become hopelessly deceitful. But God knows and judges the heart prompting the actions.

Loss of Godly wisdom caused the bad habit of blaming others to become a common practice. The worldly wisdom Adam and Eve gained originated in the realm of evil spirits headed by the devil, Lucifer. Wisdom that was worldly and pleased the flesh would be all Adam's seed would know. Adam followed in accord with his father the devil, as did his descendents after him.

With faulty reasoning some would take Adam and Eve's shame at being naked as an excuse to follow nakedness. Clothing was necessary for their sin affected all others. Naked flesh tempts the flesh to all types of defilements. Nakedness is only appropriate when babies need clean diapers, people need baths, and husbands and wives are alone together in the privacy of their own bedchamber or equivalent.

The suit, the filthy garment of sin given when the covenant with death was activated, left them inadequately clothed with leaves sewn together. Their defiled heart and outer garments would need to be replaced often. The shame of filth prevailed, beginning with Adam and Eve trying to hide from God.

Sin immediately caused destructive consequence for the first Adam. No one born of the first Adam would be qualified to deal with the sin that entered at *his fall*. The dangers of following evil voices led Adam's descendants from Genesis through Revelation into a digression with few exceptions. A digression that would only end after the one true Almighty God judged all the works of all men.

Adam no longer harmonized with Elohim. Adam's misalignment caused him to fear *the voice of the LORD God walking in the garden.* How does a voice walk? Perhaps like the wind blows. Like the sound that accompanies it's presence. Adam and Eve hid themselves from the presence of the Lord. They were separated from God, who is life. Adam died. He died quickly in his spirit, slower in his soul, slowest in his body. The natural pull of gravity took its toll. His descendants were born in sin.

Adam had activated a covenant with death. His offspring would be inclined to wallow in sin and hold onto a ragged, filthy comfort zone perverting the God-given covenant principles. Some men and women, however, would grasp blood covenant principles in faith and walk accordingly. Far too many of Adam's seed would follow after the head of their covenant. Few would not even let their eyes see any of God's intended plans for salvation. They would not let their ears hear the glorious voice of the Lord. (Genesis 2:7; 3:8, 13, 20-23; Deuteronomy 1:35-38; John 10:10; Ephesians 3:9; 6:11; Hebrews 5:14; 6:5; Titus 1:16; James 3:13, 17; 2 John 1:11; Revelation 20:12)

DISOBEDIENCE

God created Adam for plans and purposes that many theologians still debate, creating a sound much like that of war between the teachers of different doctrines. There is a major difference between covenant and dispensation theologies. It is not my intent to side with either. I have sought only to gain clarity for myself.

There is one truth. The rightly divided Word of truth as taught by the Holy Spirit of Truth is the truth I desire and attempt to relay. I have also seen from church history and current teachings how vehemently adherents feel about defending their doctrines. With daily reading over successive years, insights into the mysteries of God's plan began to pull the puzzle together for me piece by piece. After years of considering the subject of covenant and the astounding truths in blood covenant I was encouraged to resume writing. (John 1:1-14; 8:30-51; 14:6, 17; 15:26; Acts 17:11-12, 17-19; Romans 9:1; 15:8-9; Colossians 2:10; 4:12; Exodus 34:6; Deuteronomy 32:1-6)

The second and the final Adam would complete the good work begun even before the first Adam was created. Agape love would see the planned, purposed completion of the good work begun. (Matthew 4:4; John 1:1-14, 29-32; 14:24-26; Romans 5:14; 1 Corinthians 15:22, 45)

God is love. It is conspicuous that the New Covenant commandment is love. Adherents to the New Covenant of necessity must walk their talk and love one another, even as He has loved us. God so loved us that He gave His only begotten Son. Some are challenged with marriage issues and more specifically the virgin birth issues mentioned in the Bible. Churches, cults, and doctrines abound.

Judgment and rewards will come. While we wait for the Lord's return we are to wait with lamps filled with oil. We are to judge ourselves and let the chaff fly away in the wind. As one prominent Bible teacher said, "chew the hay and spite out the stubble." Hold tight to the anchor as strong, tempestuous, doctrinal winds whip around. Be assured the rushing mighty wind filling the house where believers waited is still moving today. He is still as mighty and there are a lot more believers now. Believers will continue to see the love of the Lord poured out as we continue to wait. The Lord has prepared and will return again. He will return for his bride. The wise will still be standing with oil in their lamps. (Matthews 25:1-13; John 3:16; Acts 2:2; 27:14; Ephesians 4:14; Hebrews 6:19; 13:1-9; 1 John 4:8, 16)

> In the Near East betrothal . . . is almost as binding as marriage itself. In the Bible the betrothed woman was sometimes called 'wife' and was under the same obligation of faithfulness (Genesis 29:21; Deuteronomy 22:23,24; Matthew 1:18,20) and the betrothed man was called 'husband' (Joel 1:18; Matthew 1:19).[117]

Jesus would make a way. Only the Father knew the right time. Jesus came the first time and as a display adapter, converted information from the Father. God's great love was shown to His own and then even to the world. When Jesus had ascended, the apostles preached everywhere, the Lord working with them, and confirming the word with signs following. Amen.

We are continuing to write the acts of the Holy Spirit because His great love for us motivates us to show His love to others. At His first coming, Israel was called. John the Baptist would prepare the way for his beloved. John the Baptist began preaching and proclaiming, *repent*. Jesus came fulfilling what Isaiah had spoken. He too began to preach and say, *repent*. God's great love is persistent. (Matthew 3:2; 4:17; 13:57; Mark 16:19-20; John 1:11; 3:2, 16; 2 Corinthians 11:1-4; Revelation 21:2)

If it seems like gibberish or unintelligible talk, realize Paul wrote of the mystery of Christ within. Peter said Paul, according to the wisdom given him, wrote of things hard to understand. The simplest Bible principles can be as gibberish to the unlearned or unstable. Jesus displayed God's love. His love prompted Him to personally bear our sins in His own body. (1 Peter 2:24 AMP; 2 Peter 3:15-16)

GOD'S LOVE

God is love and He is faithful to covenant. As a cheated party hurts when an engagement or marriage is broken, likewise God ached because of Adam's transgression. He also ached as Israel repeatedly violated covenant with their unfaithfulness. Gomer, Hosea's wife, who lightly considered her marriage vows and took many lovers, demonstrated Israel's philandering. Hosea, the Old Testament prophet, illustrated God's steadfast love for his unfaithful covenant partner Gomer. (Hosea 1-3)

> The relation between the prophet and his unfaithful wife, Gomer, is illustrative of the ultimate basis of the divine covenant in a deeper than legal relationship, in a love that is willing to suffer. God's love is part of His personality and cannot be swayed by passion or diverted by disobedience (Hosea 11:1-4, 7-9, RSV; this passage is as close as the Old Testament comes to a declaration that God is love). Israel's unfaithfulness can have no effect upon it, for 'I have loved thee with an everlasting love' (Jeremiah 31:3). The threat to 'love them no more' (Hosea 9:15) is best interpreted as one to be their God no more.[118]

Though Adam's transgression adversely affected his relationship with God, it did not alter God's love for Adam or Adam's descendants. Elohim's love for Adam was everlasting. The covenants God made with Adam's descendants were all initiated by love. God is love. He is permeated with compassion for man. Though God is love, He is also righteous. Because He is righteous, He could not reinstate Adam to his pre-transgression status without legal provision. That provision took thousands of years to complete. Man, left to his own devices is a slow learner. The laws God set in motion before Adam's violation could not be altered for any reason, not even for Adam. God could not compromise without becoming an unrighteous, lawbreaker Himself. A transgressed covenant demanded that the transgressor die. Without compromising his righteousness God could however provide the means for limited interaction with Adam and his descendants. (John 4:8; Psalm 119:137; 145:17)

Theories abound around the Genesis account of the creation and even of man himself. When addressing covenant, even the Bible account is not conspicuous. Neither is it completely concealed. The awful, bitter, effect of the fruit of deception includes fear. Fear is the opposite of faith in God. Fear motivates futile attempts to thwart God. In the chapters between Adam and Abraham is an account of some of the awfulness Adam's descendants were surrounded with and indulged in. Within the first few chapters in Genesis, genealogy and sins were primary topics. (Genesis 1-11).

Fear is the assurance of things dreaded, the conviction of destructive things birthed by sin and wickedness. Fear spawned lies about creation. The deceived bought lies. The deceiver was continuing to condemn them. The total fealty expected of them was kept from them. They were in a covenant with death. The small print in their covenant was hidden from them. Darkness shrouded them. They could not see. Liars and lies fed each other.

By fear, Adam and Eve anxiously clothed themselves. By fear, they blamed each other. They wore condemnation chains of serpent-worship. The lies of the slave master convinced the slaves they had greater knowledge than any declining, waning righteous preacher. Abel aggravated Cain. Ignoring the voice of the Lord, Cain opened the door to sin. Bitterness and jealousy bore thistles. The tools of the slave master prompted Cain to murder his brother. As a fugitive and vagabond, Cain wandered in fear of being slain himself.

Fear came forth from Lamech lamenting his own evil deed. He was afraid he would be avenged. If Cain was avenged sevenfold, Lamech would surely be avenged seven times over what Cain had been avenged. God's mercy toward Cain was disregarded and thorns continued to grow. The Devil did not allow heartfelt acknowledgment of God. Wickedness increased.

Enoch and Noah were irritations, annoyances. They were as threads of faith threatening filthy rags of fear. Enoch walked with God. Advancing with and caught away by God, Enoch left an impression. Methuselah had a bit of light among his children. Noah walked with God and found grace and favor with Him.

The wickedness surrounding Noah was so pronounced God was grieved. The wicked played games and ridiculed, even while God was giving instruction for the ark. A flood was brought forth wherein the breath of life was suffocated out of their soul. The flesh began to drag with a heavy burden. Adrenaline was continuously secreted. Stress was taking a toll on the bodies. Evil deeds continued. They ridiculed even as the waters began to rise.

From among the mockers Noah's family loaded the ark built as God directed. Still being ridiculed, the family went into the ark and the Lord shut the door. Noah and his family escaped. Noah did all God commanded him.

God would establish His covenant with Noah. The awesome creative power of God judged the earth. The devil lost the bodies and souls he had enslaved. The proud boasted even as the door was slammed shut. Ridicule was drowned in a flood never seen before or since. Noah had heeded the voice of God though living in the company of braggart, rebellious, and disobedient souls frolicking for the entertainment of the devil. But fear would continue to be a shield of lies, for the devil remained to tempt again.

God established His covenant with Noah and Noah's seed. Wickedness had been judged. But the covenant with death had not been annulled. Noah's family multiplied and replenished the earth. The fear and dread of Noah and the flood would be repeated with variations throughout the earth. Ham was the first to fall. Shem did not delay long. Wickedness ran rampant again. Lies and fear kept truth deflected and the devil shielded as he twisted the concept of covenant again.

Fear intensified after Noah died, lust for the power of darkness increased. Fear whipped into a frenzied body, joined together like hornets around their nest, building for a downfall. Through the power of darkness Shem by fear brought forth a proud mass. Constraining by fear of being scattered, en mass they were led by Nimrod to build a tower. Babel self-exalted, but then confounded, was indeed scattered. They left off building and followed on after the deceiver, stealing, killing, and destroying on various wandering ways.

Between Noah and Abraham, successive generations repeated the story of Noah and the flood and the wrath of God. The names were changed, but similar accounts were repeated and repeated again. The deceiver continued instilling fear without repentance so covenant known to all was twisted. The thief continued to steal, kill, and destroy. Knowledge of good and evil was promoted and twisted. Theories came forth to explain away Adam, Eve, Cain, Abel, Enoch, Noah, and all that related to them. Covenant was twisted. False gods were named and territories assigned.

Jacob came to the forefront. His son Joseph was sold into slavery. Joseph's story is a picture of what was to come. Jacob's seed found a haven in Egypt. But 400 years later they called to the God of Abraham, Isaac, and Jacob and were delivered from the slave driver. Passover was observed. Moses was given covenant commandments, which served as law and guidelines until the final sacrifice was made on Golgotha.

God's covenant with Abraham and the covenant with Moses was the beginning of covenant details that became a repetitive bone of contention in Jesus' day. The covenant stipulations given Moses were very detailed. Exodus through Deuteronomy is the account of the covenant designed by God to help His people realize His Holiness and their sin. The High Priest was no exception. Stephen called out to the high priest, *brethren and fathers, listen.* (Acts 7:1-60)

Sacrifice was always part of making blood covenant, God directed and Moses wrote the specifics. God's intention was to bring man to the realization of the awfulness of sin through the Law of Moses. Moses' law referred to the stipulations of blood covenant and the sacrifice to cover sin. (Exodus – Deuteronomy)

COVENANT SACRIFICE

Interaction between unrighteous man and righteous God was made possible by means of covenant sacrifice. Unrighteousness required a death, either of the guilty party or of a substitute, for without the shedding of blood there is no remission of sin. With sacrifices, men around the world attempted to approach God. However, man frequently approached God assuming the sacrifice itself was pleasing to God. Love, however, had no pleasure in sacrifices. (Hebrews 10:6; 1 John 4:8) God did not delight in bloodshed. Rather, His desire was that man would acknowledge and repent of his evil ways. When man acknowledged sin, sacrifice met the requirements of righteousness and sin was then remitted. Without acknowledging the unrighteousness of man and the righteousness of God sacrifice was futile. (Hebrews 9:22; 10:6; 1 John 4:8; Isaiah 1:11-18)

God had a plan of salvation that would eventually end all need for shedding the blood of sacrificial animals. His plan was for a one-time perfect sacrifice that would deal with sin forever. Jesus was the unblemished lamb for the perfect sacrifice. He was the promised redeemer. Until that perfect lamb (Jesus) came, the blood covenant was active by those who obediently continued offering animal sacrifices to cover their sins. At Sinai, when Jehovah made covenant with Israel, substitute blood was offered by Israel and accepted by Jehovah. (Exodus 24:3-8)

The declaration of Moses to Israel was: *Behold the blood of the covenant, which the LORD hath made with you.* This declaration is referred to after the New Covenant. (Exodus 24:8; Hebrews 9:18-22 NKJV) Because of blood covenant with Abraham, God was able to bring forth a second Adam that would come to complete the work the first Adam had failed to achieve.

RELINQUISHED COVENANT AUTHORITY

The first Adam was born again from life unto death. He annulled the initial steps of the covenant of life and instead began the covenant of death. The earth consequently was cursed because of Adam. He also relinquished all the authority that had been given him. Satan, the benefactor of that relinquished authority, became the god of this world. As the god of this world, Satan indirectly has been the primary source of temptation to man. It was as a tempter that Satan approached the second Adam at the beginning of Jesus' ministry.

THE SECOND ADAM—A QUICKENING SPIRIT

The first Adam was a living soul. But the second Adam was a quickening spirit, the Son of God. He was a man born without sin, who lived in a body, and lived without compromise. He did not give in to temptations even after a forty-day fast. The devil tempted Jesus when the Lord had been without food. The simplicity and pure motive of the Lord had His shield of faith in place. With a valid defensive correction the Lord nullified the devil's false assertion. Though Jesus had been close to the stage where starvation sets in, He remained strong in faith. Well-armed with the sword of the Spirit, Jesus countered every temptation. (1 Peter 2:7-8)

Jesus was approximately thirty years old when He went to the Jordan River to be baptized by John. Afterwards, led by the Holy Spirit, Jesus spent time fasting and continuing in prayer. Jesus sought time alone with his heavenly Father. Luke tells when Jesus, full of the Holy Ghost during his fellowship time with His Father, successfully wielded the sword of the Spirit. The Lord's time was intruded upon by temptation from the very source by which the first Adam had been tempted. The second Adam rightly divided the Word of God. The devil left and the angels of God came to minister to Jesus. (Matthew 4:1-11; Luke 3:21-22; 4:1-8 KJV and RSV)

Paul spoke of a mystery and told of a change that would take place in the twinkling of an eye. He admonished believers to be steadfast, unmovable, abounding in the work of the Lord. The second Adam completed and made an everlasting better covenant. (1 Corinthians 15:45-58)

Like Adam, Jesus was tempted to take authority and glory without responsibility and obedience. Satan could not have enticed Jesus with authority and glory if he lacked the ability to give possession of them. For something to be tempting it must be feasible. Oatmeal cookies do not tempt a child if possession of an oatmeal cookie is not possible. If, however, possession is possible, the temptation to eat cookies before supper is present in spite of a parental ban.

Satan's offer was tempting because Jesus did not yet have authority over all the kingdoms of the world—Satan did. Satan was authorized by the first Adam to reign. The thief that steals, kills, and destroys lived up to his name. But the second Adam came to legally regain that authority and Satan was fearful.

Since the day God had promised redemption to the first Adam, Satan had dreaded the day of incarnation. He had tried unsuccessfully to deter God's plan of salvation. But he had failed. Now the Son of God as a man had the ability to wrench from Satan his ill-gotten authority. If, however, Satan could get this Christ to give in to temptation, God's plan of redemption would be abated to the detriment of all mankind. As a tempter, Satan (Matthew 4:3; 1 Thessalonians 3:5) had caused havoc in God's original plan for man, and now he was setting himself against the second Adam. (Matthew 4:3; Romans 5:12-21; 1 Thessalonians 3:5; James 1:12-15)

Jesus was tempted in every way that all other people are tempted. Jesus was successful in overcoming the world with all its temptations. Jesus endured temptation and became the first man capable of receiving the crown of life. He was the first man since Adam who was qualified to make a covenant of life. Jesus, like no man before him, walked without having committed sin. (John 16:33; Romans 5:9-10,18-19)

Jesus was the second Adam. He personally bore our sins, yet he also lived unto righteousness all His days. He was the first righteous man to be raised from the dead because of His flawless life. Though He had been tempted in all points, he was yet without sin. Since he has suffered temptation, He is able to come to the aid of those who are tempted. John 16:33 in *The Amplified Bible* says, "For I have overcome the world. [I have deprived it of power to harm you and have conquered it for you]." (Luke 4:13; John 8:44; Acts 13:10-11; Hebrews 4:15; 2 Corinthians 4:4)

OBEDIENT

Jesus was born to make an everlasting covenant of Peace. During his ministry he lived in obedience to the Old covenant while making the

New Covenant. He ministered in the power of the Holy Spirit within the limits of the Old Covenant. He was faithful in fellowship with His Heavenly Father. He did all as a man, our representative.

The Old Covenant was an unequal suzerain-type of covenant; therefore it contained a very lengthy and detailed list of rules and regulations. That lengthy list, given by God to Moses, had been amplified extensively by many generations of scholars since they were originally written. By the time Jesus was born, covenant had come to mean almost exclusively obedience to the extensive additions made by the scholars of the Old Testament.[119] Although Jesus did not necessarily operate in complete conformity to all that had been added through the years. The leaders in Israel became irate that He did not. He did remain obedient to all God's *original* Old Covenant stipulations.

Walking in complete obedience to the Old Covenant was one of the reasons He was capable of making a New Covenant. Jesus was born and lived to fulfill the law of the Covenant. Jesus had an assignment and He pleased His heavenly Father in all He did. He fulfilled what *had been told the prophets to speak*. The prophets of the Old Testament had functioned as men sent by God to declare an admonishment formulated like a lawsuit related to covenant transgression.[120] Israel owed a debt they could not pay. Their hearts were as stone. But God in His mercy, though aching because of covenant transgressions, repeatedly spoke of the coming messiah who would establish a New Covenant. (Matthew 5:17)

> Starting with Vague Hints, there soon begin to appear Specific Definite Predictions, which, as the story sweeps onward, become more Specific, more Definite, and more Abundant.
>
> And, as Definite Predictions multiply, accompanying Symbols, Pictures, Types, and indirect Foregleams, also increase.
>
> So that, by the time we come to the end of the Old Testament, the entire Story of Christ has been Pre-Written and Pre-Figured

in Language and Symbol, which, taken as a whole, Cannot Refer to Any Other Person in History.[121]

Who believed the report of the Lord? With a strong outstretched arm God had repeatedly reached out to Israel. Jesus came but they did not know Him. He grew up in their midst and astonished them as a young man. But as He continued to grow little more was written of Him. Speculations are not worth consideration. The Bible says, "He shall grow up before Him as a tender plant. . . . He has no form or comeliness." Artists often render Jesus with halos but that is not the way He appeared. He was not a choice model for a painting. "He is despised and rejected by men, a Man of sorrows and acquainted with grief. And we hid, as it were, our faces from Him; He was despised, and we did not esteem Him," (Isaiah 53:1-3 NKJV).

BORN WITHOUT SIN

Witnesses arose. Genealogists, historians, prophets, angels, shepherds, wise men, Zacharias, Elisabeth, Mary, Joseph, Simeon, and Anna are just a few of the witnesses. They bore witness He was the Messiah, the Christ, the Savior, the Seed of David. Of all those listed here the greatest was John the Baptist. The Apostles of the Lord would further bear witness after the crucifixion. The Lord himself said there was not a greater prophet than John the Baptist.

JOHN THE FORERUNNER

Luke's gospel, beginning with a brief introduction, moves quickly to tell of an admirable high priest and his wife. They were both righteous before God. How were they counted righteous before God? They submitted to the stipulations of the Old Covenant. They yielded themselves to God's will.

Years ago I read what was described as one of the earliest definitions of righteous. *Right wise*—that is simple and applicable. Right wise conduct is possible for even unbelievers if they will simply conduct themselves after the fashion of someone who is right wise. Zacharias and his wife, Elisabeth, had walked faithfully and blamelessly in all the commandments and ordinances of the Lord. They were counted as righteous. They may have even conformed to some of the additions to the Old Covenant stipulations if it seemed right and wise to do so.

At least they remained true to the original Old Covenant because Luke's account said, "they were both righteous before God, walking in all the commandments, and ordinances of the Lord blameless," (Luke 1:6 NKJV). Abraham and Sarah had grown too old to have children naturally. Likewise, their descendants Zacharias and Elisabeth were barren in their old age. God intervened supernaturally for them also. They were enabled and had a child in spite of their age. They named their child John, which means "God is gracious." He was the forerunner of the Messiah spoken of prophetically by Malachi. Elisabeth was six months pregnant when she heard another miracle had come to pass for her cousin, Mary. (Matthew 3:3, 13-17; 4:12-14; Mark 1:1-14; Luke 1:5-6; 13-17; Malachi 4:4-6)

MARY'S OBEDIENCE

Mary, like Zacharias and Elisabeth and so many others in Israel, had been expecting Jehovah to fulfill his promise of a Messiah. Mary would be the mother of the promised Messiah and with the faith required of a covenant partner she said, "Let it be to me according to your word," (Luke 1:38 NKJV). In faithful obedience to covenant, Mary answered God's summons and consented to serve Him. Such faithful obedience was expected even in Hittite covenants centuries ago. Mary's childlike obedience to Jehovah, the covenant partner of David, her forefather, was much more profitable than obedience to the covenants of men. Mary's obedience brought about the realization of the Adamic covenant promise. (Luke 1:26-40; Genesis 3:15)

JESUS

Jesus was able to fulfill the promise of the Old Covenant because he was born without sin. He was born of a virgin. With Jesus' birth, the miracle-working Jehovah performed a miracle that still confounds even the wisest. (1 Corinthians 1:27; Matthew 1:20-23; Isaiah 7:14)

It was necessary for Jesus to be born miraculously of a virgin to be born sin-free. Sin had, since Adam's transgression, polluted even the act of procreation. Immanuel, God with us, had been born to bear our sins that we might die to sin and live unto righteousness. God with us, because of His great love and touched with the feelings of our infirmities, does over and beyond anything we could dare ask or think. (Ephesians 3:20; 1 Peter 2:24)

HIS BLOOD

If Adam's blood had been coursing through Jesus' veins, He would not have been born without sin. But Jesus never knew sin. He was one man walking this earth, like you and me in every way, except that He didn't know sin—and He didn't know sickness.[122]

Because of Adam's transgression, mankind had been handicapped by an inherited, incurable, and fatal blood disease. Sin is a blood disease that kills the spirit. The destructiveness of that disease was amplified by individual enactments of personal sins. Jesus was unique because man's sin-polluted blood did not run through His veins. The doctrine of the virgin birth is significant to the church.

Because of the virgin birth it was impossible for Jesus to have a drop of human blood. Nature dictates that when a baby is conceived it is because a male sperm has united with a female egg. It is in this way fertilized and life begins. The panorama of developing life can be witnessed in a chicken egg. When an incubated fertilized chicken egg is held against a strong light little veins of blood can be seen within a few hours after fertilization. Likewise, the human fetus begins within a few hours after fertilization to develop veins for transferring blood to the embryo. The blood will not develop in a chicken egg or in a fetus unless there has been fertilization from a male sperm.

The bloodline comes through the male. When a baby begins to grow in the womb, it is separated from the mother by the placenta. The mother's blood comes to the placenta, but stops there. It bathes the outside of the placenta; then through the wonderful process of osmosis, the necessary nutrients and oxygen go into the baby's bloodstream. But the blood itself does not go past the placenta. It circulates back into the mother's body.

The baby's blood, which is entirely its own, doesn't belong to its mother at all. The baby doesn't share one drop of blood with its mother. It receives the nutrition and the oxygen from her blood, but does not receive the blood itself. Do you know what that means? It means that if Jesus truly was born of a virgin . . . there is only one place his blood could have come from—and it wasn't of this earth.[123]

Because of the virgin birth, Jesus' blood was free of the inherent corruption of Adamic sin. Until Jesus was conceived, all men derived their bloodline from the first Adam. Jesus' freedom from sin and consequent incorruptible blood made the second Adam capable of transfusing His healthy blood to sin-sick man. To be healthy, sinful man must receive a transfusion of the healthy, sinless blood of the perfect Lamb of God. The perfect blood of Jesus carries nutrients to the new believer as the Holy Spirit quickens the regenerated man, even to the tissues in his mortal body. Thus the recreated man is redeemed with the incorruptible blood of Jesus. (Romans 8:10-11; Ephesians 1:6-7; Colossians 1:13-14; 1 Peter 1:18-21; Revelation 5:9)

The virgin birth remains an essential factor in the New Covenant. It is a factor often targeted by those opposing the gospel whether under the guise of philosophy, psychology, religion, science, or some other wile. (Ephesians 6:11)

The gospels of Matthew and Luke testify, adding theirs to other historical accounts of the miraculous birth of the Lord Jesus Christ.

> Luke is thought to have gotten his story of Jesus' birth directly from Mary herself. Matthew probably got his from Joseph. Both state plainly, explicitly, unmistakably, and unequivocally that Jesus was born of a virgin. From the beginning, in unbroken eloquence, it has been held as a tenant of the church, till the rise of modern criticism. If we believe in the deity of Jesus and his resurrection from the dead, what is gained by discrediting the virgin birth? The resurrection is the greatest of miracles. If we do believe it, then why carp at the other parts of the miraculous story? His supernatural exit from the world presupposes a supernatural entrance into the world. To call Jesus an illegitimate child is nothing less than blasphemy.[124]

Jesus' miraculous conception made him the only qualified candidate for the head of an everlasting covenant of life. The first Adam, before he sinned, had been a candidate, also. The first Adam *was the son of God*. The second Adam *was the Son of God*. They both were born without sin. Their spiritual and physical natures were free of the effects of sin. Because of their sinless natures—Adam's before he sinned and Jesus' because he never sinned—they were righteous and therefore able to make a covenant of life. Adam and Jesus, because of their unique origin, were able to walk without fault in an intimate covenant relationship with a righteous and holy God.

The first Adam was tempted and gave into that temptation, thereby terminating his ability to fellowship with God as a blood-linked sinless man. The second Adam likewise was tempted, but he never gave in to temptation and was for that reason able to continue in intimate fellowship with God. Because of his victory over sin, Jesus, the second Adam, was able to complete the work the first Adam had failed to finish. (Matthew 27:54; Luke 3:38)

QUALIFIED

Though Jesus was conceived by the Holy Spirit and born of the virgin Mary, he was nonetheless a flesh and blood man. As a man he walked throughout Judea and Galilee ministering to the blind, lame, leprous, and demon-possessed. He taught in synagogues, in temples, on mountains, and from boats on the lake of Gennesaret. He taught wherever people gathered to hear the good news. He ministered until he was physically exhausted. Though he got hungry, thirsty, and tired like other men, he never gave into temptations. He was never resentful, indignant, anxious, bitter, lustful, rebellious, or unbelieving, nor did he succumb to any of the other sins possible to man. He was born without sin and he lived without committing sin.

As a sinless man, Jesus, the second Adam, did so much more than the four gospels' authors were able to record. John concluded his gospel saying, if every one of the things Jesus had done should be written the world itself could not contain the books that should be written. The second Adam was qualified to make a better and everlasting covenant; he had conducted himself flawlessly. (John 21:25)

The second Adam qualified to legally bear the sins of man. Jesus was prepared for such a ministry because of his sinless birth and his sinless conduct. God incarnate and functioning solely as God would not have been qualified to represent man and carry his sins. A man conceived by natural means would have been disqualified from carrying the sins of others for he would have possessed inherit sin. Jesus was able to buy back the descendants of the first Adam from the clutches of the deceiver (Satan). Though Jesus had been born without sin and had lived apart from sin, it was because of sin He died. (Isaiah 59:21)

LIFE AND DEATH

Jesus was made to be sin for all people. He personally knew no sin Himself, thus making it possible by grace through faith for whosoever would receive to be made the righteousness of God. What a joy to die to sin and be able to live righteously, to be free of sin. I do not disregard the fact some chose to sin after making Jesus Lord of their lives. It is important to apply the principles of New Covenant faith in the mediator of our confession and say no to temptations and walk in faith with the Lord of Righteousness. (2 Corinthians 5:19-21; 1 Peter 2:21-24; Romans 5:2)

Peter wrote, in his first epistle, that Jesus bore our sins. The second Adam voluntarily died for the sins set in motion by the covenant transgression of the first Adam. The sins that the first Adam set in motion in the Garden of Eden were still active in the lives of his descendants.

Though Jesus had not known sin, he took upon himself the sins of all the individuals of the world. Sin, or transgression of covenant, is punishable by death. Jesus was no exception. He experienced death as our representative. It was impending death that brought him such anguish in the garden of Gethsemane. It was the horror of separation from God because of sin that caused him to call out from the cross, "My God, My God, why hast thou forsaken me?" (Matthew 26:36-39; 27:46; Mark 14:32-34; 15:34; Luke 22:39-44)

Like the first Adam, the second Adam experienced the penalty of sin. Death was his reward. Because Jesus bore our sins, he died in our place. But before taking mankind's transgressions upon Himself Jesus had obediently lived righteously and well-pleasing to God. He introduced the Covenant of Life. It was because of our sins of commission and omission and the inborn sin which came through Adam that Jesus died to bear away our sins. It was because of the New Covenant that he was resurrected. (Acts 13:26-30)

The second Adam had made a covenant of life. The blood of the covenant of life enabled Jesus to skillfully annul the covenant of death. Jesus confronted Satan, overcame him and rendered him harmless and ineffective. It was in anticipation of this day that Jesus said to his disciples, just before his crucifixion, "be of good cheer," (John 16:33 AMP).

It was, with an understanding of covenant, that the author of Hebrews wrote that Jesus, the perfect Lamb of God, could lawfully be raised from the dead. In my Bible studies on the subject of covenant, my favorite verses are Hebrews 13:20-21. Reading those verses still makes me rejoice. Through most of this book I have given Bible references and simply added some commentary of my own. But these verses so powerfully speak the heart of God for His covenant people they are quoted here from the *King James* and *Amplified* versions of the Bible.

> *Now the God of peace, that brought again from the dead our Lord Jesus, that great shepherd of the sheep, through the blood of the everlasting covenant, make you perfect in every good work to do his will, working in you that which is well-pleasing in his sight, through Jesus Christ; to whom be glory for ever and ever. Amen.*
>
> —Hebrews 13:20-21

Now may the God of peace [Who is the Author and the Giver of peace], Who brought again from among the dead our Lord Jesus, that great Shepherd of the sheep, by the blood [that sealed, ratified] the everlasting agreement (covenant, testament), strengthen (complete, perfect) ***and*** *make you what you ought to be* ***and*** *equip you with everything good that you may carry out His will; [while He Himself] works in you* ***and*** *accomplishes that which is pleasing in His sight, through Jesus Christ (the Messiah); to Whom be the glory forever and ever (to the ages of the ages) Amen (so be it).*

—Hebrews 13:20-21 AMP

The author of Hebrews, whether Paul or another, gives us remarkable insights. The Lord whose blood was shed to wash away sin, the blood that cleanses from all unrighteousness is the power that brought Jesus up from the dead. His blood sealed the everlasting covenant. Nothing can ever break that covenant. In the Old Testament, fickle hearts led silly others swayed by the wiles of the devil into covenants of death. But the wise, powerful creator of all things wisely made a covenant with men through a righteous representative—one made like ourselves. Jesus, whose name is now above all names, empowers believers through the blood of the everlasting covenant. That blood covenant to end all others is the means whereby the Righteous God of all, the God of peace has raised up my Lord Jesus.

The New Testament says of the blood of the Lord Jesus Christ:

With the precious blood of Christ we were redeemed.	1 Peter 1:18-19
Christ has purchased believers with His blood.	Acts 20:28
Through faith in His blood we are atoned.	Romans 3:25

By His blood we are justified.	Romans 5:9
His blood is the means for communion with Him.	1 Corinthians10:16; 11:25, 27
We have redemption and forgiveness of sin by His blood.	Ephesians 1:7
We are brought near Him.	Ephesians 2:13
We have redemption and forgiveness by His blood.	Colossians 1:14
We have peace with Him through the blood of His cross.	Colossians 1:20
By His blood He obtained eternal redemption for us.	Hebrews 9:12
By His blood He qualifies us to serve the Living God.	Hebrews 9:14
His blood is the blood of the Testament (Covenant).	Hebrews 9:20
Without the shedding of blood there is no remission.	Hebrews 9:22
Having boldness to enter the Holiest by the blood.	Hebrews 10:19
By His blood we are sanctified.	Hebrews 10:29
Through the blood of the everlasting covenant.	Hebrews 13:20
His blood cleanses us from all sin.	1 John 1:7
Jesus washed us from our sins by His own blood.	Revelation 1:5

His blood washes us.	Revelation 7:14
His blood and the word of testimony overcomes.	Revelation 12:11

The Lord of lords, the great shepherd of the sheep is now, currently, forever perfecting believers. Believers who have humbled themselves and submitted to the Lord are born again. The Second Adam made it possible for whosoever will to be born again. Not with corruptible things, but with the precious blood of Christ Jesus.

As a lamb without blemish and without spot He was manifest and lived among us. All are able to come to Him and believe in Christ Jesus who was raised from the dead. He reigns, supremely. His reign is everlasting. His subjects are purifying their souls by obedience to the truth with the help of the Holy Spirit. Through His Spirit, His Helper, we are able to walk with a pure heart loving Him fervently. Love for one another likewise flourishing in the camp of the Lord Jesus Christ. (1 Peter 1:18-25)

The covenant with death has lost its power over believers. Going into all the world, believers are continuing to be made perfect (mature) in every good work to do his will. Because of the better covenant, because of the precious blood, because of His loving-kindness, He is working in us that which is well pleasing in his sight. Indeed, most certainly Lord Jesus Christ, my Lord and my Savior—to you be all the glory forever and ever. Amen.

It is by the blood of the everlasting covenant all our sins are washed away. There are no more sacrifices needed. The perfection in the sinless, precious blood of the perfect Lamb of God indeed washes away the filth of sin for whosoever will receive. Such a marvelous mystery, which unbelievers cannot unravel, remains a mystery to them. They will however acknowledge the reality of the risen Lord for they will bow their knees in His presence on judgment day.

Before the "rise of modern criticism,"[125] most of the denominational hymnals and sermons included much about the shed blood of Christ Jesus. Because the PR of modern society has tried to defuse the power of the gospel with man-made traditions, seldom are the scriptures containing references to the Lord's blood preached. What a terrible thing to diminish the powerful effect of the Word of God by tradition. Supposed ministers influencing people and claiming to honor God while disregarding what is written in his Word are certainly like the proverbial "the blind leading the blind." (Matthew 15:1-18 KJV; 6-9 AMP)

The God of peace had a covenant agreement with the man Christ Jesus. For that reason God came to Jesus' defense and all the combined efforts of Satan and his cohorts with all their combined wiles were not able to restrain Jesus. Neither death, the grave, nor hell was strong enough to keep the covenant partner of God from being saved out of the clutches of the head of the covenant of death. Jesus became the first to be born again from death unto life. Jesus was the firstborn from the dead, the firstborn among many brethren. (Romans 8:29; Colossians 1:18-20)

All who are born continue to be born in sin, but the gospel truth in the written Word of God declares that they can be born again. The way of salvation is fully explained in the Bible with the epistles being especially helpful for understanding. The fullness made available through the blood of the everlasting covenant is available to any who will receive, be born again and walk with Him, if they will believe in their heart and confess with their mouth. (John 3:16-21; Romans 10:9; Colossians 2:6)

As the firstborn of a new breed of righteous men, Jesus declared himself alive for evermore with the keys of hell and of death. After his glorious resurrection from death, Jesus appeared to his disciples and told them he had been given all power in heaven and earth. There was nothing left that had not been put under the power of the covenant head of the everlasting covenant of life. All power had been given to the second Adam. The power that the first Adam had given away when he made the covenant of death was regained when the second Adam made the covenant of life. (Matthew 28:18; Mark 11:23-24; John 14:1; Romans 10:9; Revelation 1:18)

REGAINED AUTHORITY

Three years before his crucifixion, Jesus was in the wilderness waiting on His Heavenly Father while fasting and praying. The liar, Satan, came. In the Garden of Eden, the devil's trickery was sharp but generation after generation he only became more and more cunning. The liar waited thinking forty days of fasting would make Jesus easier prey.

After Jesus had fasted forty days and forty nights he was hungry. The devil began with "If you are the Son of God" in two of the three temptations. The last temptation the Devil dared to say after "showing him all the kingdoms of the world, and the glory of them",, "if you will fall down and worship me." After the Devil tempted Jesus as he had tempted Adam he waited for the answer of this one who had resisted all his previous temptations.

> *But he answered and said, It is written, Man shall not live by bread alone, but by every word that proceedeth out of the mouth of God.*
>
> *Jesus said unto him, It is written again, Thou shalt not tempt the Lord thy God.*
>
> *Then saith Jesus unto him, Get thee hence, Satan: for it is written, Thou shalt worship the Lord thy God, and him only shalt thou serve. Then the devil leaveth him, and, behold, angels came and ministered unto him.*
>
> —Matthew 4:4,7,10-11

Though the subtle wiles of the devil had been insidiously successful against the first Adam, the Second Adam was victorious. He would not compromise as the first Adam had done. Jesus would regain the authority stolen by the devil. Jesus, anointed of the Holy Ghost, brilliantly, powerfully spoke forth the Word of the Lord. Though hungry he resisted and the Devil fled. And the angels of the Lord came and ministered to Jesus. (Matthew 4:1-10)

Jesus told the truth in context without twisting the word of His Heavenly Father. The devil used the truth out of context, which made the liar sound religious. It is interesting that religion in the New Testament is mentioned just five times. Religious is mentioned 2 times. Two uses of religion purposes to correct braggarts. In James epistle he admonished the Christians to be a doer of the word, not just hearers. Hearing and not doing the word is nothing more than self-deception, usually resulting from some lie and disguised as religion or self-righteousness. Paul was testifying of his life while still being in the sect of religion before his dramatic experience on the road to Damascus. The second Adam did not come to set up a new religion. He came to destroy the yokes of bondages locked in place when the First Adam sinned. The second Adam, the Lord of lords, made it possible for 5 of 7 believers to shout with joy. "'Thanks be to God, which gives us the victory." (Matthew 4:1-11; Mark 1:6-13; Luke 4:1-13; Acts 13:43; 26:5; 1 Corinthians 15:57: Galatians 1: 13-14; Colossians 2:6-15; James 1:26-27)

> Colossians 2:15 The metaphor changes as Paul thinks of God's master-stroke in Christ. He is reminded of a conqueror's triumphal procession in which the captives of war are exhibited to enhance the conqueror's own glory. The enemies here are spiritual—*principalities and powers*—which have nevertheless been disarmed, i.e. robbed of all further opportunity to do harm. God made a *public example of them,* not only in the sense that all can see, but also as an act of defiance against those powers

> which were challenging His authority. They now presented a sorry spectacle, utterly defeated. *In him* (i.e. 'in Christ') is better than 'in it' (i.e. in the cross), since God is the subject of the whole sentence.[126]

The epistles were written for the instruction of born again believers. The second Adam regained authority. Believers are able to overcome because of the gospel of Christ for it is the power of God unto salvation to every one that believes. Paul wrote often of the mystery of Christ within. Because of the Second Adam the Better Covenant is Excellent, Established, Eternal. It is so excellent each believer by grace through faith can know the King of kings personally. It is so established that no power can shake or disannul the Better Covenant. It is an eternal unbreakable covenant. "And this is life eternal, that they might know you the only true God, and Jesus Christ, whom you have sent." What a perfect plan of salvation the only true God has set forth for all people. We can continue to go and preach the gospel that those who believe may be saved. (Mark 16:15-18; John 17:2-3, 20)

Paul wrote to the Corinthians reminding them he had declared the gospel whereby they were saved. He reminded them Christ died for our sins according to the scriptures, he was buried and on the third day he rose. He was seen of Cephas, of the twelve and then of above 500 brethren at once. After that, he was seen of James, then of all the apostles. Paul also saw the Lord. Paul indicates that by the grace of God the resurrection of the Lord was seen by more witnesses than any court would need to declare it so. (I Corinthians 15: 1 -11)

God's abundant grace was sufficient for Paul to preach the gospel in the face of any opposition. God's grace was not in vain. Because of God's saving and keeping grace, Paul labored more abundantly then others. Paul admonished the believers at Corinth to not give ear to seducing doctrines. For there were some who were teaching there is no resurrection of the dead. Paul reminded them and encouraged them not to forget the power by which the Heavenly Father put down all types of demonic and devilish rule, authority, and power. For Jesus Himself shall reign till all things are put under him including death, the last enemy.

Jesus Himself had been raised from the dead. Miracles were reported. Since His resurrection, a lame man was healed in the name of Jesus; a multitude of sick people were healed. When Peter's shadow touched the sick they were healed. The lame were healed. Unclean spirits were cast out. The Book of Acts written by Luke has twenty-eight chapters of marvelous good news reports. The gospel continues to spread as powerfully as it did in the book of Acts. The news reports still are sent out by missionaries and evangelists, those gifted and sent to preach.

The authority for believers to is still a powerful means to defeat principalities and powers and the rulers of the darkness of this world. The Gospels and Acts illustrate, the Epistles instruct. It is the believers' responsibility to be doers of the Word. (1 Corinthians 15:1-28; Acts 3:1-11; 5:12-16; 8:7; Ephesians 6:10-20)

Jesus is alive. Religion tries to keep him on a cross. Religion is a stranger to the person who has been born again, for with the witness in their spirits they know they are new. They have heard the truth. Called unto liberty daily, choices are still made. Called unto liberty, we are to serve one another with agape love. Christians are not doormats for every ungodly person insisting on remaining in covenant with death. Heartily following their Lord Jesus Christ, believers go forth ministering God's love as only the regenerated are able to do. Learning from the New Covenant and living in habitual fellowship with the Lord, they are able to rejoice always.

The law of liberty rules in the heart of those desiring to do God's will. Each day they have opportunities to overcome by the blood of the Lamb. "The God of peace brought our LORD Jesus up from the dead through the blood of the everlasting covenant." He is well able and certainly willing to help us mature in our walk with Him. "Through the blood of the everlasting covenant He works in us that which is well pleasing in his sight," (Hebrews 13:20-21)

Jesus is alive. He conquered the grave. As conqueror, Jesus has every right to call believers into active service. In unequal Hittite covenants they would have merely been vassals. In equal covenants they would simply be allies. In the better covenant the best is available to all and received by some. Believers have authority with hearts of flesh able to walk with the Lord and follow His voice. Yes they rule subordinately, with their Lord the only true God. He is wise in counsel and indeed is made unto believers their wisdom, righteousness, sanctification, and redemption. (1 Corinthians 1:30)

As God in the flesh, Jesus could have called an innumerable host of angels to assist Him. But His Heavenly Father had the best plan. Within thirty years after Jesus' death, those subordinate rulers (believers) would be referred to by their covenant partner's name—they would be called Christians. As vassals in this covenant, they would vow homage and fealty to their covenant lord while remaining accountable to him. They would faithfully go throughout the conquered area declaring the *word of their covenant partner*.

The Christians would simultaneously declare the good news around the world. Truth is still declared. The Messiah, the Christ, the Last Man had broken the chains. Bondages are broken. The lordship of a merciful and loving deliverer is to be preached. The Lord's apostles and followers in the book of Acts courageously told how Jesus is resurrection and life. (1 Corinthians 15:1-11).

They would joyfully declare how the Lord Jesus Christ had established his vassals, his believers, his covenant partners in ruling positions, and how they would now be acting as a single unit for the successful rule of the Lord of lords and King of kings. They would act as a single unit within the perfect law of liberty. They would cease to live independently and would begin functioning as a single body with Jesus as their head. He had justifiably been declared the head of the new covenant. Christians were the body of Christ and He was the head. Christians, as vassals in this everlasting covenant, would be expected to be a friend to the friends of their lord and to be an enemy to the enemies of their lord. They would be expected to hate those whom he hated and love those whom he loved. They would be expected to speak in agreement with their covenant partner, and to refrain from murmuring against their Lord. As vassals they were not to enter into alliances with other kings without the approval of their Lord and they were to answer any military summons and to engage wholeheartedly in military campaigns. (Ephesians 1:15-23; 6:10-20; 1 Peter 1:22-25; 4:1-2; 14-19)

Faithfully they would be expected to trust their Lord and to honor his word even when appearances and situations contradicted his word. They were instructed to frequently read their covenant document, the New Testament. The vassals of this New Covenant were to "Go into all the world and preach the gospel to every creature." Gospel means good news. The gospel to be preached was that by Jesus' life, death, and resurrection a better covenant had been made that returned to all men the ability to become the sons of God. The New Covenant made it possible for all men to be actively involved in the kingdom of God. The prerequisite for entry was faith that would cause a spiritual transformation referred to as the new birth. (Mark 16:15; John 1:12; 3:3,7)

The New Covenant indirectly and passively affected all men, but directly and actively affects all who believe and receive. Involvement was, and still is, necessary before the covenant benefits can be fully received and enjoyed. Some benefits may be enjoyed when born into a family who live in the fullness of what God has promised. Eternal life and full personal benefits are only available for those who personally receive Jesus as their Lord and Savior. (Romans 1:1-32; 4:1-8, 13-25; 10:5-17)

Because of covenant faithfulness, David cared for Jonathan's son. Mephibosheth had been indirectly affected by the covenant his father, Jonathan, had made with David years before Mephibosheth became directly affected. He had spent years in Lodebar completely unaware that a covenant had even been made. However, his father's covenant partner, David, had been actively seeking any descendants of Jonathan, that he might *show him kindness for Jonathan's sake*. When David's soldiers found Mephibosheth and brought him before David, Mephibosheth heard the good news that he had been provided for.

The provisions had been made available when David and Jonathan made a blood covenant. The subsequent benefits would not bless Mephibosheth, however, unless he consented to receiving David's covenant friendship. He had to believe, then he had to receive to appropriate what David through kindness was offering. There had indeed been a covenant made. With words and probably a very grateful heart by speaking of himself as subject, friend, and covenant partner of David, Mephibosheth received David's offer of friendship. Mephibosheth began actively receiving the benefits of being a friend of David and he was able to *eat continually at the king's table*. Though his fellowship with David was not without some difficulties, because of covenant David graciously continued providing for Mephibosheth. (2 Samuel 9:1,13; 19:24-30)

Jonathan and David's covenant included all their descendants. The provisions of that covenant were not automatic, however. To receive those provisions, Mephibosheth had to believe a covenant had been made, he had to receive it as his own, and he had to live in agreement and in submission with the covenant stipulations. It was only then that Mephibosheth could be actively benefited by the covenant Jonathan had made years before Mephibosheth's birth. Like Mephibosheth, many today are receiving the benefits of a covenant made even before they were born. However, there are many others who have not yet heard that a covenant has even been made that affects them. Many potential Christians are still hiding in Lodebar in bondage to a covenant with death.

Isaiah addressed proud, scornful drunkards and told them they had erred. They answered the Lord's messenger with scorn. In a braggart, self-important way they answered, "we have made a covenant with death, and with hell." They continued by saying, "we have made lies our refuge and under falsehood have we hid ourselves." It is beyond me why the Lord would not immediately hit them with lightning. A hard lesson for believers to learn is that the Lord even loves the braggart, the self-important, those who have made a covenant with death and with hell, and those who count on lies and falsehood and try to hide therein.

Each one who is a believer was loved when they were like those who have chosen to stay in the darkness. Judgment came when Jesus came. Any that believes on him is not condemned. He that believes not is condemned already for not believing. People who believe come into the light. They conduct themselves with integrity. Jesus is the light. In His presence filth is washed away. It may sound harsh when said so briefly, but it is the truth. The covenant with death and with hell has been an annulled, officially cancelled. (Isaiah 28: 14-23)

New Covenant believers trust in the Lord. To as many as received Him were given power to become sons (children) of God. He gives power to those that believe on His name. His name, His power, His love, His word convinced me. He calls me His own. His Ambassador. He is my strength and song and has become my salvation. They are heralding the good news that Jesus has died to provide an everlasting covenant for all people. They frequently share one-on-one of the unbreakable covenant in which God has provided salvation. They sometimes shout it from the rooftops, from horseback, or on journeys around the world. To mission sites, in churches the good news continues to go out. Many believe, reach out, receive and enter the kingdom of God. (John 1).

Some remain puzzled and go about their own business remaining lords of their own lives.

The covenant with death has been annulled.

The covenant with life has been established.

The decision is left up to the individuals.

And unto this people thou shalt say, Thus saith the Lord; Behold, I set before you the way of life, and the way of death.

—Jeremiah 21:8

Verily, verily, I say unto you, He that heareth my word, and believeth on him that sent me, hath everlasting life, and shall not come into condemnation; but is passed from death unto life.

—John 5:24

But is now made manifest by the appearing of our Saviour Jesus Christ, who hath abolished death, and hath brought life and immortality to light through the gospel.

—2 Timothy 1:10

And deliver them who through fear of death were all their lifetime subject to bondage.

—Hebrews 2:15

We know that we have passed from death unto life, because we love the brethren. He that loveth not his brother abideth in death.

—1 John 3:14

If any man see his brother sin a sin which is not unto death, he shall ask, and he shall give him life for them that sin not unto death. There is a sin unto death: I do not say that he shall pray for it.

—1 John 5:16

Fear none of those things which thou shalt suffer: behold, the devil shall cast some of you into prison, that ye may be tried; and ye shall have tribulation ten days: be thou faithful unto death, and I will give thee a crown of life.

—Revelation 2:10

His name is Jesus. He is my Lord and my Savior. The Second Adam is King of Kings and Lord of Lords. He finished the job given Him as a man. He has begun a good work in believers and commissioned us to go tell what good things the Lord has done. In his second epistle Peter told the believers to add to their faith through the knowledge of him that had called us to glory and virtue. In the fourth verse Peter wrote, "Whereby are given unto us exceeding great and precious promises: that by these ye might be partakers of the divine nature . . ." As the chapter continues believers are told to "add to their faith".

God has revealed His divine nature from Genesis through Revelation. I am convinced continuing through eternity we will progressively see the many faceted glory of God. Now we have His revelation of His nature in His names to sustain us even during these last days. (John 3:16-18; 2 Peter 1: 1-11; Proverbs 29:2; Isaiah 28:15; 28:18)

Chapter 8

THE NATURE IN THE NAME

Names are chosen carefully. Some are named to honor a kinsman. Some names acknowledge a meaningful site or event. Prominent names show up on school records years later. My own son was named to commemorate a prominent, valiant man. Sometimes the supernatural spirit that dwells in them, or their nature prompts a name. Names are given for any number of reasons.

From the oldest to the youngest, some families have four generations living. Each member with their own name and personality adds to the character of the family. During large group meetings, some may have trouble remembering names. Physical resemblances often remain and are discussed. At a family reunion, my mom's brother called me by my dad's sister's name and said, "you haven't changed a bit." Uncle Howard thought I was Aunt Thelma. She and I had often been told we looked like each other. Others in the family would tell me "You look just like your mom." Or "you look just like" another relative. The names may change, but family characteristics are reapplied, repeated, and reviewed at a lot of family reunions. Each member with their own individuality still bears a strong resemblance to other family members.

Families grow. Grandchildren, in-laws, and extended families bring names into families that can make it difficult to remember everyone by name. Instead of names some may be remembered by their appearances, characteristics, natures, or skills. Often older members at a reunion will tell how a child reminds them of a deceased grandparent. Families exchange tales of some attributes, events, or memories of a deceased family member. When the stories of a favorite aunt or uncle are told, memories of that person may linger in the family for another decade or so.

Soon enough, the names become a simple name, birth and death date, and one or two lines of text. Out of sight out of mind. Unless love abounds, the deceased will soon be forgotten. Others come to the forefront to spend their own allotted time. From beginning to end, choices are made that will impact the lives of their own lineage.

But men and women with excellent leadership attributes like Abraham Lincoln (1809-1865) are still remembered. Whatever his characteristics, the attributes of a mortal man seldom linger for centuries. A few, whether good or evil, may be remembered for a millennium. But there is one who is beyond man's comprehension. One whose appearance, characteristics, creations, nature, power, skills, and works have gone through millennia. Building nations, delivering from hardships, refreshing the perishing, healing the lame, setting up national leaders. His name is above all names. He is not a figment of any imagination. He is the Lord Jesus Christ.

Mortals deal with perception issues. The perceptual experience of life and death matters in all areas to all people. The spirit, soul, and body are basic components. God is Spirit. Jesus was a man and had a soul, which was exceedingly sorrowful even unto death when He went to pray in the garden. The Lord God is incomprehensible to the flesh. Those who came to Jesus belonged to a camp of Abrahamic descendents. Within that camp every one had a spirit and a soul, but lived in bodies. They dealt with perception issues. Their souls puzzled over who Jesus was.

Individually people were drawn to Jesus because their spirits longed for truth. Some were agitated by His word of truth because they wanted to stay in the darkness lest their deeds be reproved. God was manifest in the flesh, justified in the Spirit, seen of angels, preached unto the Gentiles, believed on in the world was received up into glory. Great is the mystery of godliness. (1 Timothy 3:16)

It seems Judas often became agitated after hearing the Lord teach. His flesh considered money and it provoked him to draw away. (Mark 14:34; John 3:19-21; 4:24). The flesh is dictated to by the five senses. So a person in the flesh is ineffective in perceiving what is going on in the soul and spirit of another person. The disciples did not know why Judas left. Their own flesh even wondered, "is it I?" Making decisions every moment of every day, the three parts tend to toss about with every wind of doctrine if the soul is not renewed and the spirit is not born again. The winds are quieted when the soul and spirit let their ears hear and discipline the body to be still. (John 3:3,7; Ephesians 4:14).

Every person will decide if they will follow the Lord of Lords and be set free, spiritually delivered, by an active involvement in the everlasting covenant of life. To not decide is to remain following the only alternative—entanglement in bondage. The lord of this world, motivated by hatred, fights to keep people bound in a covenant with death.

GOD IS . . .

God is the great I AM (Jehovah) the Creator (Elohim). With the spirit misaligned, the soul is inclined to believe lies and the flesh tends to follow after degradations of all sorts in a downward spiral. (Matthew 12:43; Romans 1:13-32; 6: 12:14; 8:1; 1 Thessalonians 5:23; Hebrews 11:6; Genesis 1:1; Exodus 3:6-14; Isaiah 28:15, 18)

The One true God is omni in holiness, majesty, power, presence, righteousness, abilities, willingness, and much more than can be written. Whether or not He is perceived does not alter the fact that He is who He says He is. God as revealed by God is as a puzzle piece after puzzle piece aligned according to His direction. With His names He revealed who He is. The first puzzle piece was shown in Genesis. (Genesis 1:1)

God began giving puzzle pieces to men who God chose according to their heart condition. Enoch—how could one man be not as though he were? Moses—how can the bush burn without being consumed and millions be brought out of bondage in a miraculous deliverance? Solomon—how could so much wisdom abide in one man? Jesus—how could one bear the sins of all? The records are there. The witnesses cover the earth. The works are still evident. Lives are still changed.

How can we know this One unless He tells us of Himself? He alone can reveal His attributes, character, love, and power. With His names, little by little, He began to show his creation who He is and that God is a Rewarder. Whosoever diligently seeks Him is rewarded. Those who let their ears hear and let their eyes see what He has to say are rewarded. He opens the eyes to see what He has prepared for them to see. Adam and Eve are too far removed from today, which makes it impossible to personally know them. Descendants are scattered. Without understanding they encounter each other regularly.

The born again offspring of Abraham's seed choosing to follow Christ Jesus, head of the covenant with life, bear a strong family resemblance to their covenant head. The descendants choosing to follow the devil, the head of their covenant with death bare a strong family resemblance to their covenant head.

Enoch cannot personally tell us of family resemblances. Neither can Abraham, Moses, David, or Solomon tell a niece how she resembles an aunt. Even Jesus personally as a man limited Himself. As a man He was limited to being one place at a time. He did and said as His Father said to do, as the Holy Spirit directed. He was limited in what He could do as a man to further the Kingdom of God.

After the Day of Pentecost, power was poured out on those in the Upper Room. Peter preached powerfully. Peter and John, together in the name of Jesus, reached out to the lame man. Ministering in His name became part of a distinguishing feature in members of the covenant of life. His name, His Spirit, His Lords took forth the good news, the gospel the Word of the Lord. One, the Lord Jesus Christ, name above all names became the Mediator of the New Covenant. (Matthew 6:14,26,32-33; 15:13; 18:35; Luke 11:13; Acts 3:6; Hebrews 12:24)

HIS NAMES

His names are shown through out the Holy Scriptures within immediate context for clarity and complete context (Genesis through Revelation) for more thorough clarity. What is written here is of necessity entirely too brief, but hopefully will inspire study and fellowship for personal understanding of the names of God which speak to the hearts of His covenant people.

Through His names His attributes are revealed. A glimpse of Him as omnipotent, omnipresent, omniscient is shown to His people and often even to those who oppose His people. His names include Adonai, Elohim, El-Shaddai, Jehovah. There are a number of names compounded with his name Jehovah. They include Jehovah-jireh, Jehovah-rophe, Jehovah-nissi, Jehovah-M'Kadddesh, Jehovah-shalom, Jehovah-tsidkenu, Jehovah-rohi, Jehovah-shammah. With each name his people gain more insight from God Himself who is everywhere all the time *omni*. This chapter will be far too brief to do justice to God's names, but for the sake of the primary subject covenant something needs to be said of the one who has so mercifully made covenant with mankind. He is One who is everywhere all the time omni.

Know with certainty the Lord our God is One God. Let that be an anchor as some of His names are shown from Genesis through Revelation. Covenant is the subject of this book. A thorough study of God's names is not intended. But what I have seen as it relates to covenant is included here. (Mark 12:29,32; Romans 3:3; 1 Corinthians 8:4,6; Galatians 3:20; 1 Timothy 2:5; James 2:19; Deuteronomy 6:4; Malachi 2:10)

From Genesis through the book of Revelation and even today God continues to reveal His character and attributes to those who seek Him with their whole hearts. He never changes, but individual concepts and understanding of God changes. Each generation and each society adds their own understanding. Commentaries and study aids abound. God speaks to the hearts of His people. The flesh can be blessed or cursed depending on adherence to the word of the Lord.

David was keenly aware of God's goodness and the power given Israel through covenant. God's name became a power resource for those with whom God had initiated covenant. David's insightful Psalms, still cherished by believers around the world, reflect the plans and purposes of God. David understood the merciful character of God shown forth through covenant.

THE NAME OF THE LORD

> Psalm 145:1-7. The singer praises the various qualities which unite in the name of God, i.e. his saving presence with his people (vss. 1-2; cf. vs 21). The unlimited power of his kingly majesty (vss. 1,3) is revealed in his wonderful works (vss. 4-7) an expression usually used of the exodus event (see above Ps. 136). The deeds of the Lord also make plain his goodness and his righteousness, i.e. his faithfulness to his covenant with Israel.

> 145:8-13b. The merciful character of the covenant God is reinforced by the quotation of an ancient covenant formula (vs. 8; cf. 103:8; Exodus 34:6) and by the insistence that his compassion is as wide as the world he created (vs. 8; cf. 103:8; Exodus 34:6) (vs. 9). Kingdom in vss. 11-13b is not a geographical or political unity by God's kingly authority which rules all time and space (see above on 100:3-5).
>
> 145:13c-21. Vss. 13c-20 describe God's consistency to his words and deeds of salvation and judgment: upholding the weak, feeding man and beast, protecting those who sincerely call on him, preserving all who love him, and destroying inveterate enemies against his authority. These deeds are manifestations of his justice (vs. 17; see above on 68:5-6; 112:1-4). Such a God is worthy to be praised by everything he has made, especially by the members of the covenant community (saints, vs. 10), by the singer himself, and by every human being (all flesh, vs. 21; cf. vs 6).[127]

God makes himself known by His Word, His names, His acts, and His Spirit. It is his revelation of himself via His names that will be considered here. God's names are equivalent to his very being. They reveal his omnipotence, omniscience, and omnipresence and help believers to be more specific about who He is. (Acts 2:1-14; Psalm 118:21-28)

In Hebrew a name is more than a title by which a person or thing is designated. It summarizes and contains the nature and character of its bearer.[128] With the names Adonai, Elohim, El-Shaddai, Jehovah, Christ, Jesus, and the adjective Holy, the covenant head makes Himself known to His people.

OLD TESTAMENT NAMES OF GOD

Daniel prayed for his people. The names used in that prayer included several examples of the excellence of the King James' translators. In most, if not all, translated the name Adonai as Lord, EL as God, Elohim as God, Jehovah as Lord. The names of God and the depth of their meanings is somewhat elusive. The meanings relate to people who, after Adam's fall, tended to judge more by their five senses than by the measure of faith given them. Daniel was definitely an exception. (Daniel 9)

ADONAI

In the *King James* Bible, Adonai was translated as Lord and spelled with upper case (capital) letter "L" and a lower case "ord." Jehovah was likewise translated LORD, but it was spelled with all capital letters. The Lord (Adonai) God (Elohim) was called upon when Daniel fasted and prayed. He prayed unto the LORD (Jehovah) God (Elohim), and said, "O Lord (Adonai), the great and dreadful God (El), keeping the covenant and mercy to them that love him and to them that keep his commandments." From the context of this prayer, it seems conspicuous that Adonai, Elohim, and Jehovah were names that had been revealed previously. (Daniel 9:3-5)

Jehovah was by rights Israel's covenant Adonai or Lord. Lordship was the covenant right of the Hittite suzerain just as Lordship was God's role with Israel by virtue of the covenant. Covenant transgression, such as Israel's, demanded attention. Daniel repented before the Lord for the iniquity of Israel and appealed to God's covenant mercy and love in His judgment of their transgressions.

Daniel addresses God as Adonai in his prayer for forgiveness and restoration of the people and Jerusalem. Since it is God as

Lord and Master whose will they have disobeyed, it is He to whom they must address their prayer for forgiveness, for acceptance, for restoration. Thus it is in verse 19, "O Adonai, hear; O Adonai, forgive; O Adonai, hearken and do; defer not, for thine own sake, O my God. . . . [129]

The Israelites received, with the revelation of the nature of God as Lord, the understanding of the necessity of being obedient to their covenant partner. The use of this name Adonai in the Old Testament plainly reveals the relationship, which God sustains toward His creatures and what He expects of them.[130]

ELOHIM

ELOHIM is plural and indicates trinity. Elohim has unlimited greatness and exceptional dignity. Elohim is the One in whom all powers of eternity and infinity are subject. (*The Wycliffe Bible Commentary*, p. 2) Since the plurality and one God study baffles theologians it will not be addressed here. By faith, millions move on, overcoming challenges scholars scratch their heads over. It is not impossible for the One to whom all things are possible to be who He says He is. No language exists that can adequately tell all the attributes of God. God is. Notice the period, God is.

In the beginning of Genesis 1:1, God created. It has been said if you won't believe the first verse in the Bible you won't believe the rest of the Bible. Such phrases make a point for therein is Elohim. There in the Bible's first book, first chapter, first verse, the first word is, "God," Elohim in the Hebrew language. By continuing to read, one may begin to understand and choose to believe God truly is and that He is the Creator.

God revealed much more about Himself through His names as the Holy Scriptures were written to record his attributes. The main subject of this book is covenant and His names as the means of understanding the covenant partner of the Israelites and the mediator of the better covenant is the subject of this chapter. His names reveal so much about Him.

God created. The sublime certainty of revelation is based on this one mighty assertion. God did it. Nothing more astounding could be declared. Elohim is the usual word for "God" in Hebrew, Aramaic, and Arabic. It is actually plural in form, but it is used with a verb in the singular.

Perhaps the plural is best explained as indicating "plenitude of might" or exceptional dignity and unlimited greatness. In this One are united all the powers of eternity and infinity.[131]

God revealed Himself as Elohim, the triune, mighty, and powerful creator. He proved Himself able to do what He said He would do. Elohim said and it was so as He created the heavens and the earth, the vegetation, the animals, the birds, and man. (Genesis 1:6-30) In the first chapter of Genesis the Hebrew word for God, Elohim was used at least thirty-two times.[132] The remaining chapters of the Old Testament speaks of Elohim approximately 2,500 times. (Genesis 1:6-30)

In the name Elohim there is creative power, blessing, and comfort. That name reveals God as a supreme power, as sovereign and glorious. Elohim God reveals Himself faithful to the word of His covenant. When God spoke the word the world was created. God said, and it was so.

Elohim is our covenant partner by grace through faith in our Lord Jesus Christ.

EL-SHADDAI

El-Shaddai appears first in the Bible in connection with Abram, later called Abraham. When Abram was ninety-nine years old, the Lord appeared. His name Almighty God was revealed to Abram. Abram was told to be perfect—meaning mature, upright, sound, innocent, simple, honest, and sincere, and he was to conduct all his affairs with integrity. (Genesis 17:1-2)

In many places in the Old Testament, God was translated from the Hebrew word El. Almighty was translated from the Hebrew word shaddai. So that El-Shaddai in the Hebrew language became God Almighty in the English translation of the Bible.

It was as an exceedingly abundant provider that Israel's covenant partner revealed Himself with the name El-Shaddai. God revealed Himself able to save to the uttermost. One opinion of the root meaning of the Hebrew word shaddai is one who nourishes, supplies, and satisfies and able to save to the uttermost. He is the all-sufficient one.

JEHOVAH

His people found through the name Jehovah that their God was unlike any other. With this name, Israel was shown their Jehovah being self-Existent. Jehovah needed no counsel, no support from any man. Man made crafted imitations, so-called gods. But Jehovah showed Himself strong on behalf of His people and vexed the priests of Egypt, Balak, and others. Their crafted gods were no more animated than the scraps from which they were cut. The crafters and priests in Egypt found out the hard way how powerful Israel's covenant God was against the idols made of wood and metal.

There are a number of names compounded with the name Jehovah. His name Jehovah is linked in scripture and become part of His revelation to his Covenant people. Those names include Jehovah-jireh, Jehovah-rophe, Jehovah-nissi, Jehovah-M'Kadddesh, Jehovah-shalom, Jehovah-tsidkenu, Jehovah-rohi, and Jehovah-shammah.

In the *King James Version* of the Bible, printers distinguished Jehovah from his other names. With the use of all upper case, that is, capital letters the profound significance of the covenant name LORD is emphasized. The significance of the names of God cannot be understood intellectually without the meaning made clearer by the LORD himself.

The divine name YHWH (Jehovah) appears only in the Bible. Its precise meaning is much debated. God chose it as His personal name by which He related specifically to His chosen or covenant people.[133]

Most nations had their version of elohim, the Hebrew word for god, but only Israel had a Jehovah (LORD). Jehovah belonged exclusively and personally to Israel. With the name Jehovah, God revealed His self-existent, being. With this name He also revealed His capacity to provide for His covenant people. Jehovah God revealed Himself consistently faithful to covenant. "It is as Jehovah He manifests Himself in covenants and acts of deliverance and redemption."[134]

> Jehovah, the Lord God. For the first time, the name *Yahweh*, or Jehovah (cf. Ex 6:2,3) is presented. Jehovah is the personal covenant God of Israel, who is at the same time the God of heaven and earth. The name connotes the eternal self-existence of the Author of all existence. It is expressive of God's loving-kindness, his grace, his mercy, his lordship, and his eternal relationship to his own chosen ones who are created in his image. Jehovah's special relationship to Israel would be described more distinctly when he would appear at the burning bush near Sinai. Here the Author of life is identified with the divine Creator of Genesis 1.[135]

Jehovah's name is compounded in several places in the Old Testament. Extensions were made as He progressively revealed His attributes to His covenant people. Some of his compounded names are seen below.

Jehovah–jireh, revealed after God tested Abraham's covenant commitment. Abraham had given everything to God when he covenanted with him almost fifty years before Isaac was born. Abraham and Sarah's long years of yearning for an heir promised had been fulfilled in Isaac. Isaac had been an immeasurable source of joy to Abraham. But with covenant understanding Abraham obediently went to mount Moriah intending to sacrifice his only, beloved son. All that Abraham had belonged to his covenant partner and Isaac was not an exception. With confidence in God's ability to raise Isaac from the dead if necessary, Abraham prepared an altar for the sacrifice.

It was during this test of Abraham's faith that another aspect of God's magnitude was revealed. As a result of the revelation of God as his provider, Abraham came to know God as Jehovah-Jireh. With the name Jehovah-jireh, God as covenant partner provided for Abraham. That recorded portion of the Holy Scriptures pictures the eventual sacrifice of the Son of God at Calvary. (Genesis 22:8, 12-14; Hebrews 11:17-19)

God's short-term provision was a ram to serve as a sacrifice instead of Isaac. His long-term provision was the perfect sacrifice of His own beloved son nearly two thousand years later. Abraham had been willing to give his only beloved son sacrificially to God. His heart was right in God's sight and Abraham's obedience passed the test set before him. Jehovah-jireh had provided.

> The Offering of Isaac was a Picture-Prophecy of the Death of Christ. A Father offering his Son. The Son Dead for Three Days (in Abraham's mind, 4) A Substitution. An Actual Sacrifice. And it was on Mt. Moriah, the very same place where, 2000 years later, God's Own Son was Offered. Thus, it was a Shadow, in the birth of the Hebrew nation, of the Grand Event the nation was born to bring about.[136]

Jehovah-nissi, revealed the Lord as Israel's banner. A banner was a piece of cloth, which was attached by one edge to a staff. Such a banner was used by monarchs, feudal lords and commanders as standards and as rallying points during battle. Declaring Himself as Israel's banner, God was revealing Himself as a support and rallying point during combat.

As opposing forces battled, they had standard bearers that held their lord's flag high. The troops were more likely to maintain faith and hope for victory when they could lift their eyes during combat and see their banners were still there. As long as the flags were held high, the men knew, though they could not readily see for themselves, that the battle was going favorably. The lowered banner said the battle was lost, consequently the soldiers gave up hope and cast their faith aside. This is illustrated when Israel was battling the Amalekites in Rephidim. Jehovah-nissi had sworn to protect his covenant partners. As God's banner was lifted, the battle went favorably for Israel. (Exodus 17:9-11, 14-15)

The purpose of a banner was to rally the troops for united effort against a common enemy. Jesus was lifted up on Calvary's Hill as the rallying point for all the troops of the New Testament army of the Lord. It has been maintained that the Romans, before entering battle, would routinely establish their banners and their generals on a high hill when possible, where they could readily see the ensuing battle taking place in the valley below.[137] As in Moses' day the flag would be raised or lowered indicating to the soldiers the over all battle trend. When the flag was raised the battle was going favorably, when lower the battle was being lost. When the battle was won, the flag was raised high as the general shouted, *It is finished*. The general's shout and the raised banner announced that the remaining confrontations on the battlefield were just part of the post war clean up. Jesus is God's banner held high as the post-war clean up continues yet today. (John 19:30)

Jesus shouted, for the battle was won. His shout was not the typical whispered cry of a dying man. The Roman centurion familiar with the triumphant shout of a general at the conclusion of a battle realized that Jesus was truly the victorious Son of God.

Jehovah-rapha, was translated into the *King James Version* of the Bible as "the LORD that healeth." God's ability and willingness to heal was another of His covenant revelations to Israel. Repeated in this declaration by God was the admonishment to remain faithful to covenant. For if Israel would persist in obedience to the covenant stipulations, health and healing would be the result. Jehovah-rapha's name revealed health as part of God's very being. As Jehovah's covenant partner, Israel—both nationally and individually—could assimilate into themselves the health of God.

This compound "rapha" was assigned the number 3068 by James Strong, in his concordance of the Bible. Strong did an exhaustive study of Bible words and assigned them numbers. His work is an excellent concordance and study aid. It is available to help those of us who have not studied the original languages from which subsequent Bibles were translated. His work has been referred to in many excellent study aids since Strong's initial compilation. Two other noteworthy study aids are *The Complete Word Study Old Testament* and *The Complete Word Study New Testament*.

I have chosen to show Exodus 15:26 with the numbers used in *Strong's Hebrew Dictionary of Old Testament Words*. God spoke through Moses to Israel of another Covenant name, Jehovah-rapha. *Strong's* numbers are shown below.[138]

> "And said (559), If (518) thou wilt <u>diligently (8085) hearken (8085)</u> to the voice (696) of the Lord (3068) thy God (430), and wilt do (6213) *that which is right* (3477) in his sight (5869), and wilt give ear (238) to his commandments (4687), and keep

> (8104) all (3605) his statutes (2706), I will put (7760) none (3808) of these diseases (4245) upon (5921) thee, which (834) I have brought (7760) upon the Egyptians (714): for (3588 589) I am the Lord (3068) that healeth (7495) thee."
>
> —Exodus 15:26[139]

With *Strong's* study aid, the Lord that healeth can be clarified. *I am the Lord* comes from one Hebrew word, which the number 3068 appointed by Strong's leads to the definition of Jehovah. *That healeth* is shown to come from the Hebrew word rapha or raphah, which was assigned the Strong's number 7495. For anyone interested in considering a more in depth study of God's word, short of in-depth study of ancient languages, the study aids are an excellent way to gain clarity. Consider some of the aids shown in the bibliography compiled in the writing of this book. By using *Strong's* alone it is seen that God made it clear as their Lord, He was their healer.

As shown earlier, Exodus 15:26 shows Jehovah-rapha revealed Himself as Israel's source of restoration and health, physically, morally and spiritually. Israel received their covenant partner as their healer when they received revelation of Jehovah-rapha.

Jehovah-shalom, The Lord is peace revealed Himself to Gideon and therefore to Israel. Jehovah-shalom was their freedom from the bondage of fear, their wholeness, their harmony and their means of fulfillment. Shalom was translated "peace" more than 170 times in the *King James Version* of the Bible . Shalom means more than absence of strife. It contains in the Hebrew language, the meaning of a state of wholeness and unity and of restored relationship. Truly shalom is the presence of God's presence within, and among His faithful covenant people. (Judges 6:23-24)

> And so, *shalom* is a harmonious state of soul and mind, both externally and internally (Psalm 4:8). Deuteronomy 20:11;

> Judges 4:17; and Jeremiah 9:8 demonstrate that it is a prosperous relationship between two parties or more. The "Prince of Peace" (Isaiah 9:6) is the Messiah. He was destined to usher in a government of peace (Isaiah 9:7). The new covenant would be one of *shalom* (Ezekiel 37:26). The Sept. used eirene (1515, NT), eirenikos (1516, NT), *soteria* (4991, NT), and hugiaino (5198, NT). Though *shalom* can mean the absence of strife, it usually is much more. It expresses completeness, harmony, and fulfillment. To wish one *shalom* implies a blessing (2 Samuel 15:27), but to withhold it implies a curse (1 Kings 2:6). In modern Israel the greeting is "*Mah shlomkha?*" ("What is your peace?" or "How are you doing?"). Jesus said, "My peace I give unto you; not as the world giveth give I unto you" (John 14:27). Here Jesus was clearly defining two radically different conceptions of peace. The only true source of peace is God (Psalm 85:8 [cf. 1 Chronicles 22:9, 10]). To the believer, Christ is his peace (Ephesians 2:14).[140]

God has provided within terms of covenant, a peace that passes all understanding. He will not remove His peace from His people, but they can give their peace away when their hearts are faithless, their minds waver, and their souls are not at rest. The cares of this world can be seductive and persuasive, demanding that those at peace give up peace. Those who know God personally and intimately as their covenant partner are less inclined to give away their peace. Like Gideon, they may be challenged, but like Gideon, they can be victorious in the presence of Jehovah-shalom. (Mark 4:18-20, 39-41; Judges 6:23-24)

The peace available to Israel included inter as well as intra personal peace. Theirs was a condition to be met to insure that peace, however. That condition was faithfulness to covenant. Jehovah-shalom revealed God as Israel's peace. He was their covenant God. (Isaiah 55:1-3, 12)

Jehovah-shammah, is seen in Ezekiel 48:35. The name means "the LORD is there" or "the LORD is PRESENT." Theologians and expositors have speculated too much on what God was "trying to say" through Ezekiel. That may be something that will remain for God to know and may not be a mystery explained to the Israelites, or to the Christians.

The relative lack of explanation for the name Jehovah-shammah in most study aids may be because of the tediousness of the context in which the compound name is found. Though the context in which Ezekiel 48:35 is placed is tedious and has been extensively debated, it does not remove the fact another compound name is used there. To counter speculation perhaps it would be applicable to simply say, "As for me and my house we will serve the LORD," (Joshua 24:15).

Like Joshua believers can simply walk forward in faith assured God said to do so. "The LORD is There," "the LORD is PRESENT," Jehovah-shammah is His name and He is faithful and His presence is all that is needed. His word gives victory to His faithful people. By faith believers can walk in the reality of covenant benefits. (1 Timothy 6:2; Hebrews 11:1; Joshua 24:15; Psalms 103:2; 116:12; Ezekiel 48:35; Zephaniah 1:7)

Jehovah-tsidkenu, was written "THE LORD OUR RIGHTEOUSNESS"[141] using all upper case, capital letters to honor the Lord and to strategically emphasize the Lord is the Righteousness of His covenant people. Righteousness has the double meaning of righteousness and of salvation.[142] (Romans 1:16-17; Isaiah 46:13; 51:6, 8; Jeremiah 23:6)

God's revelation of Himself to His covenant partners continued when He introduced Himself as righteous, and even more as their righteousness. There are many scriptures that speak of God's righteousness. Jeremiah recorded it beautifully. (Isaiah 46:13; 51:6,8; Jeremiah 23:6; Romans 1:16-17)

With this compound name of Jehovah, Israel realized that God's righteousness was given to them. They were in covenant with "The Lord Our Righteousness" and it was made their own by His covenant grace. Covenant faithfulness, diligence, and durability were still required, but by His grace they were enabled. Man had a choice as to which master he would serve. The author of Romans has an interesting comment on that matter.

> *"Know ye not, that to whom ye yield yourselves servants to obey, his servants ye are to whom ye obey; whether of sin unto death, or of obedience unto righteousness? But God be thanked, that ye were the servants of sin, but ye have obeyed from the heart that form of doctrine which was delivered you. Being then made free from sin, ye became the servants of righteousness."*
>
> —Romans 6:16-18

With His names, God disclosed His character to His covenant people. He revealed Himself as a powerful creator, an all-sufficient, self-existent, and ever-present provider. He also revealed Himself as their healer, their peace, their victory, their righteousness, and their lord. One could say simply that the covenant partner of Israel was extraordinary, supernaturally so.

Concerning a name and the one who bore that name, *The New Bible Dictionary* says that biblically "the name is the person; the name is the person revealed; and the name is the person actively present. . . ." The names of God express the quality and presence of God. It was by His names that God detailed the provisions available to His beloved covenant partners. Because of the revelation of God's nature through His names, Israel gained confidence in their covenant partner with whom they had entered into an unbreakable and solemn agreement. As long as Israel remained true to their covenant, all that God had was theirs and all they had was His, for covenant partners gladly share everything. They died to independent living; they were wholly committed to their partner.

God has progressively revealed himself to his people with great detail through His Old Testament names. The New Testament likewise has contributions to the progressive revelation of God.

NEW TESTAMENT

The Apostle John wrote in his gospel that the man named Jesus of Nazareth was called: the Son of God; the bread of life; the living bread; the Son of man; the Good Shepherd; the resurrection and the life; Master and Lord; the way, the truth, and the life; the true vine. John also wrote in the book of Revelation that Jesus said of Himself, "I am Alpha and Omega."

In other places in the New Testament, with names, titles, and adjectives placed alphabetically, He is called Alpha and Omega; Beginning and The End, Christ; Door of the sheep; Emmanuel; Great Shepherd; KING of kings, King eternal, King immortal, King invisible; Light of the world; Lord; LORD of lords; Mediator of a better covenant; Messiah; Savior; The only wise God; and even the Word of God. Please note that is not even a complete list of the Name(s) still referred to around the world. (John 5:43; 6:35, 48, 51; 8:28; 10:11, 14:6; 15:1; Revelation 1:8; 22:13)

All the first Christians were Jews who believed Jesus was the promised Savior, the Messiah (Christ). The resurrection was emphasized more than his death, for the resurrection demonstrated Jesus was truly God's Messiah.[143]

> Following guidelines laid down by Jesus himself, the apostles pointed to Old Testament passages which had been fulfilled in his career and in the beginnings of the church. "This is what was

> prophesied" was a phrase frequently on their lips. They used Old Testament images to describe Jesus. He was the Passover lamb, the second Adam, the kinsman-redeemer. He was the stone the builders rejected, but God chose him to be the 'cornerstone' in the construction of his church.
>
> This central concern of the earliest Christian preaching and teaching is especially emphasized in Matthew's gospel and, from a different angle, in the letter to the Hebrews. But all early Christian theology was Jewish, since language and concepts used were quarried chiefly from the Old Testament.[144]

JESUS

Jesus "was the Passover lamb, the second Adam, the kinsman-redeemer. He was the stone the builders rejected, but God chose him to be the 'cornerstone' in the construction of his church."[145] He is and was and ever shall be much more than we can ever stretch ourselves to comprehend. To learn to rest, to trust He is who He has said He is, can enable believers now. Resting in His Word and trusting in Him enabled Abraham, Noah, Moses, and others in Hebrews 11, and can likewise enable true believers today. There are so many promises and provisions throughout the Old and New Testament that can be activated by grace through faith in the name of Jesus. (Hebrews 11:1-40; John 7:17; Revelation 12:11; Ephesians 2:8)

Notice that beginning with the first book, first chapter, and first verse of the New Testament, the lineage of Jesus is documented. Its placement was important in Matthew's day and even more important in this day. Understanding of the importance of heritage, the importance of covenant descendants has waned for too many people. The emphasis and the placement of Matthew's gospel in the New Testament is very strategic. He wrote "The book of the generation of Jesus Christ, the son of David, the son of Abraham." Through the gospel according to Matthew, fulfillment of prophecy is emphasized. Jesus is Immanuel, God with us. God's presence had been with his covenant people with mighty works shown repeatedly in the Old Testament. They were recorded in the books of inspired writers from Moses through Malachi. (Matthew 1:1,23; Isaiah 7:14; 8:8)

The Old Testament books wrote of many of Jehovah's plural works, his mercies, his loving kindnesses, and his singular promised deliverer. Jesus fulfilled all the Old Testament prophecies. The New Testament told of God's faithfulness to covenant. Many came before Jesus' birth and many came afterwards promising big things and claiming to speak for God. But only Jesus was qualified and only Jesus completed what had been "foreordained before the foundation of the world, but was manifest in these last times for you." He is the Redeemer, Christ, and Lamb of God in the New Testament. His names reveal even more of the heart of God. They show the great love with which He loves us. (1 Peter 1:18-20; Revelation 5:6-14; 6:1,16; 7:9,10,14,17; 12:11; 13:8-12; 17:14; 21:22-27)

The birth of Jesus was the beginning of the realization of the promised Messiah. God came in the flesh to dwell among mankind. (Matthew 1:18-25; 1 Timothy 3:16)

> The child is to be called *Yeshua* or, in its more familiar Greek form, Jesus. The name means lit. "he shall save." In the OT the name refers, of course, to God's deliverance of his people from their enemies and his vindication of them by the establishment of his kingdom (cf. Psalm 7; 9). By adding the words save his people from their sins Matthew pictures Jesus as the one through whom the forgiveness of sins is announced. There had been no tradition in Israel for a messiah who would save from sin.[146]

Many in Israel were prepared for their deliverer. Their expected deliverer would be one of David's descendents. Zacharias and Elizabeth had a son, though they both were well-stricken in years. When their son, John, was born, Zacharias prophesied. In the gospel of Luke the expectation of Israel was recorded and seen so beautifully in what the Holy Spirit inspired Zacharias to say. John would be called "the prophet of the Highest and would go before the face of the Lord to prepare his ways." John would speak with the boldness of Elijah and be strong in spirit. He would be called the prophet of the Highest. Preaching repentance and admonishing, even to the priests, to bring forth fruits meet for repentance. John would go before the face of the Lord to prepare his ways to give knowledge of salvation unto his people. (Luke 1:5-17; 67-80; Matthew 3:8)

The plan of God initiated before the creation was continuing toward fulfillment. The law and the prophets pointed to the day being acknowledged by Zacharias. On the day his son, John, was born, Zacharias prophesied and rejoiced in God's holy covenant, *the oath which (God) sware* to Abraham. John the Baptist would grow to be the one of whom the Lord would say, "For I say unto you, among those that are born of women there is not a greater prophet than John the Baptist: but he that is least in the kingdom of God is greater than he," (Luke 7:28).

The glorious and miraculous interaction between the Lord Jesus Christ and John the Baptist becomes clearer when one begins to see the power of God even in His name(s). His names make the one true Almighty One known and they can be seen from Genesis through Revelation. Luke causes us to consider the mighty marvels of God the Awesome One, as he tells how the faithful God of the Covenant came to live as a man. More than fifty years later it was recorded, "And without controversy great is the mystery of godliness: God was manifest in the flesh, justified in the Spirit, seen of angels, preached unto the Gentiles, believed on in the world, received up into glory" (1 Timothy 3:16).

A blueprint was drawn before the creation of man. It was laid on the foundation of the Word of God for the welfare of mankind. It had been recorded, but was not yet completed when Zacharias prophesied. The finishing work of the Old Covenant was close to being accomplished and the foundation of the New Testament was beginning to be recorded. God's Word would endure throughout eternity.

When Jesus was at the well in Samaria, a woman came to know Him as the Christ as He spoke with her. She, though not a scholar, was perceptive in her spirit—even though her mind had many questions that needed answers. She had been seeking answers for a long time but was muddled with a lot of faulty doctrine. The puzzle pieces were still perplexing to her. It has been said, "it is better to be right in your head than wrong in your heart." That seems to hold true for this woman.

Jesus is the Christ. Can we believe less when we have the New Testament and the Old Testament to verify who He is? Search the scriptures, for they are true and settled. Let yourself believe His Word. Search the Word of God free of doctrines that would have you cutting out verses because of preconceived ideas. Seek the Lord for answers. He was willing to answer heart inquiries throughout the Bible. He is able and willing to show Himself true to any who call on Him. Jesus, anointed with the Holy Ghost and with power, answers the New Testament believer. He answered believers in the Old Testament and He certainly will answer New Testament believers. (Matthew 11:25; 16:17; John 14:13; 1 Timothy 1:1-2; 3:13,16; James 1:5-6; 4:2-3; 1 John 5:14-15; Psalm 91:15)

> The Messiah is Jesus of Nazareth, who at His baptism was 'anointed . . . with the Holy Ghost and with power' (Acts 10:38; cf. the implication of Jesus' quotation of Isaiah 61:1 in Luke 4:18). But He Himself rarely employed the term, no doubt because of the misunderstanding to which its employment would give rise. When Peter confessed Him to be the

> Christ He accepted the designation, but ordered His disciples not to tell anyone else (Mark 8:29 f.) In His conversation with the Samaritan woman (John 4:25f.) the term would be understood in the light of the Samaritan expectation of the *Taheb* or 'restorer,' the prophet like Moses promised in Deuteronomy 18:15 ff. When, however, He was challenged by the high priest at His trial to say whether or not He was 'the Christ, the Son of the Blessed,' He agreed that He was, and the language of His reply, with its implied claim to be the peer of the Almighty, led to a unanimous verdict of guilty on the score of blasphemy (Mark 14: 61-64). This verdict, with the ensuing death-sentence, was reversed by God, who raised Him from the dead and exalted Him to His 'right 'hand,' thus proclaiming the crucified Jesus as 'Lord and Messiah' (Acts 2:36, NEB; cf. Romans 1:4).[147]

When the scriptures are searched, we find that Jesus established an everlasting covenant of life and peace, qualifying Him to receive from God a name that is above all other names. Jesus became the covenant head of the covenant-providing life and as such his name holds infinite power and authority and dominion. As is the case in covenant relationships, the name of Jesus was made available to those that would be born again into the kingdom of God. (Mark 16:17-20; John 3:3; Ephesians 1:20-23; Philippians 2:6-9)

The Christian became a legal agent for ministering the business of Jesus, who by his birth, life, death, and resurrection became the King of kings and the Lord of lords. In the Old Testament David used the name of the Lord against his enemies by right of the authority and power available to him because of covenant. In the New Testament Jesus gave authority and power to those that dared to believe in him, as the head of the new covenant.

Twelve disciples, even before Jesus' crucifixion, had seen the power available in His name. Jesus had given them power and authority over devils and diseases. They were sent to preach the kingdom of God and to heal the sick. As they ministered, the crowds became too large for just twelve men to minister effectively. The Lord appointed another seventy. They returned joyful that devils were subject to them through the name of Jesus. But an even more glorious thing was to come.

First, what seemed a dream-annihilating tragedy was to take place. Jesus was crucified—without even defending Himself. Peter tried to defend Him when the soldiers came. Confusion, condemnation, and dismay followed. But then Jesus rose from the dead. He revealed Himself, instructed the disciples, and then ascended into the heavens. He commanded them not to depart from Jerusalem. They were to wait for the promise of the Father and be baptized with the Holy Ghost. Power would be given them to be witnesses of the Lord even all over the world. Now at peace, His disciples must still have wondered about this puzzle piece when Jesus ascended into the clouds. (Luke 9:1-2; 10:11, 17; Luke 16:31; Acts 1:1-14; 2:1-4; 1 Corinthians 15:12)

He had trained the disciples, instructed them, empowered them, gave them some on-the-job training, and had given them an example to follow. He left nothing undone. They were to go all over the world and spread the good news and in the name of Jesus offer evidence of the power and saving grace of God. This was their covenant responsibility. (Mark 16:15-20; 1 Timothy 6:15; Psalm 118:9-14; Revelation 17:14; 19:16)

From the Old had come forth the New. Like a seed that had been planted, the old brought forth sprouts that would be nourished and brought to maturity. Jesus the Word made flesh brought forth healthy branches, which bore good fruit. Clear understanding of covenant is so helpful in rightly dividing the Word of truth. Abiding in the vine is clarified with understanding covenant and the power in the name of Christ

Jesus. (John 1:12-14; 15:1-5; John 17:1-6, 14-17, 20; 1 Peter 1:9-23; Revelation 12:10-11; Hebrews 8:6-13; 9:15; 12:24; Isaiah 45:22-25)

His name in the New Testament books contains the Greek equivalents of the Old Testament names of Elohim, El Shaddai, Jehovah, and Adonai. For Elohim the New Testament uses *Theos* which is Greek for "god." Elohim throughout the Bible is used of heathen gods as well as of Israel's God. Only Israel had a YHWH but nearly all nations had an elohim. The Hebrew word Shaddai found its equivalent in the Greek word *Pantokrator,* which was translated as "Almighty." *Kruios*—Greek for "Lord"—compares to the Hebrew Jehova, Yahweh, or YHWH.

Iesous is the Greek word for "Jesus" and is the equivalent of the Hebrew word *Yehowshua,* rendered "Joshua." What Joshua is in the Old Testament, Jesus is in the New Testament. Joshua of the Old Testament walked in faith and led the Israelites into the Promised Land. Jesus, in the New Testament, walked in faith and lead Abraham's offspring into the Promised Land.

In the New Testament, Christ comes from the Greek word *Christos,* meaning "anointed." It is the same as the Hebrew *mashiyach*, which is translated "Messiah" in the Old Testament. It has to do with the humanity of Jesus Christ. As a sinless man, Jesus' victory in establishing the covenant of life qualified Him to receive from God a name that is above all other names. Jesus became the covenant head of the New Covenant and as such His name has limitless power and authority and dominion. As is the case in covenant relationships, the name of Jesus was made available to those that would be born again into the kingdom of God. (Mark 16:17-20; John 3:3; Ephesians 1:20-23; Philippians 2:6-11)

The truly born again Christian, of necessity, was to *come boldly to the throne*. It seems an official vassal was to come on official business. Approach the Son of God with wholehearted due respect. Prayerfully approach the Lord on behalf of Ambassadors in bonds that the Word of the Lord would continue to be spoken boldly. As legal agents and ministers of the business of the Lord of lords and the King of kings we are to hear, believe, go, and do as the Lord directs.

Jesus became the King of kings and the Lord of lords. God in the flesh dwelt among us. Privileged, cleansed, and properly clothed, we enter into His presence. Garments of praise glistening, we come before Him. Accessible all the time for counsel, direction, comfort, and fellowship, He even walks with us as we return to our daily tasks. *Walking by faith and not by sight* we move on from day to day. And this is love, ours for Him, that we keep His commandments. Because He first loved us, we race with our siblings from assignment to assignment joyful in mind and heart. He has given us liberty and strength to run and not grow weary. Resting the body and caring for the temple of the Holy Spirit we continue the work of the Lord. (2 Corinthians 5:7)

In the Old Testament, David used the name of the Lord against his enemies by right of the authority and power available to him because of covenant. In the New Testament, Jesus did the works of the Father by the same right of authority and power because of the Old Covenant. He came to fulfill the law and worked in obedience to the Old Covenant and abstaining from the traditions and doctrines of the Pharisees. In the New Testament, after giving His disciples what has become referred to as the "Great Commission," Jesus gave authority and power to those that dared to believe in Him, as the head of the new covenant. He had trained the disciples, instructed them, empowered them, and given them an example to follow. He left nothing undone. They were to go into all over the world, spread the good news and in the name of Jesus offer evidence and bear witness of the power and saving grace of God. This was their covenant responsibility, given as a stipulation to covenant. (Ephesians 6:20; 1 Timothy 6:15; Hebrews 4:16; 5:1-6; Revelation 17:14; 19; 16; Psalm 118:9-14)

Later, John—overjoyed with the growing realization the Holy Spirit was the one to empower believers to walk fully in power, love, and faith—would write of love and faith as being the New Covenant Commandment and Law. Believe on His name and love one another for he has commanded us to do so. John also wrote that whoever keeps these commandments abides in the Lord, by the Spirit which He has given. (Romans 3:27; 1 John 3:23-24)

THE HOLY SPIRIT

After Jesus had ascended, the disciples followed His instruction to wait in Jerusalem for the promised Holy Spirit. Believers gathered in an *upper room,* waiting expectantly for the Lord to follow through with what He had promised. They were reminded John had baptized with water, but soon they would be baptized with the Holy Ghost. Their expectation surely would have been high, though their understanding was not up to par. It was best for them then, and for all believers since, to do what He says. Since He is the Word made flesh, He will never differ with what the written Word says.

Arguments go back and forth about which version of the "Word" we are to believe. Keep your heart right in God's sight and be obedient to what He has been showing you from His Word and you will hear His voice and follow Him. John wrote in his gospel Jesus had told them, "If any man desires to do His will (God's pleasure), he will know (have the needed illumination to recognize, and can tell for himself) whether the teaching is from God or whether I am speaking from Myself *and* of My own accord *and* on My own authority," (John 7:17 AMP). Ask Him as you read for understanding. He will send the answer, not unlike how the Holy Spirit dispatched Philip to an Ethiopian who puzzled over the Old Testament book of the prophet Isaiah (Acts 8:29-40). (Acts 1:2,4,5,8; 8:29-40; John 10:26-27)

> Under the guidance of the Spirit, Philip runs after the Ethiopian's chariot (or carriage). He hears the eunuch reading, for in the ancient world reading was done aloud.
>
> After the baptism, the Spirit sends Philip on his mission. Here some manuscripts say that the Spirit came on the eunuch and the angel caught up Philip. This would indicate that the Ethiopian has received the Holy Spirit at baptism. Philip proceeds to Azotus (OT Ashdod, preaching in towns (perhaps Lydda and Joppa; cf. 9:32-43) on the way to Caesarea.[148]

Philip followed his heart and God opened a door for him to expound upon the scriptures for the Ethiopian, helping him see where the puzzle piece fit. The Holy Spirit had directed them both, and as a result God granted each of them great joy. When you are puzzled, the Lord is well able to help you. Ask Him questions. He may bring you a Philip so that you will have your questions answered. He may bring you to a verse or several verses that solve the puzzle at hand. Or He may speak to you with a still small voice as He did with Elijah.

Peter, James, and John were among the 129 believers who were obedient to the Lord. They waited for the promise of the Father—the Holy Ghost. They prayed and were in one accord when Pentecost was fully come. They saw cloven tongues like as of fire, which sat upon each of them. "And they were all filled with the Holy Ghost, and began to speak with other tongues, as the Spirit gave them utterance," (Acts 2:4). (Acts 1:13-15; 2:1-6)

> Though Peter was filled with the Holy Ghost, and spake with tongues as the Spirit gave him utterance, yet he did not think to set aside the Scriptures. Christ's scholars never learn above their Bible; and the Spirit is given, not to do away the Scriptures, but to enable us to understand, approve, and obey them.[149]

Shortly after the day of Pentecost, Peter and John went to the temple at the hour of prayer. Peter responded to a lame man's request for alms by saying, "Silver and gold have I none; but such as I have give I thee: In the name of Jesus Christ of Nazareth rise up and walk," (Acts 3:6). The power of the name of Jesus and the unction of the Holy Ghost was seen as Peter and John boldly spoke forth the name of Jesus. The better covenant had made it possible for believers to be filled with the Holy Spirit. (Acts 3:1-11,16)

> Unction (1 John 2; Joshua 2:20,27; R. V., "anointing") Kings, prophets, and priests were anointed, in token of receiving divine grace. All believers are, in a secondary sense, what Christ was in a primary sense, "the Lord's anointed."[150]

During Jesus' three years of ministry He had healed multitudes of various ailments. The disciples had accompanied Him during that time and had witnessed His compassionate nature—patience, power, righteousness, joy, peace, kindness, goodness, gentleness, and self-control. They also had noted His remarkable faithfulness. He had faithfully kept and performed His father's words. The works that God had given Jesus to do, He had accomplished, including revealing another facet of the attributes of God. Jesus revealed God as a loving and faithful Father. (John 5:36)

Now the disciples knew God as their own faithful Father and they, in the name of Jesus, were continuing the work Jesus had begun by ministering to the hurting. The better covenant had given Peter and John the power to heal as Jesus had healed. They were covenant partners with one who had the desire and ability to make them capable of doing what He had instructed them to do. God had qualified them to be able ministers and dispensers of the New Covenant of the Spirit. The people who had witnessed the miracle of wholeness being manifest in the body of the lame man were split in their reaction. Some reacted with amazement and wonder while some reacted with anger and puzzlement. (2 Corinthians 3:6)

Many were amazed at what had happened. They had known this man for years. They had seen Him daily as He sat outside the temple begging for a little money. Now this man was as sound in body as all those who crowded around the temple. And all this was in the name of Jesus. Some of them remembered Jesus as He had walked among them and performed mighty miracles. Could it really be that the love He had exhibited during His ministry was still available in spite of the fact that He had been crucified? Many were filled with awe and wonder but some were angered.

Peter and John preached the resurrection from the dead when the lame man was healed. Many listened and believed. Some simply wanted to know by what power they were able to do what they had done. Peter, filled with the Holy Ghost, said it was by the name of Jesus Christ of Nazareth, that the lame man had been miraculously healed. Then he added, "neither is there salvation in any other: for there is none other name under Heaven given whereby we must be saved," (Acts 4:12). Peter and John had spoken with such boldness and with such insights when they were perceived as being unlearned and ignorant.

The opposition marveled but chose to do nothing about it because of all the people standing around who were understandably amazed. Anger and resentfulness sprang up in the officials of the temple. The rulers, elders, and scribes had spent years preparing for their ministry. They had worked long for their positions in the temple. Peter and John had done nothing to merit this much admiration from the people at the temple entrance. Thus Peter and John were forbidden to continue using the name of Jesus. The threats did not deter them, however, for Peter and John knew the power and authority available to them in and by the name and Spirit of the Lord.

Opposition to praying, preaching, ministering in the name of the Lord Jesus Christ is still rampant among unbelievers. These end times are bringing forth multitudes like Peter and John who continue to speak forth in the name of the Lord Jesus Christ and many continue to be brought out of the covenant with death. Rebellion and unbelief tragically continue to keep some eyes and ears blind, deaf and dull to the good news going out to all. The anti-christs and the Anti-Christ have and will continue to raise their ire not knowing Christ Jesus personally as their own Lord and Saviour. Too often they refuse to repent and believe though believers continue in the Better Covenant stipulations. The name of Christ Jesus shall eternally be our birthright. "The use of another person's name to declare legal rights is called 'the power of attorney.' This is a privileged power that Jesus has delegated to us in confronting the retreating rule that sickness and Satan seek to sustain over mankind." That quote from The Kingdom Dynamics written by N.V.; Nathaniel M. Van Cleave, (B.A., Th.D., D.D.), page 1495 of the *New Spirit Filled Life Bible,* excellently clarifies the privilege of having eyes to see and cars to hear. (Revelation 2:7, 11, 17, 29, 3:6, 13, 22)

With the name of Jesus another aspect of the many-faceted nature of God was revealed. He displayed Himself as a God who was glorified by healing and prospering, i.e. saving, the descendants of the first Adam. The descendants of the first Adam, when saved, were born again into the kingdom of God and were given access to the blessings of the New Covenant through Jesus their Lord. Being born again into the kingdom of God did indeed bring abundant blessings—but it also brought responsibilities.

Each person involved in a covenant has responsibilities. There is a price to pay, benefits to receive, and work to be accomplished. The work of the New Testament believer is accomplished by faith in the name of Jesus and by walking in love. Using Jesus' name is a covenant privilege; to use it rightfully, wisely, respectfully is an obligation. The born again believer has the privilege of being part of the better covenant Old Testament believers longed to see. (John 3:3,5; 1 Peter 1:23; 1 John 3:23)

We receive power when the Holy Spirit comes upon us to be witnesses throughout the earth. Declaring the works of Jesus Christ as the head of the better covenant with boldness, believers have been empowered to go forth rejoicing in Jesus their Lord and Savior. (Ephesians 1:1-23)

> The "blood" was the seal of the everlasting covenant entered into between the Father and Son; in virtue of the Son's blood, first Christ was raised, then Christ's people shall be so (Zechariah 9:11, seemingly referred to here; Acts 20:28) everlasting—The everlastingness of the covenant necessitated the resurrection. This clause, "the blood of the everlasting covenant," is a summary retrospect of the Epistle (compare Hebrews 9: 12).
>
> Make you perfect—properly said of healing a rent; join you together in perfect harmony [BENGEL]. To do his will, working in you—(Hebrews 10:36); rather as Greek, "doing in you." Whatever good we do, God does in us, is well-pleasing in his sight—(Isaiah 53:10; Ephesians 5:10) through Jesus Christ—"God doing (working) in you that . . . through Jesus Christ" (Philippians 1:11) to whom—to Christ.
>
> The "blood" was the seal of the everlasting covenant entered into between the Father and Son; in virtue of the Son's blood, first Christ was raised, then Christ's people shall be so (Zechariah 9:11, seemingly referred to here; Acts 20:28).[151]

The God of peace raised our Lord Jesus from the dead through the blood of the everlasting covenant. It is in the name of our Lord Jesus, through the blood of the everlasting covenant, that we are enabled to do what He calls us to do. For by the same means, the name of our Lord Jesus is able to perfect and mature us in every good work to do his will, working in us that which is well pleasing in his sight. It is all because of Jesus. (Hebrews 13:20-21)

He is *the mediator of a better covenant and the high priest of our confession.* He faithfully keeps His Word. The New Covenant is the better covenant. The New Covenant is everlasting. Jesus is the Way. Whosoever shall confess Jesus before men, the Lord will confess him also before the Heavenly Father, which is in heaven. But whosoever shall deny the Lord before men, Him will the Lord deny before his Heavenly Father, which is in Heaven.

Jesus is alive. The truth of His Lordship shall reign and whosoever is with Him will rejoice. Whether decision time puts one in the service of the Lord of lords who is the mediator of a better covenant or in the company of the accuser's covenant of death, all will nonetheless be judged. (Matthew 10:32-33; Mark 6:11; Galatians 3:20; Hebrews 8:6; 9:15; 12:24)

In His name shall the Gentiles trust.
Repentance and remission of sins should be preached in His name.
Through faith in His name, the man is strong.
They commanded them not to speak or teach in the name of Jesus.
They were baptized in the name of the Lord Jesus.
For His name's sake they went forth.
Holy is His name.
Believe on the name.
Your sins are forgiven for His name's sake.
Speak boldly in the name of the Lord Jesus.
Through his name whosoever believes shall receive remission of sins.
Whosoever shall call on the name of the Lord shall be saved.
God faithfully gives the ability to do what He calls us to do.
Those of faith are blessed with faithful Abraham.
Faithful is the Lord who calls you.

—Connie Fauth

Jesus, the head of the New Covenant, makes it possible for us to walk with God as dear children. He shall establish us, and keep us from evil because the Lord is faithful. (1 Corinthians 10:11, 13; Galatians 3:9; 1 Thessalonians 5:24; 2 Thessalonians 3:3)

How can I know Him? I will get to know Him as I fellowship with Him. Reading His letters, I learn what is on His heart. He lets me ask for explanations when questions arise. He willingly fellowships with me each morning and moment by moment through each day. As I rest at night, He never slumbers. He shows his loving-kindness in the morning and His faithfulness every night. He is by far the best commentary and dictionary ever written. He is an ever-present help. His names sum up His unlimited power, His majesty, His works, His goodness, His righteousness, His faithfulness, His mercy, and His grace.

The mediator of the better covenant is the Lord Jesus Christ. *His name is above all names*. His faithfulness is beyond our comprehension. Though we are limited by mortal bodies, we can stretch ourselves to trust in Him and keep growing, for He is faithful to complete the good work in us He has begun. He is a merciful and faithful high priest in things pertaining to God. (Philippians 1:6; 2:9; 1 Thessalonians 5:24; Hebrews 2:17)

Spiritually we are able to excel and become established for the Excellent, Established, Eternal Covenant enables us to grow strong in the Lord in the power of his might. He is faithful and we are made like him by His grace and excellent workmanship. (1 Corinthians 1:30-31; Ephesians 2:10; 6:10-11; Hebrews 13:20-22)

Chapter 9

GOD'S COVENANT FAITHFULNESS

God is and always shall be faithful to keep covenant, both the Old and the New. Man has habitually broken covenant, but God can always be trusted to keep His Word and we are always expected to keep our word. Let those with little or no faith in the Lord realize the profit and value of studying the Bible. Let those who cling to the traditions and doctrines of men know the reality of redemption. God's abundant mercy is new every morning and great is His faithfulness. *His mercy endures forever*. Without compromise His righteousness remains an everlasting righteousness, and His law is truth. His grace exceeds all man's expectations. His covenant people are not to frustrate the grace of God. (2 Corinthians 9:14; Galatians 2:21; 1 Peter 1:3,5,10,12,18,19,21,23; Psalm 118:3,29; 119:142)

The Old Testament prophets inquired of and searched diligently for the grace they saw in pictures and shadows. The Spirit testified of the sufferings of Christ and the glory that would follow. The pieces, the visions, and the words they spoke and wrote are revealed to us through the Lord's apostles and disciples. Among them stood Peter, who pointed to Jesus. Peter wrote believers were to gird, secure, prepare, and strengthen the loins of their minds. Girding one's mind includes diligent Bible study and fellowship with the Lord. We are to know the better covenant stipulations and the faithfulness of God towards us and on behalf of us because of Jesus the High Priest of our profession (confession). (1 Peter 1:1-3,7,10-13)

The loins are very tender, but strategically girded the Israelites were ready for the events at the first Passover. God's army against Nineveh was told to make their loins strong, and to fortify their power. Elijah girded his loins and outran Ahab's chariots. The Messiah's righteousness was the girdle of His loins. Believers are to have their loins girded with truth. (Ephesians 6:13-18; 1 Peter 1:10-13; Exodus 12:11; 1 Kings 18:41-46; Isaiah 11:5; Nahum 2:1)

The heavenly Father keeps His word. Jesus said to the Samaritan woman, "I that speak to you am he" (Messiah). God the Father kept His Word. The Messiah had come. The Lord Jesus Christ, the mediator of a better covenant and high priest of our confession, faithfully keeps His word. God, who is a Spirit, has by the better covenant brought forth true worshippers who worship the Father in spirit and in truth. (Matthew 12:28; John 4:22-24; Isaiah 61:1-6)

The Messiah, the man Jesus, also keeps His Word faithfully. He was raised up to sit at the right hand of the Father, where He makes intercession for believers. We serve Him as an occupying army serves their commander in chief. Daily going into His presence, the throne of grace, prayer, and fellowship with direction and clarity come as we habitually walk with Him. He directs His people moment-by-moment, day-by-day throughout their stay in this world.

The New Covenant is the best. All are welcome to enter the Kingdom of God. The New Covenant is a better covenant than the Old. The Messiah has come and will come again. He is the mediator. The truth of His Lordship shall reign and whosoever is with Him will rejoice. Jesus has obtained a more excellent ministry. Jesus Christ is the faithful witness, the firstborn from the dead, the prince of kings of the earth. He loves us and cleansed us from our sins in His own blood. He has even made us kings and priests unto God and His Father. How marvelous are His ways and His works. Jesus was made a man like his brethren that he might be a merciful and faithful high priest in things pertaining to God the Father. He has made reconciliation for the sins of the people. All the more reason to come into His kingdom. Restoration is yours if you will only call on the name of the Lord Jesus Christ. He certainly is worthy of all praise. (Hebrews 2:17; 8:6; 9:15; 12:24)

God is faithful. He is altogether righteous. God told Abraham to be perfect. New Covenant believers are told not to conform to this world. New believers are born again when doing as Paul directed. We are told to be transformed, changed, regenerated—to fashion ourselves by the renewing of our mind. The spirit of a man is born again. He is raised to life by the Holy Spirit and made a new man. Indeed the Word of the Lord endures forever. Thereby we are able to prove what is that good and acceptable and perfect will of God. God is perfect and His will is perfect. The Lord is faithful. He will establish us. (John 3:3,7; Romans 10:8-13; 12:2; Genesis 17:1; Galatians 3:9; 2 Thessalonians 3:3; Titus 3:5; 1 Peter 1:23)

GOD'S FAITHFULNESS

The Apostle Paul wrote, "God is faithful, by whom ye were called unto the fellowship of his Son Jesus Christ our Lord," (1 Corinthians 1:9). God is faithful to his children and they are called into the fellowship of His Son Jesus Christ our Lord. Paul wrote using "our" as a possessive adjective because of covenant. By faith Paul had been born again. By faith he had been filled with the Holy Spirit and spoke in tongues. He continued his instruction to the Corinthians by saying "I speak in tongues more than you all." It seems probable the mysteries of Christ were revealed to him as he fellowshipped with the Lord while praying in the spirit—a lot. (1 Corinthians 14:18)

To be faithful is to be full of faith, steadfast, and loyal. A faithful person is trustworthy, loyal, and conscientious. Their word is good. What they say they have done, they have done. What they say they will do, they will do. Stephen is a biblical example of one *full of faith and of the Holy Ghost*. He was in the ministry of helps to the twelve apostles and the disciples. They had chosen seven men full of the Holy Ghost and wisdom and appointed them over the matters of daily ministration—even to serving tables when needed. Being faithful to the Lord included serving where needed, and Stephen did. Full of faith and power he did great wonders and miracles among the people. (Acts 6:1-8)

Faithfulness is a rarity in man, but God is always faithful. He keeps His Word and does not break covenant. He is faithful to the head of the covenant, to the offspring of the covenant, and to the blood of the covenant. Being faithful to covenant Himself, God expects faithfulness from His covenant friends, co-workers, and covenant partners who are instructed to imitate Him. (1 Corinthians 1:12-15: Ephesians 5:1 AMP; Psalm 119:89-90; 132:12-15)

"Faithful" or "faithfulness" comes from the Hebrew word *aman*, used on twenty-one occasions in the Old Testament. The word *aman* or *amen* is definitely a covenant word. (Deuteronomy 27-28)

> Heb. Amen, 'surely,' from a root meaning 'to be firm, steady, trustworthy; cf. emuna, 'faithfulness', emet, 'truth.' Rendered also in AV 'truth' (Isaiah 65:16 twice, lit. 'God of Amen') and 'so be it' (Jeremiah 11:5). The Gk. Word is a transliteration of the Heb. And is rendered 'verily' in the frequent formula, 'Verily, verily, I say unto you.'
>
> It is used: (a) as a responsive formula with which a listener acknowledges the validity of an oath or curse and declares himself willing to accept its consequences (Numbers 5:22; Deuteronomy 27:15, etc.; Nehemiah 5:13; Jeremiah 11:5); (b) to

> welcome an announcement or a prophecy of good (1 Kings 1:36; Jeremiah 28:6); as an expression of agreement with a doxology or benediction, and often duplicated for emphasis (1 Chronicles 16:36; Psalm 41:13, etc).
>
> In the New Testament the ascriptional use is frequent, although several instances are additions by a later hand. In Revelation 1:7, 22:20 it expresses confirmation of the writer's hope in the parousia. Christ's use of it is unique and seems to imply that He is endowing His words with His own (messianic) authority, a thing no scribe or Rabbi would ever have done. That is why in Him the promises of God are authoritative and will undoubtedly be fulfilled (2 Corinthians 1:20): He can therefore be called 'the Amen' (Revelation 3:14), and if the MT is correct the same meaning must underlie the description of God in Isaiah 65:16. J.B.Tr.[152]

According to Matthew's gospel, Jesus told His disciples not to use vain repetitions, as the heathen do. The disciples were not to be like them. The example Jesus gave of how to pray began with honor. *Our Father* is a possessive adjective. "Our" indicated the disciples would become children of the Father by faith in the covenant head of the better covenant. It was covenant related when the Lord said, *Thy kingdom come*. The kingdom of God, which is not meat nor drink, would be a kingdom of righteousness, peace, and joy. Those attributes reflect character development in the people of God who habitually fellowship with the Lord.

Helped by the Holy Spirit and praying according to the guidelines written in Matthew's gospel, out of the abundance of the heart peace would reign in their lives, homes, communities, and in their villages and cities. He instructed them to end prayer by saying *Amen*, which means *so be it*. Too often speakers and congregations utter *Amen* with little or no understanding of the covenant-related word. They often are actually saying *so be it* following some idle chatter that comes closer to being a curse birthing a lie than a blessing based on truth. The Lord of the better covenant honored His own covenant partner, His Heavenly Father and told the disciples to do likewise when they prayed. *Our* in the context of Matthew 6 is a covenant related word and amen likewise is covenant related. (Matthew 6:7-15; John 8:32,45; 2 Corinthians 13:8; Deuteronomy 27:15-26)

Faithfulness applies to God and expresses His total reliability. It describes Him—His works and His words. When seeking to understand His faithfulness, simply remember God is faithful to keep covenant. Of course there is more to be said of Him, but in love for us He sought for a man that could make up a hedge and stand in the gap before God for the land, that he could not destroy it. He found none in Ezekiel's day. Therefore He poured out His indignation upon Judah. They had broken covenant. Nevertheless, God remembered His covenant with them. Repeatedly in the Old Covenant the people of God—those with whom He had a covenant through Abraham, Isaac and Jacob—had broken covenant. Yet God remained faithful. (Ezekiel 13:1-23; 22:24-31)

Hosea's prophetic marriage covenant illustrated the Lord's own heartache over Israel's covenant unfaithfulness. The Lord has always been faithful to covenant because of His great love for us. People were born in sin and lived in sin, but God's love implemented a way to minister to them using covenant. His everlasting covenant continues to be everlasting whether it is believed and received by individuals or not. No theory, no doctrine, no man, not even the most learned theologian is able to alter the fact that the Word of the Lord God Himself has uttered His *Amen* to the better covenant. (Mark 16:20; Revelation 1:5,6,18; 3:14; 5:14; 7:12; 19:4; 22:20; Ezekiel 16:8, 59-62; 22:30; Hosea 1-14)

The head, offspring, blood, and word of the covenant with all its facts, provisions and promises are like an intimately intertwined rope. The clever, the studied, the knowledgeable and even the godly and insightful cannot adequately relay with any language the magnitude of God's perfect plan of salvation. Nevertheless, in an attempt to understand God's faithfulness to covenant, it is needful to at least look at some of these different areas. May the Spirit of the Lord bless His Word and my attempt to expound on the subject of covenant and His faithfulness to keep covenant. Amen, and amen. *God is and He is a rewarder of those that diligently seek Him.* (Hebrews 11:6)

FAITHFUL TO HIS WORD

The Lord (Jehovah) God (Adonai) never changes. He is and always shall be faithful to all that he promised. He always has and always shall watch over His Word to perform it. He has sent His Word to us. He has blessed us with freedom of choice, whether our nation acknowledges His God-given freedoms or not. We are to abstain from slothfulness and be faithful and patient in all the principles of the doctrine of Christ. Many have heard of the doctrine of Christ, but many have not. Some have received His Word, but many have not. Yet God remains faithful—believe it or not. God is not dictatorial. He is good and all together righteous.

Faithfully God keeps His Word. He knows what is needed for the well-being of His people who are so inclined to want to do their own thing. With self-deceptive thinking they are inclined to think they are able to do anything. Along that broad way they easily fall prey to the one who is so apt at stealing, killing, and destroying. Listening to the thief, people are inclined to disobey the better covenant stipulations, guidelines, accounts, promises, and provisions written in His Word. Fickle, foolish, greedy, and selfish, too many people slide into the mire and cannot find an escape route. Ignoring detours they usually arrive at dead ends, or rush into ditches.

HIS WORD

God's written Word shows the problems, the answers, and examples of defeat and victory experienced by those bound by both the Old and New Covenants. With the help of the Holy Spirit, He gives wisdom from His Word for how to change course and clean up the mess made from going the wrong way to whosoever will let their eyes see and whosoever will let their ears hear. His Word read, rightly divided, and obeyed makes a new man of one that was dead. (James 2:26; Ephesians 2:1; 1 Peter 4:1-19)

Missing the mark is much more consequential in spiritual matters than in target practice. We are to be keenly aware of the Word of the living God and alert to the wiles of the devil. When in trouble, calling on the name of the Lord activates Him and puts fear in the thief intent on stealing, killing, and destroying. The Lord Jesus Christ has made a way for believers to overcome. The better covenant enables us to be born again and gives us a heart able to walk in close fellowship with our Lord and Savior. Obedience or disobedience determines the rise and fall of individuals and nations. (Mark 10:45; Romans 3:3-4,24; 6:23; 7:14; John 8:34; 10:10; 1 Corinthians 6:20; Galatians 3:13; 5:1; Exodus 6:6; 21:28-30; Judges 3:9; 3:15; 2 Samuel 22:2; Psalm 77:14-15; 78:1-72; 97:11-12)

> *Then said the Lord unto me, Thou hast well seen: for I will hasten my word to perform it.*
>
> —Jeremiah 1:12

> *Then said the Lord to me, You have seen well, for I am alert* ***and*** *active, watching over My word to perform it.*
>
> —Jeremiah 1:12 AMP

He remains faithful and will not deny what He has said. *He even hastens His word to perform it* according to the *Amplified Bible*, or *hastens to perform His word* according to the *King James Version* of the Bible. Rather than try to figure out which version is best, I simply believe the goodness of the Lord is shown in both translations. God is good and the devil is evil. The verse certainly is good and in context, even when considering it contextually from Genesis through Revelation. The admonishments of the Lord given in His Word are not to be disregarded.

God's admonishment is to not be slothful, lukewarm, slow, or sluggish. In addition, believers are told that through faith and patience, they could inherit the promises. His word is for whosoever believes and does the Word of the Lord. It is the privilege of believers to be part of the Kingdom of Heaven walking with the Lord of hosts and with the mighty men of valor. The Lord has shown us what he requires of us. We are to do justly, love mercy, and walk humbly with the Lord in the covenant of the Lord, the berith of Jehovah. (Galatians 3:1-9; 1 Timothy 2:13; Hebrews 6:12-14; Numbers 10:33; 1 Kings 8:56; Jeremiah 1:12 AMP; Micah 6:8)

God will continue to be faithful for He has made a blood covenant and taken an oath, made an everlasting solemn agreement with man's representative, the Lord Jesus Christ. By grace, through faith we can enter into that everlasting solemn agreement. For God to break the Word of the covenant would be for Him to deny Himself. God made covenant promise to Abraham and swore to keep it. There was no one else greater than Himself whereby he could swear when he made covenant with Abraham.

God is always true. God cannot deny himself. For God to break the Word of the covenant would be for Him to deny Himself and to become a liar like man. Breaking His Word would cause Him to receive the curse that is the inheritance of all covenant transgressors.

That realization emphasizes Jesus' strategic victory when tempted of the devil during the Lord's fast in the wilderness. It also emphasizes the greater one who submitted himself to his Heavenly Father and walked in complete obedience, fully completing the better covenant.

Jesus is indeed the mediator of a better covenant, better than the Adamic, the Noahic, the Abrahamic, the Mosaic, and the Davidic Covenant. Unlike the former heads of covenant, Jesus as head of the better covenant will never perish, will live eternally, and His covenant will never be broken. Faith in Him may foolishly be denied by people, but He will never deny Himself and will always remain true. Man can deny Him, but God's promises will not be broken. Man can refuse to walk in the covenant and when he dies physically, will go through judgment and then endure a second death. There will be no hope of every having another opportunity to be born again, no hope of ever seeing the kingdom of God in all it's glory. For all of eternity, sinners will endure awfulness, which will be a thousand times worse than their worst time on planet Earth. It has often been said, "There is a heaven to gain and a hell to shun." Christ Jesus is indeed the only way. (Matthew 4:1-3; Romans 3:3-5; 2 Timothy 2:13; Hebrews 10:29; 12:24; 13:20; Deuteronomy 17:2; Joshua 7:11,15; 23:16; Judges 2:20; 2 Kings 18:12; Isaiah 24:5; Jeremiah 34:18 AMP; Hosea 6:7; 8:1; Amos 1:9)

People have not always been loyal to covenant but the Lord God has remained trustworthy in His covenant commitments. His word is conclusively resolved. (Isaiah 34:16; Isaiah 11:3-4 *The Jerusalem Bible*; Isaiah 55:10-11; Mark 13:8,31)

In the Hittite nation, the word of a covenant partner was to be honored in spite of appearances to the contrary. The Hittites nor their vassals could not, however, have the confidence in the word of their covenant that Christians are able to have in the word of their covenant. For the power of the Hittite ruler to back his word was limited and the history of their kingdoms is seldom even remembered.

There is no limit to the power of God to guarantee His Word. God's (Adonai's) power, evident as God created the worlds, is available to fulfill the word of the better covenant. Consequently Christians do, with varying degrees of faith, believe that God will do what He says He will do. It is so important to let yourself believe the word, the logos, the rhema, and the agape of God. With the detail available and the victories possible in the blood of the everlasting covenant, how can it be surprising we are to meditate on the words of faith and of good doctrine, and give ourselves wholly to the godly doctrine of the only true and living God? He is the Savior of those that believe. These things Timothy was told to command and teach. (1 Timothy 4:6-16)

We are not only to trust (have faith) in the Word of God as true, but we are to trust in Jesus who is the living Word. The written Word of God and the living Word of God, are united in perfect harmony in an unbreakable covenant. It is a privilege to be born again and see his kingdom and being born again enter his kingdom. What a privilege offered to all. Who will choose to believe? (John 3:16; Romans 3:21-26; 1 Thessalonians 2:13 AMP; Hebrews 11:1)

> WORD. Yahweh's word is an extension of the divine personality, invested with divine authority, and is to be heeded by angels and men (Psalm 103:20; Deuteronomy 12:32); it stands forever (Isaiah 40:8), and once uttered it cannot return unfulfilled (Isaiah 55:11). It is used as a synonym for the law (tora) of God in Psalm 119, where alone its reference is to a written rather than a spoken message.
>
> In the New Testament it translates two terms, *logos* and *rhema*, the former being supremely used of the message of the Christian gospel (Mark 2:2; Acts 6: 2; Galatians 6:6), though the latter also bears the same meaning (Romans 10:8; Ephesians 6:17; Hebrews 5:5, etc.). Our Lord spoke of the word of God (in the parable of the sower, Luke 8:11; see also

> Mark 7:13; Luke 11:28), but in the Synoptic Gospels He always used the plural of His own message ('my words', Matthew 24:35 and parallels; Mark 8:38 Luke 24:44). In the fourth gospel, however, the singular is often found. To the early Church the word was a message revealed from God in Christ, which was to be preached, ministered, and obeyed. It was the word of life (Phillipians 2:16), of truth (Ephesians 1:13), of salvation (Acts 8:26), of reconciliation (2 Corinthians 5:19), of the cross (1 Corinthians 1:18).[153]

Jesus, the head of the better covenant is the Word of God (Adonai) powerfully personalized. During His sojourn here, Jesus demonstrated God's power, love, and faithfulness to the descendants of Abraham. The Word of God was manifest in the person of Jesus as the subject of God's loyalty.

BETTER COVENANT PROMISES AND PROVISIONS

A promise is primarily a law term, denoting a summons to proclaim and announce. It is a summons to undertake, do, or give something. It often signifies a gift bestowed, not a pledge secured by negotiation, according to *Vines Expository Dictionary*, page 891.

Provisions are plans or arrangements, made in preparation for some undertaking. There was a world to be reached. Jesus lived, died, rose, delegated authority, ascended, and intercedes today so that the plans and arrangements made for the salvation of mankind could be heard around the world. Preparations for the Passover were made, His blood was shed, and the feet of the saints were to be shod with the preparation of the gospel of peace. Provisions were made for them to go around the world and preach the gospel. (Matthew 27:62; Mark 15:42; 16:9-19; Luke 23:54; John 19:14,31,42; Ephesians 6:15)

The promises of the Old Covenant were fulfilled in Jesus providing salvation for whoever will believe. A provision is a preparation made beforehand or something for which preparation has already been made. The New Testament provisions summarized are salvation and the indwelling Holy Spirit. These provisions are the fulfillment of the Old Testament provision/promises. The provision of salvation and the indwelling Holy Spirit has made re-creation of man possible. It has made righteousness, wisdom, sanctification, and redemption available. (Luke 24:49; Acts 1:4; Acts 2:33; 23:21; Romans 9:4; 1 Corinthians 1:30; 2 Corinthians 5:17; Ephesians 1:13; Galatians 3:14; Hebrews 6:12; 8:6; 11:17; 9:15)

David wrote of his delight in doing God's will and prophetically wrote of the wonderful works of the "Lord my God" as being more than could be numbered. John concluded his gospel by saying if everything Jesus had done were written, surely the world could not contain all the documents, the books. (John 21:25; Psalm 9:1; 28:5; 33:4; 40:5; 107:31)

His redemption from the curse and the blessings is explained beautifully in the gospels, and in the acts of the Holy Spirit's work with and through the first believers; the epistles and the revelation of Jesus Christ.

> Redemption from the curse of the law comes through Christ (cf. Romans 7:24-25a) in whom the blessing of Abraham has been fulfilled. This blessing is identified with the Spirit coming through faith. The statement that Christ has become a curse for us is prompted by the words of Deuteronomy 21:23, interpreted as a reference to the Crucifixion, than it is by the logic of Paul's own argument in this passage. He probably has in mind the general idea that Christ bore man's sins "in his body on the tree" (1 Peter 2:24; cr. Roman. 8:3).

> Here is Paul's chief explanation of how Christ redeems man from the curse of the law. He uses the illustration of a legal testament of will, basing his argument of the coincidence that the Greek word used in LXX for God's covenant with Abraham also had this meaning. That covenant remains valid, he claims, because a will can be neither nullified nor supplemented. In Genesis 12:7, as in Deuteronomy 21:23 cited earlier, Paul finds a reference to Christ. This time he takes advantage of the noun offspring, which though plural in meaning is singular in form. The offspring is Christ, in whom is the fulfillment of God's covenant with Abraham, and by whom one is redeemed from the curse of the law.
>
> Paul's employment of OT proofs is continued as he points out that chronologically the covenant and its promise preceded the giving of the law, and that the law in no way suspends or supplements the prior arrangement. God's covenant is embodied, not in the law, but in the promise fulfilled in the law, but in the promise fulfilled in Christ. Therefore when the prophet says, 'He who through faith is righteous shall live' (vs. 11), he bears witness to the necessity of believing in Christ as opposed to doing works of the law.[154]

The fulfillment of the Old Testament promise in Jesus becomes the New Testament provision. God desires and has provided for all men to be saved. The New Covenant provisions include eternal life, the indwelling Holy Spirit, health, prosperity, power, comfort, peace, joy, answered prayer, love, and much more than I will expound on here. (Matthew 13:17; Romans 10:1-21; Ephesians 6:10-20; 1 Timothy 2:1-6)

The disciples were blessed to see the New Covenant activated. They were able to receive the benefits of the provisions and promises of the Better Covenant. Though somewhat repetitive, emphasis may help make the point. Repetition with variation can sometimes help the eyes see a mundane matter as a piece of art and help the puzzle pieces be arranged correctly.

Promise looks to the future. It is sent forward sometimes verbally and sometimes as a written agreement giving a basis for expectation. "A promise is a word that goes forth into unfilled time."[155] A promise offers hope for the future. So throughout the Old Testament our Lord God Almighty gave promise of the Messiah who would be the Savior.

> The noun ***provision*** is a settled, finished stipulation. It refers back to something promised and then provided, prepared, supplied, and assembled for future needs. "It is a preparatory arrangement or measure taken in advance for meeting some future need."[156]
>
> It (provision) 1. A providing, preparing, or supplying of something; 2. (a) something provided, prepared, or supplied for the future; (b) [pl.] a stock of food and other supplies assembled for future needs; 3. a preparatory arrangement or measure taken in advance for meeting some future need; 4. a clause, as in a legal document, an agreement which stipulates or requires some specific thing.[157]
>
> The adjective ***proviso*** is a condition or stipulation.[158]
>
> The verb form ***provide***, which though rarely used anymore, means to get ready beforehand, make available a supply as a condition a stipulation prepared for some probable situation or occurrence. Provision, proviso, provide, provided becomes a furnished means of support; a conjunction on the condition, understanding of that and if.[159]

Provision, as used in the context of the subject covenant, refers to all things settled, finished by the death, burial, resurrection and ascension of the Lord Jesus Christ. The provisions and the promises throughout the Holy Scriptures (Genesis through Revelation) are without comparison in all the books ever authored otherwise. (Matthew 11:27; 19:26; 28:20; Mark 4:34; Acts 1:1-5; 1 Peter 2:24; Acts 15:4; Acts 8:28; 2 Corinthians 5:17,18; Ephesians 1:11,22; Titus 1:15; 2:7; Hebrews 1:2-3; 2:8,10)

The provisions of the better covenant addressed above are harmoniously linked to the promises. Because much has already been included in previous chapters, a review will not be included here. It is sufficient to state that the covenant God made with sinful Adam contained the promise of a redeemer as did the covenant with Abraham. (Genesis 3:15; Psalm 105:42; Romans 16:20; Hebrews 2:14)

The Old Testament promise to *put enmity between you and the woman, and between thy seed and her seed* offered hope both to Adam, Eve, and their descendants who trusted in God to fulfill his promise.

> The allegiance recently transferred to Satan will be again reversed. Though the woman would realize pain and toil for her decision, God assured her she and her descendents would realize reconciliation. Beyond the woman, the whole family of the true humanity, becoming her spiritual seed by faith, will stand in continuing conflict with those descendants of a fallen Adam who obdurately manifest spiritual son ship to the devil. (cf. John 8:33,44)[160]

By submitting to the thief, the liar, the deceiver, the accuser, the tempter, covenant stipulations were disobeyed and thus the covenant was broken. (Genesis 3:13-15)

The covenant with Adam contained the promise of a redeemer. In the covenant with Noah, a picture—a shadow—of a redeemer was seen when God promised that he would never again flood the entire earth.

The redeemer was pictured in the Abrahamic Covenant. Even in the law of the covenant given through Moses, the redeemer was promised. David was promised one of his descendants would rule and establish God's kingdom. There are so many other promises in the Old Testament fulfilled in the Lord Jesus Christ who is the Lord of lords and the King of kings. (Acts 4:25-26; 1 Timothy 6:14-16; Revelation 11:14-16)

The promises by means of covenant began in Genesis. The hope, the faith in the promised redeemer was as a scarlet thread, a line reaching out to whoever would open the door to the Lord God Almighty. Many would not heed or take the time extended to repent and would remain in their sins. The Lord God's perfect plan of salvation brings his perfect plan reachable to any who will humble themselves and repent. (Matthew 11:20-21; 18:4; Luke 18:14; Acts 5:32; 11:18; Romans 2:4; 2 Peter 3:9; Revelation 2:5,16, 21-22; Revelation 17:1-18; Genesis 38:28-30; Joshua 2:18; Micah 6:8)

God (Adonai) was responsible for fulfilling the Old Covenant promises through the Lord (Jehovah), likewise he is responsible for His New Covenant promises. The one true Lord God Almighty with too many attributes to be listed has mercifully and with great grace made a way for sinful man to be redeemed, to be made new. His name was a means for Him to display His marvelous character. Those Old Testament promises were fulfilled in Jesus, who proceeded to make New Covenant promises. The better covenant promises and provisions are numerous. Some are conditional and some are not.

UNCONDITIONAL

The unconditional promises include the second coming of Christ Jesus. His second coming will be in like manner as that seen when He ascended. The angels will announce and attend Him at His second coming. He will come back unexpectedly, suddenly. As a ruler, a King, greater than King David, Jesus will return and establish His kingdom physically. (Matthew 16:27-28; 24:27-30; 36-39; Mark 13:25-27; Luke 17:26, 27-30; Acts 1:10-11; 2 Thessalonians 2:8; 2 Peter 5:4)[161]

> The second coming of Christ is inseparable from His ascension and heavenly session, for it discloses His present lordship to the world and be the means by which every knee shall finally bow and every tongue acknowledge His lordship (Philippians 2:10f.).[162]

In addition to these New Covenant promises there is the unconditional promise that the entire earth will be made new. (2 Peter 3:10-14; Revelation 21:1-4)

Believe it or not, He will return. Sooner than all believe. His return is not a conditional matter. It has been settled by the perfect work of the perfect Lamb of God who is returning as the Lion of the tribe of Judah, the Lord Jesus Christ, Lord of lords and King of kings. No man, no devil, no deception can prevent His return.

CONDITIONAL

In addition to the unconditional promises, there are conditional promises in the New Covenant. A conditional promise is one in which certain prerequisites must be met in order for the promise to take place.

Answer to prayer is a conditional promise. Praying according to the will of God is one of the conditions that must be met in order to have prayer answered. There are subdivisions of God's will, or perhaps better stated, greater aspects of God's will that include (1) praying to God the Father in Jesus' name; (2) remaining in close fellowship with Jesus, praying in the Spirit. It is also very important to pray in faith. (John 15:17-18; 16:23-24; Ephesians 6:18; 1 John 5:14-15; Hebrews 11:6; James 4:1-3,7; 5:15; Jude 20)

Salvation is a New Covenant conditional promise. "It means the action or result of deliverance or preservation from danger or disease, implying safety, health and prosperity."[163] Salvation affects man's spirit, soul, and body. Placing confidence in the covenant head of the better covenant is the condition to be met in order to receive the conditional promise of salvation. One must confess and believe Jesus as their Lord to be saved. This initial step of salvation is frequently made with a prayer similar to the one shown here. (Romans 10:9-11; 20:9-11)

> God, forgive me for sins of commission and of omission. Jesus, I believe you died in my place and you were resurrected and are now seated at the right hand of God. Jesus I choose to receive you as my Lord, Savior, Healer, Baptizer, and Deliverer. I confess you as my Lord now. I will confess you unashamedly to others knowing that as I do so you will unashamedly confess me before God. Through you, Lord Jesus, God is my Heavenly Father. Make me a new creation, Lord Jesus. I ask for wisdom and the power of your Holy Spirit to help me walk right in your sight. Thank you for loving me enough to go through the pain of death to make a better covenant that included me even before I knew you. Jesus, my Lord, it is in your name I pray. Amen.

Salvation has been made available to all and is personally activated when received. Salvation necessitates a personal relationship with the covenant head, Jesus, and willingness to do what God says. It is not by works however, but by grace through faith—a principle which cannot be understood until after an individual is made new. What God has said is His will regarding matters. His will is made clear in the Holy Scriptures. Within the Holy Scriptures the New Testament contains the gospels, the Epistles, and the Revelation of Jesus Christ shown to and recorded by John the apostle and disciple.

Those books give forth the stipulations of the better covenant. I believe John's Holy Spirit-inspired insight into the love of God was a major contributor to his longevity during the horrors of persecutions inflicted during the early church history. Many of the disciples perished during that time, but John survived. He writes more about love than any of the others in the New Testament. Agape is the God-kind of love mankind does not realize as fully as it truly is, nor does any understand the fullness made available to all men through Jesus Christ. Only when we receive Him can we begin to fully know the Lord God's love. (1 John 3:23; 4:21; 5:2-3; 2 John 1:5-6)

> Galatians 3 is occupied with showing that the promise was conditional upon faith and not upon the fulfillment of the Law. The Law was later than, and inferior to, the promise, and did not annul it, ver. 21; cp. 4:23, 28. Again, in Ephesians 2:12, "the covenants of the promise' does not indicate different covenants, but a covenant often renewed, all centering in Christ as the promised Messiah-Redeemer, and comprising the blessings to be bestowed through Him.[164]

JESUS—HEAD OF THE COVENANT

Headship indicates superiority of rank and authority—the final authority. The parties actively involved in making a covenant are the heads of the covenant. Jesus, the living Word, is the head of the New Covenant. As the head of the New Covenant He is the source of life, or union with God, for the Christian. By "Christian" it needs to be understood the necessity of the new birth qualifies one as one being in Christ.

Jesus, the holy righteous man, shed His blood for the purpose of making a blood covenant that would serve as an instrument of blessing for all men. Of all relationships that of blood covenant partners is the most sacred and intimate. Nothing can dissolve the intermingling of the lives of God the Father, the Holy Spirit, and Jesus the Christ and the transformed believers. Theologians will vary in definitions and theories until the Lord judges all the Earth, but God will not be moved. Jesus will remain the eternal head of the everlasting covenant though agreements and disagreements continue until the day He returns. (Philippians 4:7; Colossians 3:15 KJV & AMP; 1 Timothy 3:6)

The better covenant is a contract made as a result of love and trust between God the Father and Jesus the Christ. God the Father will eternally show Himself faithful to Jesus, the head of the New Covenant, by whom the Christian has access to God. In Jesus *all families of the earth* are blessed because of blood covenant and God's faithfulness. But not all are blessed with the fullness available to the one who has followed the Lord's stipulations. It is the New Covenant believer that can be blessed beyond comprehension because of God's faithfulness to Jesus the covenant head. The triune Godhead worked together even before the creation of man to complete an excellent plan. No one, no angel, no principality, power, or ruler of the darkness of this world would ever break the covenant. It was a perfect design and perfect plan built on a perfectly sure foundation. (Galatians 3:15-17,29)

"God is faithful, by whom ye were called unto the fellowship of his Son Jesus Christ our Lord," (1 Corinthians 1:9). It is the New Covenant believer that is blessed beyond comprehension because of God's faithfulness to the faithful man Christ Jesus the covenant head. God will always remain loyal to Jesus who is our representative. Because of faithfulness to Jesus, God is actively enforcing the New Covenant and establishing the New Covenant believers.

Descendants of the Lord Jesus Christ of a necessity must become alive to Him. "Born again not of corruptible seed, but of incorruptible, by the word of God, which lives and abides forever," (1 Peter 1:23). Born again they become children of the Most High God.

COVENANT DESCENDANTS

Descendants are individuals with the same nature as the one from whom they are born. Christians, born again into the family of God, are recreated in the image of God through Jesus Christ their Lord. The supernatural work of the Father, the Son, and the Holy Spirit has worked awesomely so that multitudes still marvel. Each that has been supernaturally born again has a witness of the reality of that simple phrase.

As Jesus is wise, righteous, sanctified, and redeemed, those that are born again are, in Christ Jesus made wise, righteous, sanctified, and redeemed. (2 Peter 1:2-4; 1 Corinthians 1:30; 1 John 3:2-3; Psalms 107:8,15,20-21,31)

Being faithful to the head of the New Covenant, to the Word of the better covenant, God is also faithful to the offspring of the head of the New Covenant. God is faithful to the New Testament believers, who have been born again of the incorruptible Word of God. God is in the process of perfecting the offspring of the head of the better covenant through the ministry of apostles, prophets, evangelists, pastors, and teachers. The ones gifted of God and truly called of God, minister the rightly divided Word of the covenant, in love and in the power of the Holy Spirit. They are like the heralds that proclaimed the covenant news of the Hittite covenants, and the kings they represented expected the heralded messages to be adhered to. (1 Corinthians 10:8-9; Ephesians 4:11-16; Hebrews 10: 14-17)

Much more than any man, God is faithful and confirms His Word with signs following. For more than 2,000 years, the personal witnesses of the goodness of God continue to go according to Mark's gospel. Churches continue to be built, prophets still speak forth, evangelists still herald the news, teachers still expound the written word, disciples still hear and do the good news of the Lord. God continues to confirm His Word with signs following. Amen. (Mark 16:15-20)

When the Hittites had conquered a land and made a covenant, they appointed men to rule subordinately under them. Part of the duties of an appointed subordinate was to distribute their lord's news, his covenant specifications, his commitments, and his expectations. Appointed heralds posted bulletins authorized by the suzerain. Bulletins would be posted in some previously designated public place in every city and village. Sometimes the heralds would stand in the town or village and shout out the suzerain's latest new release.

Being thus informed by the heralds, the entire kingdom would be liable to the suzerain's heralded word. The Hittite suzerain lacked the ability to walk in close fellowship with each of the people in his kingdom. He could not be everywhere at all times. He was limited to intimate fellowship with only a few of his vassals.

Jesus understood covenant. He had been there before the worlds were created. Man created in the image of God was introduced to the principles of covenant in Genesis. God expounded on covenant through the eras of Noah, Abraham, Moses, and David. Man is without excuse. The Lord God is omnipotent, and well able to live in close fellowship with everyone that desires to do His will. (John 7:17 AMP; Romans 1:20-22); Philippians 1:3-6)

God has always been and will always be faithful to covenant. Because of His faithfulness, Christians will always be able to maintain confidence that God will live up to His covenant responsibilities as they move out in faith to accomplish their assignments. (Psalms 89:34-36) Fully committed to keeping covenant, God gave His Son. What more could He give to prove His steadfast covenant love? Jesus the Son lived, died, was raised again, and now sits as mediator between God and man. (Hebrews 9:15-18 AMP; Galatians 3:19-22)

THE BLOOD OF THE COVENANT

The God of peace raised Jesus from the dead through the blood of the everlasting covenant. Jesus, the perfect Lamb of God, the perfect sacrifice, died as a man bearing our sins. Jesus legally represented us before the judge of all the earth. (1 Peter 2:24)

Because of our sins Jesus died. Because of the blood of the everlasting covenant He was resurrected. Death could not hold the covenant head of the better covenant. Jesus' covenant partner had sworn to defend Him. Swiftly the God of peace came to His defense because of covenant faithfulness.

Jesus had conducted Himself flawlessly during His sojourn here. While walking the dusty paths throughout Israel and Judah, He obediently completed the steps required to make the everlasting covenant as man's representative. Jesus' obedience caused Him to taste death for every man. It was through death that Jesus destroyed Satan's power and redeemed man from bondage. God raised Jesus from the dead. It was for our offenses that Jesus had died and it was for our justification that He was raised from the dead. Because of the blood of the everlasting covenant, Jesus' resurrection was possible. (Hebrews 2:9; Psalm 92:15 AMP)

> Then our Master, Head, and Lord did the amazing thing found first in Hebrews and then in Colossians. He met the adversary who had reigned over the human race for more than four thousand years. He stripped him of his authority . . . He entered the home of the strong man and conquered him, defeated him, broke his dominion over the human race. What an hour it must have been! What a thing it must have been when Jesus actually paralyzed the death dealing power of Satan! Revelation 1:18 became a fact: "I am he that was dead, and, behold, I am alive for evermore and I have the keys of death and of Hades."[165]

War had been declared on Satan and the blood covenant partner of the God of Peace would not allow Jesus to remain a prisoner of war. The power of the Holy Spirit of God by Jesus' faith and obedience in the covenant of life and because of the blood of that covenant He raised Christ Jesus from the dead. That miraculous resurrection because of the blood of the covenant is still affecting believers today. The same Spirit that raised Christ from the dead is available to believers today and He desires to indwell the born again descendants of the covenant head of the everlasting covenant of life. (Romans 8:11, 14-17)

The blood of the everlasting covenant of life is still powerfully raising the spiritually dead to life in Christ Jesus when they act on the measure of faith allotted to them. Now, because of the completed work of the Second Adam, people can be made new after the image of God. God's first covenant was fulfilled in Jesus. Though the enemy of man's soul, Satan, tried, he was not successful in keeping Elohim from creating man in His own image. When Jesus supernaturally shouted from the cross, "*It is finished!*" the perfect, one of a kind, blood covenant was completed and man was freed from the fear of death. The everlasting covenant with life was activated and the covenant with death was annulled through Jesus, the head of the better covenant.

> *By him therefore let us offer the sacrifice of praise to God continually, that is, the fruit of our lips giving thanks to his name. But to do good and to communicate forget not: for with such sacrifices God is well pleased.*
>
> *Obey them that have the rule over you, and submit yourselves: for they watch for your souls, as they that must give account, that they may do it with joy, and not with grief: for that is unprofitable for you. Pray for us: for we trust we have a good conscience, in all things willing to live honestly. But I beseech you the rather to do this, that I may be restored to you the sooner.*

Now the God of peace, that brought again from the dead our Lord Jesus, that great shepherd of the sheep, through the blood of the everlasting covenant, Make you perfect in every good work to do his will, working in you that which is well-pleasing in his sight, through Jesus Christ; to whom be glory for ever and ever. Amen.

And I beseech you, brethren, suffer the word of exhortation: for I have written a letter unto you in few words. Know ye that our brother Timothy is set at liberty; with whom, if he come shortly, I will see you. Salute all them that have the rule over you, and all the saints. They of Italy salute you. Grace be with you all. Amen.

—Hebrews 13:15-22

Now may the God of peace [Who is the Author and the Giver of peace], Who brought again from among the dead our Lord Jesus, that great Shepherd of the sheep, by the blood [that sealed, ratified] the everlasting agreement (covenant, testament), Strengthen (complete, perfect) and make you what you ought to be and equip you with everything good that you may carry out His will; [while He Himself] works in you and accomplishes that which is pleasing in His sight, through Jesus Christ (the Messiah); to Whom be the glory forever and ever (to the ages of the ages). Amen (so be it).

—Hebrews 13:20-21 AMP

God is faithful to covenant stipulations, to the better covenant, to His family and to all that is His. When people hear His call for the blind, the lame, even for the people which were not His people, they come by the thousands. His people are told to *go into all the world*. All are called to go. (Mark 16:15-20)

How can they call on Jesus when they have not heard of Him? Whosoever calls on the name of the Lord shall be saved. But how can they call on him if they have not heard that they might believe? How shall they believe Jesus of whom they have not heard? How shall they hear without a witness, a preacher, a teacher of God? We have been called to go and tell. Some have been sent but all believers are to go. (Romans 10:14-17)

Accusations have been aimed at those who have gone but supposedly did as much, or more, wrong than right. They will answer for what they have done and so will everyone else. Have the stipulations of the better covenant been followed. Have they ever been born again is for God to judge. There is only one Commander in Chief, the Lord Jesus Christ, King of Kings and Lord of Lords. There are times when we are to judge. However, the biggest share of the time judgments are made by people out of order. The sin of disorderliness often has simply found a scapegoat.

Unlike Adam, people behaving in such a manner cannot break covenant. They simply do not stay where God can bless them. They make moves in darkness and reap bitter fruit. They puzzle over troubles without calling on the name of the Lord for wisdom. And if they continue to follow the accuser, the tempter, they waste their own lives and lead many in a wrong direction.

The Old Covenant and the New Covenant complement each other. The Old Covenant abounds with rules because of the flesh pressured by the covenant with death. Covenant was needed for dealing with the sinful nature of the natural man. The New Covenant abounds with good news of freedom from sin. The rules are minimal. The Law of the Spirit of life in Christ Jesus has set people free from the law of sin and death. (Romans 8:2) The power of death has been broken.

Understand the *perfect law of liberty* addresses matters that deal with the flesh because the devil is still around. As believers we are to be led by our spirit, not by our flesh. The Holy Spirit is our Helper when we step out in faith with our spirit. He helps us resist the temptations. The devil in the garden succeeded and caused the downfall of Adam and his descendents. The Lord Jesus Christ succeeded and freedom rang. Joy fills the heart. Why in the world would anyone return to the lust of the flesh rather than walk on resisting the devil, having on the full armor of God? (Galatians 5:13; Ephesians 6:10-19)

The covenant principles we've studied in this book have hopefully helped you to realize that lives can be changed when life and death issues are addressed. There are more with us than those who are against us.

Look into the perfect law of liberty and continue in that. Don't be forgetful of His perfect and much better covenant. Be a doer of the work of the Lord following the stipulations of the New Covenant. (James 1:25)

The better covenant overflows with life and the covenant with death is an empty cup of dross. The lust of the flesh is a fishhook disguised according to the allure that tickles your fancy. Don't bite into the lies of the devil that tempt according to your weakness. Choose to grow strong in the Lord and in the power of His might.

The better covenant is available to all who will come to the Mediator of this excellent covenant. If you hearken diligently to the voice of the Lord God, you will be blessed. A curse belongs to those who have chosen to remain in a covenant with death rather than repent and come out into the light. (Galatians 3:1,13-14; Deuteronomy 28:1-14)

Remember God is good all the time—even into eternity. The most pleasant thing you have ever known will be immeasurably better in Heaven. You cannot even begin to know what is good on earth unless you have seen that God is good. Clarity comes through His Word and His Spirit and the peace that passes all understanding follows afterwards.

The devil is evil and destined for an eternal torment. You don't want to go there. Be assured evil is an ugly hook below an alluring lure and an ugly demise. The second death will be worse than the physical death and immeasurably worse than anything ever experienced anywhere for anyone. Getting hooked in the covenant with death leads to misery, death, judgment, and a second death. (Revelation 20:7, 14; 2 Thessalonians 1:9-11)

Jesus did not come to condemn the world He came to save. Heaven is real and eternal. Hell is real and eternal. Those who continue to love darkness and their evil deeds will hold fast to their lies, like an injured vicious animal biting the hand of one trying to help.

Following are a few noteworthy aspects of an outgrowth of misconceptions about *the record of the word of God, and of the testimony of Jesus Christ*. (Revelation 1:2) Ungodly world religions formed covenants in deference to those testified of in the Old and New Testament accounts of Judeo-Christian history and faith. Hebrews I I is one chapter that summarizes the Judeo faith. New Testament Believers have been provided a better covenant whereby *God has provided a better thing for us, that they without us should not be made perfect*. (Hebrews 11:40) The Apostle John wrote *the Revelation of Jesus Christ given to him things, which were to come to pass*. (Revelation 1: 1)

People around the world have held fast to the chains binding them though they are often hurting. They often bite the hand that tries to help them like wild animals caught in traps. Be mindful a true believer is not to be religious. Rather he should be a reflection of the One True Almighty God by grace through faith in the Lord Jesus Christ.

In Merrill C. Tenney's book *New Testament Survey Revised,* pages 65-78, the following quotes summarize an interesting account of THE RELIGIOUS WORLD.

The Graeco-Roman Pantheon – Each small farmer worshiped the gods of his own farm and fireside, which personified for him the forces with which he had to deal in living his daily life.

Emperor Worship – Although the worship of local deities persisted, the growing cosmopolitan consciousness in the empire prepared the way for a new type of religion, the worship of the state.

The concentration of the executive functions of the Roman state in the person of one man had vested him with powers unprecedented in the history of the world. The fact that he was able to utilize those powers for the good of the empire created the feeling that there must be something divine in him.

The Mystery Religions – While all of them differed from each other in origin and in detail, all were alike in certain broad characteristics. Each had a ritual or formulas, symbols and of secret dramatic representations of the experience of the god, by which initiates were inducted into an experience, and presumably rendered a candidate for immortality.

The Worship of the Occult – Akin in many ways to the mystery religions was the occultism of the day, the superstitious observances and regard of the masses for the powers of the universe, which they could not understand but which they could vaguely feel. For them the entire world was inhabited by spirits and demons who could be invoked or commanded to do one's bidding if only one knew the correct rite or formula to use.

The Philosophies – When religion degenerates into empty ritualism or ignorant superstition, thoughtful people may abandon it altogether because they feel it has no real satisfaction to offer them. Philosophy is an attempt to correlate existing knowledge about the universe into systematic form and to integrate human experience with it. Philosophy has always assumed the potential adequacy of humans to understand their world and decide their fate.

If I am found guilty when I stand before those who oppose faith in my Lord Jesus Christ, I long to be found guilty of witnessing too boldly and of praying too often and of trusting the Lord fully. I desire to do God's will in all areas of my life because I love Him. The God of peace, that brought again from the dead my Lord Jesus, that great shepherd of the sheep, through the blood of the everlasting covenant, make me able and willing to grow mature and strong in Him. He is well able to keep us and He is very willing to do so.

Before the first inevitable physical death there is a choice to be made. There is a heaven to gain and a hell to shun. Moving from death to life begins with calling on the name of Jesus. Gospel tracts can give you a jump start. The water of the Word will cleanse you. The milk of the Word will give you strength to grow strong. The meat of the Word will strengthen you for a healthy walk in the better covenant.

Know that God loves you and may His Grace be with you always. Amen.

ABOUT THE AUTHOR

Connie Fauth is a minister, writer, and a studio 2d artist. She has served the Lord, beginning in 1976, testifying and teaching in a Reformed Church. Her preaching includes numerous denominational and independent churches. Connie attended Rhema Bible Training Center for two years and graduated in 1991. As an assistant minister from 1991-1996 she helped in the work of her pastors. Her heart led her to found and serve as Senior Pastor of Princeville Church of Hope. Later renamed Romans 1513 Ministries, she continued as senior pastor from 1996-2005.

Connie was writing before she was born again and writing is still part of her life. As a minister, sermon preparation was the major part of her writing endeavors. Preparation was a joy. The written word of God encouraged, strengthened, and prepared her heart to preach the gospel, the good news. Connie continually communed with the Holy Spirit. She prepared to address listeners with God's Word on the matters of life.

Both graphic design and fine art are still part of her life. She earned her Associates Degree in Applied Science specializing in Graphic Design in 1986. In addition, between Illinois Central College and Bradley University, she has 94 hours in fine art, specializing in studio painting. On canvas Connie reflects her love for the Lord.

Since 1975, Connie's life has centered around her Lord, her family, and her friends, with the most devotion to her Lord. She has experienced sunshine and rain, and has found God in both places. To live for God has required many sacrifices. With her heart motivated to give God first place, the benefits that she has received have been noted to inspire her readers. The inspiration is of a heavenly nature, not of an earthly nature. Her gratitude is expressed daily to her Lord for his wisdom and his grace.

END NOTES

1 *The Interpreter's One Volume Commentary of the Bible,* Charles M. Laymon, Editor; Tennessee, The Parthenon Press, p. 1012.

2 *The Interpreter's Dictionary of the Bible,* New York, Abington Press, p. 714.

3 *Ancient Near Eastern Texts Relating to the Old Testament,* New Jersey, Princeton Press, p. 199.

4 *The Illustrated World History,* New York, Wm. H. Wise & Co., p. 54.

5 *The Interpreter's Dictionary of the Bible,* p. 714.

6 *Webster's New Collegiate Dictionary,* p. 199.

7 *Ancient Near Eastern Texts Relating to the Old Testament,* p. 204.

8 Ibid.

9 Ibid, p. 205.

10 *The Interpreter's Dictionary of the Bible,* p. 66.

11 Ibid, p. 714.

12 *The New International Dictionary of Biblical Archaeology,* p. 138.

13 Bobbie Gay, Graduate of Illinois State University, Ancient History Major.

14 *The International Law and Custom of Ancient Greece and Rome,* Phillipson, Coleman, London, Macmillan and Co., Limited, p. 118.

15 Ibid.

16 *Webster's New Twentieth Century Dictionary of the English Language,* Unabridged Second Edition, New York, World Publishing Co.

17 *The International Law and Custom of Ancient Greece and Rome,* Phillipson, Coleman, London, Macmillan and Co., Limited, p. 117-118.

18 Ibid, p. 119.

19 Ibid, p. 119-120.

20 Ibid, p. 120.

21 *The Blood Covenant,* H. Clay Trumbull, Missouri, Impact Books, Inc.

22 Ibid, p. 298.

23 *The Blood Covenant,* E.W. Kenyon, Kenyon's Gospel Publishing Society, p. 9.

24 Ibid, p. 10.

25 *Stanley's Africa,* Rafaello Busoni, New York, The Viking Press, p. 143.

26 Ibid, p. 145.

27 Ibid, p. 146.

28 Ibid, p. 147.

29 Ibid, p. 173.

30 Ibid, p. 195.

31 Ibid, p. 275.

32 *The Blood Covenant,* H. Clay Trumbull, Missouri, Impact Books, Inc., p. 72.

33 Ibid, p. 75.

34 Ibid, pp. 235-236.

35 Ibid, pp. 340-341.

36 *My Father's Names,* Elmer L Towns, p. 17.

37 *Eerdmans' Handbook to the History of Christianity,* paraphrased, p. 76.

38 *Names of God,* Stone, Nathan J., Illinois, Moody Press, p. 12.

39 *God's Plan For Man,* Dake, Finis Jennings, Georgia, Dake Bible Sales, Inc., p. 480.

40 Ibid.

41 *Names of God,* Stone, Nathan J., Illinois, Moody Press, pp. 14-15.

42 *Youngs Analytical Concordance to the Bible,* Robert Young, LL.D.; Wm. B. Eerdmans Publishing Company, Grand Rapids, Michigan.

43 *Names of God,* Stone, Nathan J., Illinois, Moody Press, p. 15.

44 *Webster's New Collegiate Dictionary,* Massachusetts, G. & C. Merriam Company, p. 756.

45 Ibid, p. 74.

46 *God's Plan For Man,* Dake, Finis Jennings, Georgia, Dake Bible Sales, Inc., p. 113.

47 *The New Thayer's Greek-English Lexicon of the New Testament,* Indiana, APXA, p. 5-6.

48 *The New Bible Dictionary,* pp. 1146-47.

49 *Halley's Bible Handbook,* Henry H. Halley, Michigan, Zondervan Publishing House, p. 59.

50 *Webster's New Collegiate Dictionary,* Massachusetts, G. & C. Merriam Company, p. 981.

51 *The Exhaustive Concordance of The Bible,* James Strong, S.T.D., L.L.D.; Distributors, A Division of Baker Book House Grand Rapids, Michigan 49506, p. 984.

52 *Ancient Near Eastern Texts Relating to the Old Testament,* New Jersey, Princeton Press, p. 204.

53 *The Interpreter's One-Volume Commentary on the Bible,* Charles M. Laymon, editor, Abingdon Press, Nashville, Tennessee, p. 4.

54 *God's Plan For Man,* Dake, Finis Jennings, Georgia, Dake Bible Sales, Inc., p. 140.

55 *The Covenants of God,* Lester Sumrall, Indiana, Lesea Publishing Company, p. 13.

56 *A Faire and Easie Way to Heaven,* Connecticut, Wesleyan University Press, p. 82.

57 *The New Bible Dictionary,* p. 1027.

58 *The New Bible Dictionary,* pp. 1164-1165

59 Ibid, p. 85.

60 Ibid.

61 *The Wycliffe Bible Commentary,* Illinois, Moody Press, p. 8.

62 *The New Bible Dictionary,* p. 307.

63 *The New Bible Commentary,* p. 85

64 *Nelson's Expository Dictionary,* Merrill F. Unger, editor, Nashville, Thomas Nelson Publishers, p. 234.

65 Ibid.

66 Ibid.

67 *The New Bible Commentary,* p. 85.

68 Ibid, p. 84.

69 *Analytical Concordance to the Bible,* Young, Robert, (Michigan, Wm. B. Eerdman's Publishing Company, p. 70.

70 *New Spirit Filled Life Bible, The Holy Bible, New King James Version,* copyright 1982 by Thomas Nelson, Inc., Kingdom Dynamics Malachi 2:13-16, p. 1270.

71 *The Blood Covenant,* H. Clay Trumbull, Preface v,vi, dated August 14, 1885.

72 *The Blood Covenant,* H. Clay Trumbull, Appendix, p. 335.

73 *The New Scofield Reference Bible,* New York, Oxford University Press, 1967, Genesis 17:1 footnote, p. 25.

74 *The New Bible Commentary Revised,* Michigan, Wm. B. Eerdman's Publishing Company, 1979, p. 95.

75 *The New Bible Dictionary,* J.D. Douglas, M.A., B.D., S.T.M., Ph.D., (Wm. B. Eerdmans Publishing Co., Grand Rapids, Michigan, p. 27

76 *The New Bible Commentary,* p. 97.

77 *New Spirit Filled Life Bible,* Exodus 4:24-26 footnote.

78 *Haley's Bible Handbook,* p. 111.

79 *New Spirit Filled Life Bible,* pp. 85-86 footnotes.

80 *The Interpreter's One-Volume Commentary of the Bible,* p. 53.

81 *Encyclopedia Judaica,* New York, The Macmillan Company, pp. 1019-1020. Also seen at www.netzarim.co.il/Shared/Glossary/Glos)A-D.htm

82 *The New Bible Dictionary,* p. 283 manuscript 3.19 of 21.

83 Moore Life Ministries, Keith Moore, Branson, Missouri.

84 *The New Bible Commentary Revised,* p. 241.

85 Ibid, p. 243.

86 Ibid.

87 *Blood Brothers in Christ,* New Jersey, Fleming H Revell Company, 1975, pp. 21-27.

88 *New Spirit Filled Life Bible,* Copyright 1982 by Thomas Nelson, Inc., p. 383, 1 Samuel 18:1 margin note; 1 Samuel 18:1-4 footnote.

89 Ibid, footnotes p. 413.

90 Unconditional Love Int'l, Malcolm Smith; P.O. Box 1599, Bandera, TX 78003; formerly or DBA Malcolm Smith Ministries, P.O. Box 245, NY 10992.

91 Ibid.

92 Ibid.

93 Ibid.

94 *The Wycliffe Bible Commentary,* Illinois, Moody Press, Pfeiffer, Charles T. & Harrison, Everett, editors, p. 1142.

[95] *The New Bible Commentary Revised,* Michigan, Wm. B. Eerdman's Publishing Company, 1979, p. 985.

[96] *The Wycliffe Bible Commentary,* p. 1142.

[97] *Vines Expository Dictionary of New Testament Words,* W.E. Vine, M.A.; Iowa, Riverside Book and Bible House, p. 568.

[98] *The New Bible Commentary Revised,* p. 1143.

[99] *The Blood Covenant,* H. Clay Trumbull, Missouri, Impact Books, Inc.; Published first in 1885, p. 211.

[100] The *New Spirit Filled Life Bible,* pp. 96-97, Exodus 15:26 footnote, Kingdom Dynamics, Nathaniel Van Cleave.

[101] *Halley's Bible Handbook,* Henry H. Halley, Michigan, Zondervan Publishing House, p. 69.

[102] *The New Bible Commentary,* Revised, p. 357.

[103] *The New Bible Dictionary,* Revised, pp. 966-67.

[104] *Great People of the Bible and How They Lived,* pp. 356-357

[105] "*The Blood Covenant,*" Leonard Gardner,(Michigan, Zion Tape Ministries, Tape #12.

[106] *Great People of the Bible and How They Lived,* p. 328.

[107] *The Wycliffe Bible Commentary,* Illinois, Moody Press, p. 1077.

[108] *The New Bible Commentary Revised,* pp. 948-949.

[109] *The New Bible Dictionary Revised,* pp. 966-967.

[110] *The New Bible Dictionary,* p. 509.

[111] *The Wycliffe Bible Commentary,* p. 1217.

[112] *The New Bible Commentary Revised,* p. 944.

[113] *The Illustrated Bible Dictionary Part 1;* p. 329.

[114] Ibid.

[115] *The Interpreter's One-Volume Commentary of the Bible,* p. 986.

[116] *The Interpreter's Dictionary of the Bible,* p. 722.

[117] *The New Bible Dictionary,* p. 788.

[118] Ibid, p. 752.

[119] *The Interpreter's One-Volume Commentary of the Bible,* p. 986.

120 *Encyclopedia Judaica,* Vol. 5, p. 1019.

121 *Halley's Bible Handbook,* p. 387.

122 *The Blood Speaks,* pp. 39-41.

123 Ibid.

124 *Halley's Bible Handbook,* p. 488.

125 Ibid.

126 *The New Bible Commentary Revised,* p. 1147.

127 *The Interpreter's One-Volume Commentary on the Bible,* p. 301.

128 *The Interpreter's One-Volume Commentary on the Bible,* p. 263.

129 *Names of God,* p. 50.

130 Ibid, p. 45

131 *The Wycliffe Bible Commentary,* p. 2.

132 *Names of God,* Stone, p. 12

133 *Expository Dictionary of the Old Testament,* p. 28.

134 *Names of God,* p. 28.

135 *The Wycliffe Bible Commentary,* p. 4.

136 *Halley's Bible Handbook,* p. 101.

137 "The Blood Covenant," Leonard Gardner tapes.

138 *The Complete Word Study Old Testament King James Version,* p. 189.

139 Ibid.

140 Ibid, Lexical Aids, p. 2374.

141 *The Holy Bible* Containing the Old and New Testaments, Jeremiah 23:6.

142 *The Wycliffe Bible Commentary,* p. 673.

143 *Eerdmans' Handbook to the History of Christianity,* p. 96-97.

144 Ibid, p. 97.

145 Ibid.

146 *The Interpreter's One-Volume Commentary on the Bible,* p. 611.

147 *The New Bible Dictionary,* p. 818.

148 *Interpreter's one-Volume Commentary,* p. 739-740

149 *Matthew Henry's Concise Commentary,* Acts 2:14-36.

150 *Easton Dictionary of the Bible,* Unction.

151 Jamieson, Fausset, and Brown Comment, Hebrews 13:20-21.

152 *The New Bible Dictionary,* Amen, p. 29-30.

153 Ibid, Word, p. 1337.

154 *The Interpreter's One-Volume Commentary on the Bible,* pp. 829-30.

155 *The New Bible Dictionary,* p. 1036.

156 *Webster's New World College Dictionary* Fourth Edition, p. 1155.

157 Ibid.

158 Ibid.

159 Ibid.

160 *The New Bible Commentary Revised,* p. 85.

161 Bible Gateway, http://www.biblegateway.com/; Nave's Topical Bible Topical Index search.

162 *International Standard Bible Encyclopedia:* E-J, p. 139.

163 *The New Bible Dictionary,* p. 1126.

164 *Vines Expository Dictionary of New Testament Words,* p. 891.

165 *Advanced Bible Study Course,* E.W., Kenyon, p. 150.

BIBLIOGRAPHY

A Faire and Easie Way to Heaven, Connecticut, Wesleyan University Press.

A Merriam-Webster, Webster's New Collegiate Dictionary, (Massachusetts: G. & C. Merriam Company).

Advanced Bible Study Course, E.W., Kenyon, (Kenyon's Gospel Publishing Society, Washington).

"Amazing Grace: The Story of John Newton" by Al Rogers; http://www.anointedlinks.com/amazing_grace.html

Analytical Concordance to the Bible, Young, Robert, (Michigan, Wm. B. Eerdman's Publishing Company)

Ancient Greece, http://ancientgreece.me/2012/03/government-and-diplomacy-in-ancient.html

Ancient Near Eastern Texts Relating to the Old Testament, (New Jersey, Princeton Press).

Assyrian-Hittite Treaty; Translator: Treaty Between Mursilis And Duppi-Tessub Of Amurru [a] Texts: Akkadian version: KUB, III, 14. Hittite version: KBo v, g; KUB, 111, 119; KUB, XIV ,5; KUB, XIX. Literature: J. Friedrich, Staatsvertragc des Hatti-Reiches in hethitischer Sprache (MVAG, XXXI, I926), 1-48. E. F. Weidner, Politische Dotumente aus Kleinasien (Boghazkoi Studien, VII 1923), 76-79. http://toplumvetarih.blogcu.com/evlilik-bosanma-ve-antlasma-kayit-lari-3/9137862. The'Eternal Treaty' from the Hittite perspective; www.thebritishmuseum.ac.uk/issue6/bryce.html; Trevor Bryce.

"Away Here in Texas," Article "Amazing Grace: The Story of John Newton" by Al Rogers, July-August 1996 issue; reprinted by http://www.anointedlinks.com/amazing_grace.html

Blood Brothers in Christ, New Jersey, Fleming H Revell Company, 1975.

Cambridge Dictionary, The Cambridge Advanced Learner's Dictionary & Thesaurus © Cambridge University Press; Cambridge Dictionaries. Online!http://dictionary.cambridge.org/dictionary/british/antidisestablishmentarianism

Easton Dictionary of the Bible, Bible Reader for Mac Reader Version 7199591.

Eerdmans' Handbook to the History of Christianity, ©1977 Lion Publishing, Icknield Way, Tring., Hertfordshire, England; Wm B Eerdmans Publishing Co., 225 Jefferson S.E., Grand Rapids, Michigan 49503, USA BR146.E35 270 77.5616; ISBN 0-8028-3450-7.

Encyclopedia Judaica, New York, The Macmillan Company.

Expository Dictionary of the Old Testament, Merrill F. Unger, Williams White, Jr., editors, Nashville, Thomas Nelson Publishers, 1980.

God's Plan For Man, Dake, Finis Jennings, Georgia, Dake Bible Sales, Inc.

Great People of the Bible and How They Lived, Ernest C. Wright (Editorial Consultant), New York, The Reader's Digest Association, Inc., 1974.

Halley's Bible Handbook, Henry H. Halley, Michigan, Zondervan Publishing House.

International Standard Bible Encyclopedia: E-J, By Geoffrey W. Bromiley, Wm. B. Eerdmans Publishing Co., Grand Rapids/Cambridge.

Jamieson, Fausset, and Brown Comment, BibleReader, www.olive-tree.com/BibleReader/

Malcom Smith, Unconditional Love Int'l, PO Box 1599, Bandera, TX 78003. In 1984 permission was granted for me to refer to his teaching on Blood Covenant. I have paraphrased his rendition of the David,

Jonathan, Mephibosheth accounts in I & II Samuel and added many of my own notes from studies of those Scriptures.

Matthew Henry's Concise Commentary, BibleReader™ for Mac, Reader Version: 7199591, com.olivetree.BibleReaderMac, copyright © 1998-2012 Olive Tree Bible Software

My Father's Names, Elmer L. Towns, Regal Books, A Division of GL Publications, Ventura, California U.S.A. Printed in U.S.A., ©1991 by Elmer L. Towns, All rights reserved.

Names of God, Stone, Nathan J., Illinois, Moody Press, copyright 1944.

Nelson's Expository Dictionary, Merrill F. Unger, editor, Nashville, Thomas Nelson Publishers.

New Spirit Filled Life Bible, The Holy Bible, New King James Version, copyright 2002 by Thomas Nelson, Inc., Footnotes, Kingdom Dynamics, and Word Wealth.

New Testament Survey, by Merrill C. Tenney, © copyright 1985, Wm. B. Eerdmans Publishing Company, Wm. B. Eerdmans Publishing Company, Inter-Varsity Press.

Spirit Filled Life Bible, The Holy Bible, King James Version, General Editor Jack W. Hayford, Litt.D.; Copyright 1991 by Thomas Nelson, Inc.

Richards Expository Dictionary of Bible Words, Lawrence O. Richards; Regency Reference Library, Copyright © 1985 by The Zondervan Corporation, [Grand Rapids, Michigan, USA] Regency Reference Library is an imprint of Zondervan Publishing House, 1415 Lake Drive, S.E., Grand Rapids, Michigan 49506.

Stanley's Africa, Rafaello Busoni, New York, The Viking Press.

The Amplified Bible, copyright 1987 by Zondervan Bible Publishers, Grand Rapids, Michigan.

"The Blood Covenant", Leonard Gardner, Series of 12 tapes, (Michigan, Zion Tape Ministries).

The Blood Covenant, E.W. Kenyon, Kenyon's Gospel Publishing Society.

The Blood Covenant, H. Clay Trumbull, Missouri, Impact Books, Inc.; Published first in 1885.

The Blood Speaks, Larry Huggins, Oklahoma, Harrison House, 1965.

The Chronological Bible © Edward Reese, 1977; E.E. Gaddy & Associates, Inc., Publishers, P.O. Box 8411, Nashville, TN 37207.

The Complete Word Study Old Testament King James Version, 1994 AMG International, Inc., D/B/A AMG Publishers, Chattanooga, TN 37422, U.S.A.

The Covenants of God, Lester Sumrall, Indiana, Lesea Publishing Company, p. 13.

The Exhaustive Concordance of the Bible: showing every word of the text of the common English version of the Canonical Books, and every occurrence of each word in regular order; together with Dictionaries of the Hebrew and Greek Words of the original, with references to the English words: by James Strong, S.T.D., LL.D.; Distributors, A Division of Baker Book House Grand Rapids, Michigan 49506.

The Holy Bible Containing the Old and New Testaments, with notes and annotations by the Rev. Mr. Ostervalid, professor of Divinity, at Neutchatel, in Swisserland; (J. Heming, High-Street, 1807). "The whole forming a complete edition of the Holy Scriptures, calculated to enlighten the Understanding, purify the Heart, and promote the cause of virtue and Piety; and thereby establish the Happiness and Peace of Christian Families in this World, and secure their eternal Salvation in the next." This Bible was part of the personal collection of John Richard Williams. His family Bible, cherished by John, included family event records dating as far back as "Edwin Charles Williams, born April 14, 1844 died Jan. 3, 1909, buried Jan. 5, 1909 at Woodlawn Cemetery."

The Illustrated Bible Dictionary Part 1; Tyndale House Publishers.

The Illustrated World History, New York, Wm. H. Wise & Co.

The Interpreter's One-Volume Commentary on the Bible, Edited by Charles M. Laymon, Abingdon Press, Nashville, Tennessee.

The Layman's Bible Encyclopedia; Martin, Williams C., M.A., B.B., Tennessee, The Southwestern Company.

The New International Dictionary of Biblical Archaeology, E.M. Blaiklock, and R.K. Harrison, Editor, Grand Rapids; Zondervan Publishing House, 1983, Michigan, Regency Reference Library.

The Interpreter's One-Volume Commentary on the Bible, Charles M. Laymon, Tennessee, The Parthenon Press, 1982.

The New Bible Commentary Revised, Michigan, Wm. B. Eerdman's Publishing Company, 1979.

The New Bible Dictionary, J.D. Douglas, M.A., B.D., S.T.M., Ph.D., (Wm. B. Eerdmans Publishing Co., Grand Rapids, Michigan).

The New Spirit Filled Life Bible, Executive Editor Jack W. Hayford, Litt.D., (Thomas Nelson Bibles; a Division of Thomas Nelson, Inc.); www.thomasnelson.com.

The New Scofield Reference Bible, (New York, Oxford University Press, 1967).

The New Strong's Exhaustive Concordance of the Bible, James Strong, LL.D., S.T.D.; Thomas Nelson Publishers, Copyright© 1984 by Thomas Nelson Publishers.

The New Thayer's Greek-English Lexicon of the New Testament, Indiana, APXA.

The International Law and Custom of Ancient Greece and Rome, Phillipson, Coleman, London, Macmillan and Co., Limited.

The Interpreter's Dictionary of the Bible, quoted in Chapter 4, The Sabbath, Good News of Belonging, Samuel Bacchiocchi, Ph. D., Andrews University; footnote 23.

The Interpreter's Dictionary of the Bible, New York, Abington Press.

The Interpreter's One-Volume Commentary of the Bible, Charles M. Laymon, Editor; Tennessee, The Parthenon Press.

The Preparation of Sermons, Andrew Watterson Blackwood, Abingdon Press, Nashville, Tennessee.

The Theological Wordbook of the Old Testament, Laird R. Harris, (Illinois, Moody Press, 1981), Vol. 2, pg 930-31.

The Triumphant Church, Keneth E. Hagin, Kenneth Hagin Ministries, Konosha, Oklahoma.

The Wycliffe Bible Commentary, Illinois, Moody Press, Pfeiffer, Charles T. & Harrison, Everett, editors.

Vines Expostiory Dictionary of New Testament Words, W.E. Vine, M.A.; Iowa, Riverside Book and Bible House.

Webster's New Collegiate Dictionary, (Massachusetts, G. & C. Merriam Company.

Webster's New Twentieth Century Dictionary of the English Language Unabridged Second Addition, New York, World Publishing Co.

Webster's New World College Dictionary Fourth Edition, Michael Agnes Editor in Chief, David B. Guralnik Editor in Chief 1951-1985; copyright © 2008 by Wiley Publishing, Inc., Cleveland, Ohio.

Youngs Analytical Concordance to the Bible, Robert Young, LL.D.; Wm. B. Eerdmans Publishing Company, Grand Rapids, Michigan.